From
Comet
to
Cal Mac

Ferry
Publications

Published by:
Ferry Publications, PO Box 33, Ramsey, Isle of Man IM99 4LP
Tel: +44 (0) 1624 898445   Fax: +44 (0) 1624 898449
E-mail: ferrypubs@manx.net   Website: www.ferrypubs.co.uk

Introduction

A purposeful, modern ferry in her lively Caledonian MacBrayne colours of black hull, white superstructure and red funnels with lions rampant, motoring through a dramatic landscape of soaring mountains and sea lochs, is one of the iconic images of modern Scotland. Whether one stands at Ardrossan, watching the *Caledonian Isles* as she approaches from Arran and surges in through the narrow harbour entrance, or gazes at the *Isle of Lewis*, inbound from Stornoway, as she sweeps suddenly and majestically into Ullapool, the supremacy of the ferry on today's sea-routes is more than evident.

In the modern car ferry, several aspects of the Scottish seagoing experience are fused together. Registered in Glasgow, and sometimes built at Port Glasgow, the ferry and its associated shore-based infrastructure represent industrial Scotland. It was from Port Glasgow that the world's first sea-going steamship, Henry Bell's *Comet* of 1812, made her maiden voyage on the Clyde. Shortly thereafter, she became the very first West Highland steamer, bravely reaching Fort William in September of that year. Thereafter development was rapid. In subsequent decades, steamers transformed the world as the unpredictability of a course dictated by the vagaries of the wind was replaced by the predictability of a straight line cut through the sea. Distances shrank rapidly and, as a result, Britain – the first industrial nation – became the era's global superpower. In Scotland, the steamship had profound cultural implications. All of a sudden, what had been fairly 'remote' communities around the Firth of Clyde became easily accessible pleasure spots for holidaymakers and for day-trippers, eager to escape the daily urban grind for a few hours.

Modern Caledonian MacBrayne car ferries sail in the wake of the *Comet*, efficiently connecting communities and enabling a greatly enhanced quality of life and economic opportunities for islanders. Yet, these ships are also part of another romantic Scotland, bringing tourists to witness picturesque and sublime vistas of mountain and sea, and offering a very high level of hospitality, comfort and service. Indeed, for the past two years, Caledonian MacBrayne has been voted by the discerning readership of **The Guardian** newspaper as Britain's best ferry company. Tourists and local people alike enjoy freshly cooked food, often

The *Finlaggan* speeds past Port Askaig, Islay in November 2011 with the mountains of Jura forming a dramatic background. *(Bruce Peter)*

using local ingredients, well-stocked bars, comfortable lounges and sun decks – and the ships' crews are notably friendly and professional. Such high standards do not come cheaply, however, and in order to offer relatively low fares, based on road-equivalent pricing, the ferries are heavily subsidised. Yet, their main costs are staff wages and fuel, neither of which allows for obvious savings.

The experience of a sea voyage to Scotland's Clyde and Hebridean isles is usually a pleasure – but it was not always so. Indeed, it may be observed that the state of Scotland's domestic shipping services closely reflects that of the wider nation. During the 1930s-80s period, steamer and ferry operations fell far short of the best international standards and perhaps reflected a parochial belief that the most basic service level was good enough. Looking further back to Scotland's industrial 'golden age' from the mid-nineteenth century until the First World War, First Class travellers experienced steamers of remarkable opulence, complete with fine dining in ornate saloons, German bands to play the latest waltzes and polkas and, in one case, even the provision of salt-water baths. Yet, these vessels carried, in close proximity, larger numbers of mainly working-class deck passengers who could catch only glimpses of First Class luxury. In that sense, these vessels too closely reflected Scottish urban life in that period.

Since the *Comet* first sailed in 1812, the provision of shipping services on the Firth of Clyde and Hebrides has come a very long way. Caledonian MacBrayne's modern fleet is vital to the economy of the West Coast and to national life as a whole. The creation of this fine fleet, however, has entailed immense effort, and there have been failures as well as successes, along the route. The authors hope that readers will enjoy the two hundred year-long narrative from *Comet* to CalMac.

Donald E. Meek and Bruce Peter
November 2011

Contents

Published by Ferry Publications trading as Lily Publications Ltd 2011
PO Box 33, Ramsey, Isle of Man, British Isles, IM99 4LP
Tel: +44(0) 1624 898446
www.ferrypubs.co.uk

Chapter One
The Steamship Pioneers

Glasgow is unique in the British Isles in being a large commercial and industrial city located in close proximity to an area of such scenic beauty and variety as the Firth of Clyde. Within only an hour's sailing time from the bustling city centre, travellers find themselves surrounded by soaring mountains, quiet sea lochs, peaceful villages and secluded islands, the waters of the estuary sheltered from the stormy Atlantic Ocean by the Kintyre Peninsula. Nineteenth-century industry found in the Clyde a highway to the markets of the world, and schemes by far-sighted Glaswegians converted the shallow tidal river into a wide and deep ship canal. Trade flourished and, within a few decades, the city became Scotland's commercial capital and the Second City of the British Empire. As Charles Oakley observes, Glasgow owed its burgeoning wealth partly to its inventors, entrepreneurs and engineers, people 'who lived in the Age of Progress and Prosperity, who believed that they were making their way to an Elysium on earth of perpetual content and happiness, and the Later Victorians, who were less sanguine and less satisfied about their world, but who nevertheless lived in times of expansion and did not comprehend how very different things were going to be for the next generation.'[1] Equally, the city's wealth was earned from the hard labour of the working classes, whose lives were often short and squalid.

As industry developed, and as the Clyde was widened and deepened, Glasgow became a communications hub of national and international significance. Routes by road, rail and canal, as well as by sea, converged on the great city. As the writer of the Glasgow entry in the *New Statistical Account of Scotland* noted for 1834:

'The intercourse with Glasgow by coaches, steam-boats, track-boats, and rail-roads, is so great that it almost exceeds belief. As some of the coaches and steam-boats depart and arrive more than once a-day, and the mail-coaches every day, the following may be

taken as a low average of passengers by stage-coaches, and steam-boats; while the others are from the books of the respective companies. During 1834, 61 stage-coaches, each averaging twelve passengers, arrived and departed during 313 lawful days. This gave 458,232 persons in the year. By steam-boats, 25 passengers each, 579,050; by the swift boats on the Forth and Clyde Navigation and Union Canal, 91,975; by the light iron boats on the Paisley Canal, 307,275; by boats on the Monkland Canal, 31,784; and by the Glasgow and Garnkirk Rail-road, 118,882; the gross number of passengers amounting to 1,587,198.[2]

As this writer recognised, crucial to Glasgow's progress was the development of the steamship, which was able to sail to relatively reliable schedules, irrespective of wind and sea conditions. The first regular steamship service in Europe was provided by the *Comet* of 1812, conceived and owned by a local entrepreneur Henry Bell (1767-1830).

Bell was born in Torphichen, West Lothian, the fifth son of Patrick Bell and Margaret Easton. The Bell family firm were well-known millwrights, builders and engineers whose work included the design and construction of dock facilities and bridges. Henry Bell was educated at the local parish school then apprenticed to a local stonemason in 1780. Three years later, he worked with his uncle, who was a millwright. Subsequently, he learned ship modelling in Borrowstounness (Bo'ness) – a busy port on the River Forth engaged in the export of coal to Scandinavia and the Baltic. Thereafter, in 1787, he pursued his interest in mechanical engineering in Bellshill with the engineer James Inglis. This was followed by three years spent in London. In 1790, Bell returned to Scotland, his intention being to establish himself as an engineer. His fertile imagination apparently caused him to be unable to concentrate on any one particular project for long; as his varied early career trajectory shows, he dabbled in many trades, but appeared to master none.

The pioneering sea-going steamship *Comet* intrudes upon a picturesque panoramic depiction of the Firth of Clyde by the renowned nineteenth-century landscape painter John Knox. *(Glasgow Museums and Art Galleries)*

By the turn of the century, however, he decided to focus his attention on persuading the British authorities that steam represented the future for ship propulsion.

Steam navigation had already been attempted in Scotland by William Symington (1764–1831), who was born in Leadhills, a mining village in Lanarkshire where his father worked as a mining mechanic. Although his parents hoped that he would become a minister, in 1875 he moved to Wanlockhead in Dumfriesshire, where his brother George had established a small engine works to manufacture steam engines using James Watt's patent. Symington's work ethic and ability as an engineer greatly impressed the local mining company manager Gilbert Meason – so much so that he paid for him to attend lectures in science at Edinburgh University for a few months in 1786. Thereafter, Symington worked to improve and simplify Watt's design by making use of a second piston to force out condensing steam when fresh steam entered the cylinder. The power piston was thereby enacted through atmospheric pressure on the vacuum caused by the condensing steam.[3]

Symington decided to carry out a trial in order to demonstrate that a steam engine would safely work on a boat without it catching fire. He chose for this experiment a pleasure craft on Dalswinton Loch on the Dalswinton estate near Dumfries. This had been built in 1785 and Symington fitted it with paddles and a steam engine. The trial took place on 14th October 1788 and did ultimately demonstrate that a steam engine would work on a boat.

Next, Symington commissioned a larger engine for testing in a boat on the Forth and Clyde Canal in December 1789. This was unsuccessful, as the engine was too large and powerful and so the paddle wheels disintegrated. A second, more substantially constructed, boat was therefore commissioned from John Allan, a shipbuilder in Grangemouth on the Forth, with a steam engine supplied by the Carron Company of Falkirk, both working to designs prepared by Symington. This was given the name *Charlotte Dundas* in honour of a daughter of the Lord Dundas, the Canal Company's Chairman.[4]

The *Charlotte Dundas* made her first trip on 4th January 1803, with Lord Dundas on board. This was deemed a success and, after Symington made some adjustments, a second more ambitious trial was made on 28th March. On this occasion, the *Charlotte Dundas* towed two loaded barges through the canal, covering 18 miles in 9 hours. Although the *Charlotte Dundas* proved herself, to Symington's disappointment Lord Dundas decided to retain horse-drawn barges rather than switching to steam. Symington therefore failed to capitalise on his inventions and died in poverty.

Symington's achievements in inland waterways were well known to Henry Bell, who in 1800 wrote to Lord Melville, hoping to persuade him that the Royal Navy should adopt steam propulsion at the earliest opportunity. He was rebuffed, but three years later he tried again with the same result. Even the emphatically supportive intervention of the celebrated Lord Nelson could not persuade the Admiralty to co-operate with Bell in adopting steam propulsion and so, having failed to obtain the support of the British establishment, Bell concentrated instead on America, where he found a more receptive and progressive mindset than in the British Admiralty. In 1807 the first American river steamboat appeared, the *North River of Clermont*, devised and built by Robert Fulton. He had previously visited Scotland where he met Symington (and possibly experienced a sail on the *Charlotte Dundas*). As a result, it is likely that Fulton

1 Oakley, 1946, pvi.
2 New Statistical Account, Vol. 6, pp205-6.
3 Bowman, 1989; Symington, 2003.
4 Bowman, 1989; Symington, 2003.

The replica of the *Comet*, which was launched on 1st September 1962 from Lithgow's East Yard, Port Glasgow, the spot where Bell's *Comet* of 1812 took to the water, attracts considerable attention from rowers and those enjoying modern pleasure craft. *(Jim MacIntosh)*

The 1962-built *Comet* replica chugs out of Lithgow's basin. Behind is the Lyle Shipping iron-ore carrier *Cape Howe* - then the largest bulk-cargo vessel ever built by Lithgow's. The warship is the U.S.S. *Roy O. Hale*. *(Jim MacIntosh)*

'absorbed' Symington's techniques, and applied them to his own vessel, thus beating Bell in producing the world's first commercially viable steamship.[5] Fulton's *North River of Clermont* was however a riverboat, operating mainly between New York and Albany, rather than in more exposed waters.

With the Denholm cargo liner *Clarkforth* fitting out ahead, the *Comet* replica is prepared at Lithgow's shipyard for a sail on the Clyde in 1962. *(A. Ernest Glen)*

In 1808, Bell moved to Helensburgh, where he involved himself in the development of a public baths and an adjacent hotel, the Baths Inn, while he continued to work on his steamship design proposals. This work resulted in the commissioning of the *Comet*, a 28-ton wooden-hulled vessel measuring 45 feet in length built by John Wood & Co of Port Glasgow, directly opposite on the Clyde's South Bank. The *Comet* was propelled by a 3-horsepower steam engine designed and manufactured by John Robertson and a boiler made by David Napier, both important Glasgow engineers. The engine was placed on her port side and the boiler to starboard. (The design of the engine may have been influenced by Bell's experience of a small steam engine previously supplied by Napier to pump water into Helensburgh Public Baths.) Two sets of radial paddles were initially fitted, mounted on detached arms on each side of the vessel and driven though spur gearing. The arrangement gave trouble, however, and so single paddle wheels on each side of the hull were substituted. This solution became standard on the majority of Clyde steamers built in the *Comet*'s wake. A yardarm was attached to the tall, thin funnel to enable a sail to be hoisted when there was a following wind. (Incidentally, the name *Comet* was inspired by the visibility of a comet in the night sky for several months in 1811-12.)

David Napier (1790-1869) and his cousin, Robert (1791-1876), are widely recognised as having laid the foundations of marine engineering and shipbuilding on Clydeside. David Napier was an engineer of considerable talent and ingenuity, whose career began in his father's engine works at Camlachie in Glasgow. Robert Napier was born in Dumbarton, the son of a blacksmith and initially he followed in the family business, setting up a foundry in the East End of Glasgow in 1815.

The first commercially successful marine steam engines were adapted directly from James Watt's beam engine which, in turn, stemmed from Newcomen's engine. The machinery built for the *Comet* was an early version of the side-lever engine which, in essence, provided the pattern for a multiplicity of engine types which followed over the next few decades. As paddle wheels were then the only method of converting the power of the engine into motion, developments of the side-lever engine were concerned with maximising the relationship between engine and paddle wheel. Largely due to David Napier's efforts, a series of improved engines was developed from the side-lever engine. Indeed, Napier's steeple engine, in which the piston operated more directly and with fewer moving parts than the side-lever, was soon widely adapted.[6] (This design also had the commercial advantage of occupying less space.)

An unidentified early steamship chugs past Dunglass Castle in this circa 1820 painting by an unknown artist. The sailing ship to the right represents the old order on the Clyde. *(Glasgow Museums and Art Galleries)*

Another picturesque depiction of the Clyde estuary by John Knox, this time an 1820s view from Dalnottar Hill with a steamer in the middle-distance. By then, steamship services had proliferated on the river's firth. *(Glasgow Museums and Art Galleries)*

In August 1812 the *Comet* made her historic inaugural sailing, taking three and a half hours to steam from Port Glasgow to the Broomielaw in the City Centre, then from there downriver to Greenock, making five knots against a head-wind. Bell advertised in local papers:

'THE STEAMBOAT COMET BETWEEN GLASGOW, GREENOCK AND HELENSBURGH FOR PASSENGERS ONLY

The subscriber, having at much expense, fitted up a handsome vessel to ply upon the River Clyde from Glasgow, to sail by the power of air, wind and steam, intends that the vessel shall leave the Broomielaw on Tuesdays, Thursdays and Saturdays about mid-day, or such hour thereafter as may answer to the state of the tide, and to leave Greenock on Mondays, Wednesdays, and Fridays in the morning to suit the tide.'

The fare was four shillings in the vessel's cabin, located aft of the engines and fitted with wooden benches and a table, and three shillings on deck. Thus, even in terms of layout and fare structure, the *Comet* prefaced the generations of Clyde steamers shortly to follow.

Thereafter, the *Comet* offered a passenger service between Glasgow, Greenock and Helensburgh three times a week, returning on alternate days – making her the first commercial steamship in Europe and the prototype for nearly all Clyde steamers built thereafter. In September 1812, the *Comet* visited the West Highlands for the first time, sailing to Fort William via Tarbert, the Crinan Canal, Oban and Port Appin. Four years later, once other steamers were built for Clyde services, Bell switched the *Comet* to the Forth where there was less competition. Bell subsequently had the *Comet* lengthened and re-engined and, in August 1819, she returned to the West Coast, inaugurating a regular service between Glasgow to Fort William which continued until she was lost the following year. In *The Clyde Passenger Steamers* (1904), Captain James Williamson records that:

'On 13 December 1820, on the passage from Fort William to Glasgow, she was caught by the strong tide-race and easterly wind, and wrecked on Doras Mor, outside Crinan. The after part of the

vessel drifted towards Corrievreckan, but the fore end, from which Henry Bell and the crew and passengers scrambled ashore, remained on the rocks, and from it the machinery was afterwards removed.'[7]

The recovered engine was sold for static use, powering machinery in MacLellan's Coachworks in Glasgow. Later, it performed a similar role in a Greenock brewery before being purchased in 1862 by Robert Napier & Sons, whose apprentices restored it for presentation to the South Kensington Museum in London; it is now on display in the Science Museum there. Bell unquestionably gave Britain its lead in steam-powered maritime enterprise; as none other than the great English engineer Isambard Kingdom Brunel wryly noted, 'Bell did what we engineers all failed in – he gave us the sea steamer; his scheming was Britain's steaming'.[8]

As well as designing and building steam engines and ships, David Napier was also heavily involved in the expansion of steamship services to coastal and international routes. The first such service was inaugurated between Greenock and Belfast in 1818 by Napier's *Rob Roy*, built by William Denny of Dumbarton and powered by an engine designed and built at Camlachie. After two seasons, she was sold for service on the Dover Strait and Napier introduced a second, larger steamer, the *Ivanhoe*, built by Scott's of Greenock, between Holyhead and Dublin. In 1822, Napier was involved in the establishment of the City of Glasgow Steam Packet Company, which subsequently introduced a Liverpool-Greenock-Glasgow coastal steamer service and he also invested in a Leith-London route.

All of these early ships were made of wood, but this crucial shipbuilding material had to be imported either from Canada or the nations surrounding the Baltic. Glasgow was, however, surrounded by coalfields and deposits of iron ore – both vital materials in modern engineering and manufacturing processes. At that time, the many shipyards around Britain's coasts built wooden ships. It was not existing shipbuilders, but rather manufacturers of steam engines who viewed iron hull construction as a natural extension of their existing working techniques and practices.[9] (The first iron ship was the *Vulcan*, a canal boat built in 1819 at Faskine on the Monkland Canal by a carpenter, Thomas Wilson, who owned a small shipyard there.)

In 1821, David Napier moved from Camlachie to set up a new engine

5 This is well discussed, using Symington's own commentary, in Fox, 2005, pp23-27.
6 Johnston, 2000, p21.

7 Williamson, 1904, p12.
8 Osborne, 2001, p36.
9 Johnston, 2000, p17.

The second Clyde steamer named *Eagle* to be operated by Captain Buchanan was delivered in 1864 from Charles Connel & Co's shipyard, her predecessor having been sold to American Confederates for use as a blockade runner in the Civil War. The 1864 *Eagle* was notably successful, continuing in Clyde service until 1894 and thereafter serving a further five seasons on the Manchester Ship Canal. The distinctive black funnel livery with a white hoop of Buchanan Steamers Ltd was familiar to generations of Glaswegian excursionists. *(Glasgow Museums and Art Galleries)*

works and shipyard at Lancefield Quay on the north bank of the Clyde, west of the City Centre. His existing works was taken over by the equally talented Robert (who built his first marine steam engine there in 1823 for the paddle steamer *Leven*). At Lancefield, Napier began to construct complete ships, including in 1827 the *Aglaia*, a steamer built to ply Loch Eck, the hull of which had an iron bottom and wooden sides. In 1831, the first ship built in Glasgow of entirely iron construction, the *Fairy Queen*, was delivered from John Neilson & Company's Garscube Road foundry. Crowds cheered loudly as she was transported slowly through Glasgow's streets to the Broomielaw, where she was launched into the Clyde by a steam crane.

In 1835, David Napier purchased a shipyard at Millwall on the River Thames and so he abandoned Clydeside for London and Robert took over his Lancefield premises. Robert Napier's involvement in ship design, construction and operation spanned 50 years and, more than any other single individual, he established Glasgow and the Clyde as the world's leading centre for shipbuilding in the mid-nineteenth century. Indeed, at the time of his death in 1876, one third of all British tonnage was Clyde built.

In 1839, Robert Napier was introduced to Samuel Cunard, who had arrived in Britain from Nova Scotia to tender for a potentially lucrative Admiralty contract to carry the Royal Mail to America. Having won the contract, Cunard was faced with the problem of fulfilling its terms. Napier advised him that larger ships would be required than those he had specified and so, to provide the necessary extra funding, Napier introduced Cunard to two business partners, George Burns and David McIver. Together, the three established the first trans-Atlantic mail steamer service, which later became the Cunard Line, inaugurated by the steamer *Britannia*, engined by Napier and built by John Wood.

In order to expand iron shipbuilding, Napier purchased McArthur and Alexander's shipyard at Govan in 1842. This followed the receipt of an order from the Admiralty to build a pioneering ironclad warship – the *Vanguard*, delivered in 1843. Fulfilling this order was a great achievement for Napier and the result of vociferous lobbying on his part, as hitherto all Royal Naval vessels had been built in the dockyard towns of Southern England. Another

achievement for Napier's diplomacy was Lloyd's agreement in 1844 to grant A1 certificates to iron ships.

The Napiers' early successes in steam engine manufacture and iron shipbuilding encouraged other entrepreneurs to do likewise. Indeed, the Napiers' works were training grounds for a number of talented engineers and shipbuilders – David Tod, John McGregor, William Denny, John Elder and James and George Thomson.[10] By the 1860s, Clyde shipbuilding was transformed into a vast industry of global importance.

As the Clyde's shipyards grew in number, competition for orders between relatively small yards was intense and this gave rise to a rapid development in the design and technology of Clyde steamers. Paterson observes that these vessels,

'…built for passenger service in the shallow waters of the firth [were] unusually good-looking, often very beautiful, and above all, speedy and manoeuvrable. Development of the type reached a high point in late 1850s and some of the better known shipyards produced vessels which were intended primarily as advertisements for their builders.'[11]

The principal builders of these vessels at that time were Tod & McGregor of Partick, James & George Thomson of Govan, Henderson of Renfrew and Blackwood & Gordon of Port Glasgow.

Against this background of a rapidly expanding industrial base and a parallel increase in mercantile wealth, Glasgow's population grew four-fold from 101,000 in 1812 – the year of the *Comet*'s maiden voyage – to 448,000 in 1861. As Charles Oakley records in *The Second City*,

'The picturesque little town of closes could not accommodate such numbers, and old houses, which had looked rather charming in their day, now became shockingly overcrowded. And some of the people who moved to Glasgow made matters even worse by being dirty and verminous in person and unclean in habit. Never was there such a breeding place for disease. Indeed, in 1831 and 1832 such severe outbreaks of typhus and cholera occurred that special ground had to be purchased for the burial of the victims.'[12]

The social and economic impact of the steamship

In the first 30 years or so of the nineteenth century, the steamships which served the Firth of Clyde and the Highlands and Islands were usually owned by wealthy individuals, commonly entrepreneurs of various kinds, industrialists and landlords, or by relatively small steamboat companies, which accumulated the capital to build and sustain a steamboat by bringing interested and well-heeled parties together. The *Britannia*, built in 1815 by John Hunter, Port Glasgow, for example, was owned principally by 'Archibald McTaggart, who was also the first distiller in Campbeltown, and great-grandfather of Mr Dan McTaggart, present [in 1904] Procurator-Fiscal at that place.' Later, after trading to Campbeltown via Rothesay, she passed into the ownership of 'Messrs Alex. A. Laird & Co., of the Londonderry fleet, and was the first steamer owned by that old and energetic firm'.[13] Shipbuilders, such as David Napier, built vessels like the Loch Lomond steamer *Marion* for their own companies. The celebrated baggage-carrying steamboat *Industry* of 1814 was constructed by William Fyfe of Fairlie, whose family later became world-renowned for yacht-building, 'with oak grown in his native parish of Kilbirnie, for a small syndicate of far-seeing speculators belonging to Beith.'[14]

Gradually, through mergers and the pooling of resources, larger companies were formed, like those of George Burns (later to become part of the 'old and energetic firm' of Burns & Laird) and Thomson & McConnell. The latter developed an important and highly influential Highland department, which honed the initial managerial skills of later shipowners like Martin Orme. From 1851 David and Alexander Hutcheson, who had learned their trade within the Burns empire, laid the foundations of what was to become, from 1878, the famous fleet of their erstwhile junior partner, David MacBrayne. MacBrayne was descended from a Gaelic-speaking family who had migrated from mainland Argyll to Glasgow in the late eighteenth century and had joined the mercantile elite. MacBrayne and his company served chiefly the Hebridean islands closest to the mainland, although their ships, which were primarily passenger vessels, also sailed from Portree to Stornoway, as part of a round trip from Glasgow.[15] The outer (western) fringe of the Inner Hebrides and also St Kilda became the territory of other companies, such as the Great West of Scotland Fishery, whose principal concern was the conveyance of cargoes, including fish. The Fishery's steamship manager, Martin Orme, later established his own well-known company with Hebridean concerns. The steamship business attracted 'far-seeing' individuals and syndicates of many different kinds, who were alive to the enormous potential of 'steam navigation'. Even shipmasters were enticed into the business as 'Masters and owners', most notably from the exceptionally talented Williamson and Young families, with their distinguished fleets of Clyde steamers in the second half of the nineteenth century and the early twentieth (in the case of the Williamsons). Shareholding records (as yet seriously under-researched) show a fascinating interaction of investors across the years, and often reveal the all-important contribution of the Glasgow mercantile class as the 'principals' within the industry, who were happy to spread their capital across several different, competing companies.

The development of the steamship and the interests of business, industry, and urban 'energy centres' intersected at many points besides ownership. The steamship helped to create these 'energy centres', and was then sustained by their demands within an ever-expanding network of opportunities, from trade to holiday traffic, as Glasgow well illustrates. With massive in-migration from the Scottish Highlands, Ireland, Italy and Central Europe, the city became notably cosmopolitan. The wealthier of its inhabitants gravitated to the Western suburbs, where the air was cleaner due to the prevailing wind, while the urban poor lived in a belt of slum housing encircling the city centre and in the East End. While the Clyde provided Glasgow with its main artery for international commerce, the river also provided the city's inhabitants with their means of temporary escape to the fresh air, spaciousness and scenic splendour of the river's Firth and so, in the wake of the *Comet*, a large number of entrepreneurs introduced steamer services from the Broomielaw to the attractive watering places downriver.

The extent of public confidence in those early steamships – given the likelihood of wreckings, boiler explosions, collisions, stormy seas and many other unanticipated dangers – is remarkable. Steamboat services had reached Rothesay as early as 1814, and Campbeltown and Inveraray by 1815. As early as 1816, James Cleland, Superintendent of Public Works in Glasgow and an avid statistician, noted that, in less than four years, the volume of passenger traffic between Glasgow and Greenock had risen tenfold.[16] He continued:

'Owing to the novelty and dangers of the passage in the Firth below Dumbarton, the numbers of passengers were at the outset but small. The public, however, having gained confidence by degrees, the watering places all along the coast have been crowded with company beyond all former precedent, in consequence of steam conveyance.'[17]

In 1826, the Prussian architect, Karl Friedrich Schinkel, 'found on his visit to Glasgow…that there were no fewer than 60 to 70 steamboat advertisements posted up in George Square, most of which were offering pleasure trips either to the Scottish lochs or to Staffa and Iona.'[18] He regarded the steamships as having a 'civilising role', and noted:

'These boats are always full of people, Scots going South to have a look at the new splendours of Glasgow and Edinburgh, or Southerners seeking the Highlands out of curiosity.'[19]

By the mid-1830s, more than three-dozen steamers were sailing to the Firth of Clyde and other destinations as far away as Stranraer, Ayr, Campbeltown, Arrochar and Lochgilphead. In 1836-39 the writer of the relevant section of the *New Statistical Account* waxed lyrical in his description of shipping in the vicinity of Bowling:

'After passing the village [of Old Kilpatrick], the house of Glenarbuck is seen imbedded in trees, giving the idea of all that is peaceful and sheltered, and retired; and then not far off at the river's edge, is Bowling Bay, at the mouth of the Forth and Clyde Canal, with its basin and docks, and all the bustle of merchandize and ship-building. Beyond this, rise in great beauty the hills and woods of Auchentorlie. To complete the view, there is often a multitude of vessels in sight; the ferry-boat crossing with its load of carts and carriages, and live-stock of all kinds, the gay steamer with decks crowded, flags flying, and band of music playing, the powerful tug with her steam and smoke, dragging her half dozen of vessels, with yard and sail, some of which have probably come from the most distant parts of the world; and sailing vessels of all descriptions, making their way up or down, as wind and tide serve their purpose.'[20]

10 Johnston, 2000, pp16-17.
11 Paterson, 1972, pp13-14.
12 Oakley, 1946, p47.
13 Williamson, 1904, p29.
14 Williamson, 1904, p24.

15 Robins and Meek, 2006, pp48-49.
16 Durie, 2003, p48.
17 Durie, 2003, p48.
18 Durie, 2003, p50.
19 Durie, 2003, p50.

The scenic splendours and bracing air of the Firth of Clyde continue to provide a pleasant backdrop for travellers on the modern-day car ferries of Caledonian MacBrayne. Here, the versatile 1974-built *Jupiter* approaches Gourock in early 2009 towards the end of her long Clyde career. She was subsequently sold for scrapping in Denmark. *(Bruce Peter)*

The variety of shipping, which was to increase dramatically during the following century, is immediately apparent. Cross-river and upriver communications were transformed by such activity. 'The town of Dumbarton,' enthused the same writer, 'is distant from Glasgow about fifteen miles, and from Greenock about seven. There are two steamers belonging to a company in Dumbarton, which sail to and from each of these places twice a day…The chief means of travelling are the steam-boats on the Clyde, which pass up and down almost every hour of the day.'[21] The writer of the Roseneath entry similarly noted that:

'Not many years ago, an open packet boat from the Row and Kilcraigin ferries was the ordinary mode of conveyance to Greenock; often against wind and tide would hours be spent in crossing the frith [*sic*]; now, there are two or three steam-boats at all seasons, and in summer, arrivals and departures at the Gareloch ferry seven or eight times a day.'[22]

With such regular steamship services now prevalent, it was inevitable that the complexion of the communities of the lower firth would be transformed. The writer of the section describing the united parish of Dunoon and Kilmun drew attention to the remarkable change in its 'territorial aspects…by the erection of villages and by agricultural improvements', in 'so brief a period as little more than twenty years'. This, he observed,

'must be attributed to the wonderful powers of the steam-engine applied to the purposes of navigation. Previous to the era of this

discovery (not of steam power, but of steam navigation,) the access from this parish and from the neighbouring districts to the low country and towns on the Clyde was tedious, uncertain, and sometimes dangerous.'[23]

The transforming power of the steamship was also felt in Bute. The writer of the *NSA* entry for Rothesay was struck by the increase in the speed and power of the steamships since 'the first steamer reached Rothesay quay in 1814; [when] its speed was six miles an hour':

'Seven steam vessels ply regularly to and from Glasgow, of from 80 to 100 tons each, exclusive of engine space. Their power of steam from 50 to 70 horses each, and their speed eleven miles an hour. Their value from £3000 to £5000 each. Fares to or from Glasgow,

cabin 2s., steerage 1s. 6d. They are navigated by 70 men, steward's department included.'[24]

The writer of the entry for the Arran parish of Kilbride went beyond his own day, and donned the mantle of a prophet, as he gladly envisaged the arrival of long-stay summer tourists and the building of holiday-homes, as a result of enhanced steamship communications:

'Whitingbay [*sic*], to the south of Lamlash, is here entitled to its own share of notice. It wants the bold features of the scenery further north; but it presents many spots of soft and romantic beauty, more especially about the glen of Ashdale. Here, as well as elsewhere along the coast, most eligible spots for neat and elegant villas are continually meeting the eye; and if it suited the views of the

20 New Statistical Account, Vol. 8, p16.
21 New Statistical Account, Vol. 8, p12, 30.
22 New Statistical Account, Vol. 8, p127.

23 New Statistical Account, Vol. 7, p608.
24 New Statistical Account, Vol. 5, p111.

proprietor to grant building-leases, all these would soon be occupied. Opulent individuals from Glasgow and Ayrshire would in a few years ornament the whole line of coast from Sannox to Largiebeg, with a succession of neat summer habitations for themselves and families, and make Arran the most attractive island in the West Highlands.'[25]

The steamship opened new opportunities for trade too, including the conveyance of cattle. 'There are no market-towns either in the parish or island,' wrote the scribe for Kilbride, continuing:

'The people carry their cattle and produce to market in the different towns in the mainland; principally Saltcoats and Ardrossan; with which there is regular steam communication throughout the year. The Isle of Arran steam-packet plies between Arran and Ardrossan, twice a-week during the winter and spring months, and in summer daily. From the beginning of June till the end of September, the steam-boats of the Castle Company ply regularly between Glasgow and Arran twice a-week.'[26]

The benefits of sending livestock and other produce to Lowland markets by steamship were noted by the minister of Lochgoilhead and Kilmorich, Argyll, who was able to write approvingly in the *New Statistical Account*:

'But the most striking variation between the present state of things and that which existed a few years ago, is occasioned by the arrival of steam vessels in the parish itself, and in the neighbourhood. Black-cattle and sheep, instead of being driven a long distance,

greatly to the deterioration of their condition, are put on board a steamer, and arrive in a few hours in Greenock and Glasgow. The herrings fished near the head of Lochfine, instead of being 'carried in creels to Lochgoil-head, a distance of eight or ten miles, and injured by frequent handling,' are now sent in boxes by steam to the market, which they reach on the same day they are caught.'[27]

By the 1830s, villages and towns in the lower Firth of Clyde and in the Clyde estuary were building piers to facilitate loading and unloading. One of the first towns to do so was Largs, as the writer of the entry in the *New Statistical Account* relates:

'When steam-boats began to ply between Glasgow and Largs, the want of a harbour was much felt in the landing of passengers and goods. Upon application to Sir Thomas Macdougal Brisbane, Bart., he agreed to give the ground for a pier, to take shares for the price, and to extend the boundaries of the harbour from Haylie to Noddleburn; a subscription was entered into; an act of Parliament applied for, and obtained in May 1832; the foundation stone laid with masonic honours, 10th January 1833, after the work was in considerable progress. It was first used, 1st December 1834. The cost was £4275, which is held in £50 shares. The number of shareholders is 31. The average revenue, for the last six years, has been six per cent. The benefit it affords, in landing and shipping passengers and goods &c. is very great.'[28]

When the occasion demands, Caledonian MacBrayne's ferries are used for special excursions. Here, the *Saturn* is dressed with signal flags and well loaded with spectators to witness the final visit to the Clyde of the famous Cunard trans-Atlantic liner *Queen Elizabeth 2* on 5th October 2008. *(Bruce Peter)*

The West of Scotland climate is notorious for its high rainfall - a circumstance which must have made travel on the early Clyde steamers an uncomfortable experience. In contrast, today's large and well-appointed ferries provide agreeable crossings even in poor weather. When the sun breaks through, the ships and scenery appear particularly dramatic, as the Arran ferry *Caledonian Isles* demonstrates when approaching Ardrossan in May 2008. *(Bruce Peter)*

The writer for Dunoon and Kilmun reported similarly:

'...it may be noticed, that to obviate the inconvenience of landing from steamers in open boats, a private joint-stock Company was entered into in the year 1835, for the object of erecting a pier or jetty, at which steamers might touch at all states of the tide. The object has thoroughly succeeded. The jetty extends 130 yards from the shore into about 4 fathoms water, and has seven feet water at its extremity at the lowest tide. A pontage of one penny is levied on every passenger landing or embarking, and proportional rates upon goods, furniture &c. Though requiring extensive repairs annually, it is understood to yield a good return for the capital invested. It is an immense accommodation and benefit to the village and parish. A more substantial quay, of solid masonry, has been erected by Mr Napier at Kilmun, rendering the landing there easy and comfortable at every state of the tide.'[29]

As these entries indicate, steamships were not only changing the fabric of society, they were also offering new economic opportunities to communities in and beyond the Clyde estuary. Their overall effect on the region, particularly in stimulating the tourist trade, is well summarised by Alan J.S. Paterson in his *Victorian Summer of the Clyde Steamers*:

'...Every corner of the firth resounded to the beat of paddles and a veritable fleet of ships linked the city to the quiet communities of the estuary. Glasgow had discovered the Clyde and in the abiding affections of generations of her citizens for the scenic glories of the Firth there began a love affair that has lasted into modern times. Nourished by frequent and cheap services, traffic to the coast expanded mightily; quiet villages such as Rothesay and Dunoon grew into prosperous towns, to which thousands were glad to escape from the claustrophobic background of Victorian Glasgow. The well-to-do early appreciated the advantages of living at the coast and travelling daily to the city on business and took their families to Clyde resorts for the summer. Ground was feued in many places, and imposing villas built for the successful businessmen whose employees need be content with day trips from up the river. There came the cult of the coasting 'season' and the annual ritual of the Glasgow Fair when the whole population, or thus it seemed, made for the Clyde.'[30]

As steamship services radiated progressively outwards from Glasgow's famed Broomielaw and from other harbours along the banks of the Clyde, that same revolution soon reached the more distant Hebrides and the northern Highlands. In the Highlands and Islands, as well as in the Lowlands, the steamship lay at the very heart of Improvement, as Henry Bell recognised from the outset.

25 New Statistical Account, p5.
26 New Statistical Account, p32.
27 New Statistical Account, Vol. 7, p718.

28 New Statistical Account, Vol. 5, pp804-5.
29 New Statistical Account, Vol. 7, p618.
30 Paterson, 1972, pp13-14.

Chapter Two

Hebridean Steamers, Modernity and Romanticism

Henry Bell was immensely perceptive in his understanding that the steamship was about to transform the world beyond anyone's reckoning. He forecast that it would open new opportunities for the Highlands and Islands, and did his utmost to enlist the support of Highland landlords, most notably MacKenzie of Seaforth, telling Seaforth bluntly in 1820:

> '…You landed Gentlemen ought to dow a grate deal more than you dow in forming improvements in your Ilands and coast of the Highlands…the most pairt of the land gentlemen is so much taken up with politicks, gamblin and other trifling amusements that they both neglect their own Intrest and the Intrest of their countray.
>
> … What a grat Diffrance would be if each landowner war coming forward with marchants, stor ceapers [store-keepers] and fisherman in small improvements for the good of the Countray – it wold go forward with a quite Diffrant spirit for they wold be saying our laird is taking an intrist in this …'[31]

According to Bell, participation in his great 'scheme' of steamship services would give the landowners a golden opportunity to redeem their tarnished image. Although MacKenzie, an old-style patriarchal figure, appeared reluctant, and generally landed interest in such vessels was somewhat tardy at the outset, patterns were altering by the 1840s as Highland and Island estates changed hands. James Matheson, who was also known as 'MacDrug' because of his opium-trading in the China Seas, succeeded Mrs MacKenzie of Seaforth as proprietor of Lewis in 1844. He initiated steamship services to Glasgow with the assistance of the Duke of Sutherland, and so too did John Ramsay of Kildalton, Islay, who had a deep

The Skye ferry service from Kyle of Lochalsh to Kyleakin operated until October 1995 when a new bridge opened. As the final generation of ferries, consisting of the *Loch Fyne* and *Loch Dunvegan* dated only from 1991, both were re-deployed on other Caledonian MacBrayne routes. *(Bruce Peter)*

commitment to Islay's whisky industry.[32] Both Matheson and Ramsay, who co-operated in the provision of steamship services to the Outer and Inner Hebrides, represented the new class of nouveau riche island landlords who had made their money in Lowland industry, and had bought out earlier patriarchal landowners.[33] Aware of the central importance of transport to economic progress because of their own industrial ventures, they were more anxious than their predecessors to improve their estates by encouraging 'steam navigation'. Such navigation belonged to the same spirit of Improvement as had created the Crinan and Caledonian Canals, which were to be of strategic significance in the development of early steamship routes. By means of the steamship, Bell hoped to '…Obtain the grate object of cheap and expedishous conveyance of cattle pipale and goods between the western Ilands and the low country…'[34]

His vision came to pass in large measure before his death in 1830, at least for 'pipale and goods', but new opportunities also posed new challenges, and, even in the 1820s, the transformation wrought by the steamship could be inimical, as well as beneficial, to the areas it served. As an English tourist, John Eddowes Bowman, noted perceptively as early as 1825, a mere five years after Bell had written to Seaforth:

> 'These steam vessels have opened so frequent, so expeditious, and so easy a communication between Glasgow and the whole of the Hebrides and the western coast of Scotland, that they are effecting considerable changes in those remote places.'[35]

Tourists and sight-seers

The first steamships from the Clyde to reach the Highlands and Islands were patronised, in the main, by well-to-do tourists who were under the spell of popular literary works which were based on the Gaelic poems of the legendary blind bard, Ossian, but which reflected all too clearly the creative hand of their translator James Macpherson (1736-96).[36] The fact that they were prepared to risk their lives on board these relatively small and recently built vessels is testimony to the romantic magnetism of Highland myth and mist. From at least 1818, tiny ships like the *Highland Chieftain*, with flimsy paddles and spindly 'funnels' which doubled as masts, were battling their way northwards through the Crinan Canal, and into the land of Ossian. By the mid-1820s, the second generation of such vessels, represented by the *Maid of Morven*, built in 1826, were able to impart the full grandeur of the Ossianic experience to finely attired ladies and monacled gentlemen with telescopes and drawing-paper at the ready.[37]

The Rev. Dr Norman MacLeod ('Caraid nan Gàidheal'), a nationally important Gaelic-speaking clergyman and writer who was latterly minister of St Columba's Church of Scotland, Glasgow, had his family roots in Morvern. Like others of his kind, he was fully aware that a powerful new means of propulsion had indeed entered the Highlands, and that its success was inevitable. In his Gaelic account of rustic Highlanders travelling to Glasgow on the *Maid of Morven* in 1829, his mouth-piece, Finlay the Piper, is able to observe a deck-load of posh tourists:

> 'Cò bha an deireadh na luinge ach Alasdair Ruadh mac an Abraich, Tighearna Cholla. Mhothaich e dhomh fhèin, agus smèid e orm – cha robh math a dhiùltadh – bha mòran uaislean shìos leis air clàr deiridh na luinge; Sasannaich, Goill, agus Frangaich. Cuid dhiubh a' leughadh, cuid nan cadal, cuid a' miananaich, cuid ag ithe. Fear dhiubh le gloinn'-amhairc fhada, rìomhach ra shùil, mar gum biodh e dol a losgadh air Caisteal Dubhaird; mhothaich mi fear fada, caol, glas-neulach le speuclair air a shròin, is bioran ruadh na làimh leis an robh e tarraing dealbh a' chaisteil. Bha baintighearna mhòr, rìomhach nam measg, agus measan leibideach de chù beag, mollach na h-uchd, ris an robh i a' brìodal, agus ga phògadh; agus dà mhaighdinn òg leatha, air na robh rud nach faca mi riamh roimhe, brigisean geala anairt, fon chuid eile dan aodach. Thug mi fhèin a-mach a' phìob mar a dh'iarr iad, ach a' chiad sgal a thug i, theich gach aon diubh ach aon Sasannach mòr, reamhar, a shuidh mum choinneamh le dhà mheur na chluasaibh, agus sgraing air mar gum bithinn a' dol ga ithe.'

'Who was in the stern of the ship but Red-haired Alasdair mac an Abraich [lit., 'son of the Lochaber man'], the Laird of Coll. He noticed me, and he beckoned to me – I did not dare to refuse him – there were many toffs down there with him on the quarter-deck of the ship: English folk, Lowlanders and French folk. Some of them reading, some sleeping, some yawning, some eating. One of them [had] a long, fancy telescope to his eye, as if he were going to fire at Duart Castle; I noticed a tall, thin, sallow-complexioned man with a monacle on his nose and a red stick in his hand with which he was drawing a picture of the castle. There was a large, posh noblewoman among them with a poor, wee, hairy yapper of a dog on her lap, which she was fondling and kissing; and there were two young maids with her who wore something that I had never seen before, white trousers of linen, under the rest of their clothes. I myself brought out the pipes as they asked, but the first blast they gave, all of them fled except one big, fat Englishman who sat in front of me with his two fingers in his ears, and with a scowl as if I were going to eat him.'[38]

Descriptions of fellow passengers are set pieces in writing of this kind. MacLeod's depiction can be paralleled, from the tourist's perspective, in a journal written by John Eddowes Bowman, who, with his friend, John Dovaston, sailed from Glasgow via the Crinan Canal to Staffa on the *Highlander* in 1825. According to Bowman, 'The passengers on board [the

Oban's busy port has long been the 'Gateway to the Isles' and, today, three of Caledonian MacBrayne's most important ferries operate from there. In this early summer scene dating from 2008, the Oban-Craignure ferry *Isle of Mull* is passing the inbound *Lord of the Isles* in Oban Bay, the latter serving Barra, Colonsay, South Uist, Coll and Tiree. *(Bruce Peter)*

Highlander] were very numerous, but being exclusively a ship of pleasure, they were all people of respectability, some indeed of superior understanding and manners; many of them English, but chiefly Scotch or Hebrideans.'[39] Bowman's learned friend, Dovaston, had the knack of pouring forth knowledge, spouting 'Ossian' and attracting the attention of travellers (often females), to the extent of upsetting 'the proper equilibrium of the vessel'. In addition, as they were of the right social class (as retired lawyer and banker respectively), he and Bowman had access to persons of considerable social status.

Clearly, such ships were patronised at this stage pre-eminently by well-to-do tourists, who were desperately anxious to meet 'respectable' people of their own kind, and not 'rustics'. MacLeod's clever narrative, however, reverses the standard 'flow', and makes MacLean of Coll shake hands with an ordinary man of the Highlands, rather than a well-to-do tourist. It also suggests that, in certain cases, local dignitaries were willing to countenance the 'lower classes', particularly if there was a 'professional' interest of some kind, such as piping or poetry. This encouraged a narrowing of social

distance, even if that was only temporary. For the 'ordinary' passenger, 'being noticed' by the chief or laird may have added some glamour to the transition to urban squalor, or it may have offered an 'introduction' to the Ossianic Highlands, just as 'sitting at the Captain's table' not only reinforced the Captain's rank, but also offered a 'feel-good factor', as well as an introduction to the 'high command', for passengers in class-conscious liners (and MacBrayne vessels) at a much later stage. Indeed, Finlay writes home proudly about his encounter with the Laird of Coll. The ship may thus have acted initially as a means of reinforcing 'respectability', and as a vehicle for a small degree of social integration, by bringing the different classes together on the same deck.[40]

The romantic cultural mist, enveloping early nineteenth-century Highland adventure tourism, is well captured by Bowman:

'I scarcely know how to describe the scenery which surrounded us as we steered westward for the shores of Mull. Before us was a fine expanse of water, guarded by the venerable ruins of ancient castles, and hemmed in by bleak hills, above which rose the pale

peaked tops of Mull, Morvern, Appin, and Lorn, forming a circular back screen of great magnificence and grandeur. We are now in the regions and scenes of Ossian; 'and the silence of noon sleeps on an hundred isles, the sun glitters fervid on the curving sea, yet desolate is the dwelling of Morna', and we called up in our fancy the deeds of other days, a tale of the times of old…The mind was quite bewildered by the sublimity of the scenery, and the multiplicity of objects that pressed upon our attention – Dunolly, Duart, Aros, and Dunstaffnage castles were all in sight; while the pale ghosts of Ossian slept up on the hills of Morvern and of Lorn – every name, every object, awakened some recollection, enshrined in history or embalmed in song.'[41]

A year later, the Sound of Mull was visited by what was probably the largest European steamship to date – the *United Kingdom*, a representative of the aptly named 'Leviathan class', built by Robert Steele of Greenock in 1826, with two 100-horsepower engines.[42] Her maiden voyage from Greenock took her round the Mull of Kintyre, through the Sound of Mull (with similar evocations of 'the mists … on the hills of Morven'), westwards to Staffa, north-eastwards to Rum and then across to the Outer Hebrides and Stornoway.[43] By all accounts, the ship was luxuriously appointed – 'The unpleasant tremor and periodical stroke, which shakes most steam vessels, were scarcely perceptible when the ear was close upon

30 Paterson, 1972, pp13-14.
31 Osborne, 2001, p153. The spelling remains Bell's.
32 Ramsay, 1969, pp29-31. Ramsay's first vessel was the *Modern Athens*, which he was encouraged to buy by Walter Frederick Campbell of Islay. Thereafter he became, with Charles Morrison of Basildon, half-owner of Campbell's former steamship, the *Islay*, which included Port Rush in Ireland on its itinerary between Islay and Glasgow. Campbell of Islay, who represented the older class of patriarchal landlords, had thus invested in steamships before he became bankrupt in 1848. Ramsay maintained his interest in shipping until his death in 1892.
33 Devine, 1994, pp63-83.

34 Osborne, 2001, p154.
35 Bowman, 1986, p124.
36 Gaskill, 1996.
37 Meek, 2008, pp67-71.
38 Meek, 2008, p68.
39 Bowman, 1986, pp91-92.
40 MacLeod's account suggests that the stern or quarter-deck of the *Maid of Morven* accommodated the 'better class', while the rustics were given the midships section.
41 Bowman, 1986, pp99-100.
42 Gardiner, 1993, p15, p27.

Viewed from the pier at Port Askaig on Islay, the 1985-built *Hebridean Isles* departs for Kennacraig in autumn afternoon sunlight. Whisky exports and whisky-related tourism form a major part of Caledonian MacBrayne's trade to and from the island. *(Bruce Peter)*

the pillow…'[44] A good time was obviously had by all of the 120 or so passengers:

'We anchored off the village of Tobermory at four o' clock, having run about 240 miles, with the wind unfavourable the whole way, in 21 hours. The dinner was a most plentiful one. The liquors provided were excellent of their kind, Champagne, Claret, Madeira, Port, and Sherry; not to omit some beautiful old rum, which, with the aid of good lemons, limes, and iced water, was converted, by the hands of the Glasgow connoisseurs, into equally beautiful rum punch. Some gentlemen, who went ashore after dinner, preferred Tobermory whiskey, and returned quite loquacious in its praise. The crops in Mull are far advanced, and generally excellent. There is, indeed, throughout the whole of the western islands, every prospect of an abundant harvest.'[45]

In Stornoway, the *United Kingdom* attracted great attention, hardly surprisingly:

'In a few minutes the village seemed to have emptied itself of its inhabitants, for every boat that could float bore groups of men, women, and children, to behold what the greater number had never seen before, namely, a steam-vessel. Captain Oman gave orders that their curiosity should be gratified to the fullest extent.'[46]

From Stornoway, the great ship sailed round Cape Wrath to Orkney, anchoring in Stromness Bay, where she was also regarded with amazement. Re-crossing the Pentland Firth to Wick, the *United Kingdom* proceeded down the east coast of Scotland to Newhaven, where her voyage

terminated. Such immense ships, which foreshadowed the cruise liners of the twentieth century, fitted the Hebrides into the wider geography of sea-borne tourism, and introduced islanders to steam power on a very large scale (by the standards of the time).[47] Curiosity on the part of tourists viewing 'sublimity' was more than matched by curiosity on the part of the islanders, when such 'wonders' appeared on their coastlines.

In the context of tours which aimed to explore the land of Ossian, however, St Kilda had climactic significance. Its particular remoteness, off the western edge of the Hebrides, and its towering pinnacles inspired even greater sentiments of awe and terror and sublime beauty than Staffa or any other island. The thrill of reaching St Kilda must have been enhanced by the dangers inherent in sailing into the 'liminal' and the 'unknown' on an early steamship.

The first steamship to reach St Kilda is said to have been the 131-ton *Glen Albyn*, which left Glasgow on 21st July 1834, 15 years after Henry Bell's *Comet* of 1812 had established a passenger service between the Clyde and Fort William. The *Glen Albyn* was owned by the Glen Albyn Steamship Company. Her complement of some 50 or 60 people consisted of well-to-do travellers, including Sir John and Lady Ord, 'a few young Englishmen and foreigners', and a group of geologists. The journey from Tobermory to St Kilda proceeded by way of the Spar Cave in Skye and Loch Bracadale.[48]

The pattern of 'steamer tours to St Kilda' was now established. In 1835, the Glasgow publisher W.R. McPhun produced a notice of steamship services which included the following paragraph:

'All the Steam Vessels call at Greenock and Port Glasgow both going and coming. The *Glen Albyne* [sic], *Foyle* and *St Columb*, during the summer months make some delightful pleasure excursions round all the West Coast, stopping a few hours for the accommodation of tourists at each place. No person who comes to Scotland for pleasure should lose the opportunity thus afforded them of viewing at little cost and in little time the most delightful scenery in Scotland. These vessels touch at St Kilda, Iona, Caulin Hills, Spar Cave, Skye, Giant's Causeway, Campbeltown, Jura, Islay, Sound of Mull etc, etc.'[49]

McPhun's advertisement suggests that at least three steamships were capable of reaching St Kilda in 1835. However, the second ship to reach the archipelago is said to have been the 214-ton *Vulcan*, which made harbour in Village Bay on 28th July 1838. Normally on the Liverpool service, she belonged to the Glasgow Steam Packet Company. Leaving the Broomielaw on 25th July, she sailed via the Giant's Causeway, Staffa, Iona, Loch Scavaig, Loch Coruisk and Lochmaddy – the beauty-spots of the standard 'Ossianic tour' of the time, which suggests that admirers of the Sublime were on the passenger list.[50]

The *Vulcan*'s real purpose, however, was rather more mundane, as she functioned largely as a cargo-ship, carrying 'furnishings' for 21 new houses being built in St Kilda. Her passengers included the Rev. Neil MacKenzie, the minister of St Kilda, who had obtained the 'furnishings' in Glasgow, and the Rev. Dr Norman MacLeod who had apparently helped to meet the cost of these items. On arrival, MacLeod preached to the islanders and celebrated communion.[51]

The use of the steamship to convey tourists, cargo and ministers to St Kilda very neatly summarises the potential of such vessels to change aspects of life as fundamental as the housing-stock of the Highlands and Islands. This same prescription of tourists and cargo, with a few passengers, was to serve St Kilda until its evacuation in 1930. Likewise, the presence of the Rev. Norman MacLeod on the *Vulcan*, and his role in providing 'furnishings', hints at the potential importance of religiously based philanthropy in developing the role of steamships, and in contributing to the increasingly evangelical ethos not only of St Kilda, but also of the Hebrides as a whole.

Seasonal and long-term migration

The Rev. Dr Norman MacLeod argued that Highlanders would benefit from the steamship when they had come to terms with it and learnt how to use it. There would, however, be losses as well as gains to the people and their region – loss of dignity, as Highlanders became part of the industrial machine, and loss of cultural identity and time-honoured customs, as new fashions from the Lowlands displaced traditional Gaelic practices. For migrants from the Highlands, there was also the danger of contamination by, and potential absorption into, the great cities of the south, as the first vessels commonly sailed to and from the Clyde.[52]

From the mid-1820s, it is clear that the steamship was indeed being used to convey Highlanders and Hebrideans to Lowland harvest-fields. The *Inverness Courier* reported that in the first two weeks of August 1827:

'Upwards of 2,500 Highland shearers [i.e. reapers and harvest

workers] passed through the Crinan Canal for the South, in the steamboats Ben Nevis, Comet and Highlander, from the islands of Mull, Skye, etc.'[53]

The Outer Hebrides also contributed to this important seasonal, and thus temporary, migration. James Matheson, proprietor of Lewis, built the iron paddle steamer *Mary Jane* in 1846, and circumstances soon encouraged him to use her for the public good. In February 1847, Matheson employed the *Mary Jane* to transport, free of charge, seasonal migrants from the Hebrides to the Broomielaw – between 200 and 300 young men from Lewis, Harris and Skye:

'The steamer returned over a month later with a further 400 passengers, about a quarter of whom were 'females desirous of obtaining country service', and the rest were men recruited by the railway companies. By August 1847 the vessel had brought 2256 individuals to the Clyde ports from the Hebrides.'[54]

By the end of the nineteenth century, men from Mingulay were prepared to sail their skiffs south-eastwards across the Minch to the island of Coll, where they met the *Dunara Castle*, which transported them to the mainland for seasonal work.[55] Herring-girls too were normally conveyed by steamship from the Outer Hebrides to the mainland and Orkney and Shetland, as the 'silver darlings' worked their way eastwards round the Scottish coast, and southwards to East Anglia. Special sailings by company steamers, or diversions from normal routes, were sometimes arranged for the benefit of herring-workers. Coming to the aid of seasonal sportsmen likewise from at least the 1860s, the steamships, with appropriate route diversions, worked in association with fishing lodges, such as Finsbay in Harris.[56]

In travelling to seasonal and potentially long-term employment in Glasgow and beyond, Highlanders and Islanders would get their first experience of the great city, its opportunities – and dangers. In his 1829 essay, the Rev. Dr Norman MacLeod was at pains to warn 'innocent' Gaels of what might await them on their arrival at the Broomielaw, and how they ought to find lodgings with friends:

'*Air an là màireach ràinig sinn Glaschu, àite ris an canar am Broomielaw; b' e sin ceidhe na h-ùpraid. Luingeas na smùide a' falbh agus a' teachd làn sluaigh, mar gum biodh an saoghal a' dol do Ghlaschu, agus an saoghal a' teicheadh às. O nach d'fhàs mi bodhar leis a' ghleadhraich a bha 'm chluasaibh, cha chùram leam gun caill mi mo chlaisteachd tuilleadh. Bha sreath dhaoine (portairean a' cheidhe) air an tarraing suas fa chomhair nan soithichean le ball cainbe mu ghuala gach aoin diubh, agus bràiste rìomhach air uchd. Bha iad seo a' smèideadh oirnn mar a bha sinn a' dol gu tìr, a h-uile beul fosgailte mar gum biodh iad a' cur fàilte oirnn; gach làmh sìnte, agus gach sùil siùbhlach mar gum biodh iad ag iarraidh luchd-eòlais. Bha aon fhear gu h-àraidh a shocraich a shùil orm fhèin, agus air dhomh amharc air gu geur, a dh'fheuch an cuimhnichinn cò e, chuir e làmh ra aid, agus chrom e cheann cho modhail, shìobhalta, 's nach b' urrainn domh gun an fhàilt a fhreagradh; ann am priobadh na sùla bha e air clàr na luinge, agus thog e leis bocsa mo phìoba agus màileid Phara Mhòir, cho èasgaidh 's a ghlacadh gàidsear Thobar Mhoire buideal uisge-bheatha, gun chuireadh, gun*

43 The Kaleidoscope, August 1826. We owe this very important, and hitherto unnoticed, reference to Dr Donald William Stewart.
44 The Kaleidoscope, August 1826, p42.
45 'The Kaleidoscope, August 1826, p42.
46 The Kaleidoscope, August 1826, p43.
47 Robins, 2008, provides a valuable overview of patterns of maritime cruising in and from the United Kingdom from the nineteenth century to the present day.
48 Robson, 2005, pp337-8.
49 McPhun, 1835.

50 Robson, 2005, pp344-8.
51 Robson, 2005, pp344-8.
52 Meek, 2008.
53 Osborne, 2001, p185.
54 Devine, 1988, p159
55 Storey, 2007, p26
56 For an account of Finsbay Lodge, see Gardner (forthcoming), and for details of the Youngs, see Meek (forthcoming)

Streaks of sunshine flash across the village of Tarbert, Harris, where Caledonian MacBrayne's ferry *Hebrides* is berthed at the linkspan. Operating the 'Uig triangle' routes from Skye to North Uist and Harris, the ferry was built in 2000 by Ferguson Shipbuilders on the Clyde and is a near sister to the *Clansman*. *(Bruce Peter)*

chead. 'Air d' athais,' arsa Para Mòr. 'An cuala tu riamh, mo ghille math, mar a thuirt Clag Sgàin, "An rud nach buin duit, na buin da"?' 'Leanaibh mis', a dhaoine uaisle,' ars an duine, agus e falbh ceum romhainn. ''S ann sa bhaile mhòr fhèin,' a deir mis', 'a tha 'm modh. Is fhad' on a chuala mi gum bi gill' aig an fheannaig fhèin san fhoghar.' Dh'iarr sinn air e gar toirt gu taigh Eòghainn Oig, far an d'rinn iad ar beatha gu cridheil.'

'The next day we arrived in Glasgow, [at] a place that they call the Broomielaw; that certainly was the quay of commotion. Steamships going and coming full of people, as if the world were going to Glasgow, and the world escaping from it. Since I did not become deaf with the clamour in my ears, I have no fear that I will lose my hearing ever again. A row of men (dock porters) were drawn up before the vessels with a hemp rope about the shoulder of each of them, and a fancy badge on his chest. They were waving to us as we were going ashore, every mouth open as if they were welcoming us; every hand stretched out as if they were looking for acquaintances. There was one man particularly who settled his eye on myself, and when I looked closely to see if I could recognise him, he raised his hand to his hat, and he bowed his head in such a mannerly, genteel way that I could not but respond to his welcome; in the twinkling of an eye he was on the deck of the ship, and he took away my pipe-box and Para Mòr's bag as nimbly as the Tobermory gauger would

confiscate a cask of whisky, without invitation, without permission. 'Take it easy,' said Para Mòr. 'Have you not heard, my fine lad, what the Bell of Scone said, "The thing that has nothing to do with you, do not take anything to do with it"?' 'Follow me, gentlemen,' said the man, as he took a step ahead of us. 'It is in the big city,' I said, 'that one really finds manners. It is a long time since I first heard the saying that even the hoodie crow itself will have a servant in autumn.' We asked him to take us to Young Eòghann's house, where they gave us a hearty welcome.' [57]

The description of Glasgow, and particularly of the Broomielaw, offered in this concluding section of Finlay's letter catches the atmosphere and activity of the famous quay, traditionally thick with people, smoke and steamships. The implied contrast with Finlay's secluded home area is well made. The reference to Eòghann Og acknowledges the existence of a colony of urban Gaels with local segments, whose members provide a 'home from

home' for recent Highland immigrants. That is one kind of welcome. Of more significance, however, and much less friendly in tone is the characterisation of the 'welcoming' shore porters as exploitative and devious, always on the lookout for 'innocents' whom they can waylay. Their practice may have called to mind an even more notorious convention, involving 'crimps', whose role is explained as follows by Nicolette Jones:

'Crimps were swindlers who would take advantage of the system by which sailors were paid in advance, and would swarm aboard ships as they came into port, collecting sailors' bags together and taking them off to their lodging houses, where the men had no choice but to follow. By various inducements they would part them from their money and then pass them on, as drunk as it was possible to make them, to any old ship in need of men, in exchange for their advance pay on the grounds that it covered their debts.' [58]

A more general picture of Glasgow as the 'alien other' and as a city of

The long-serving 1984-built *Isle of Arran* manoeuvres in Oban Bay in May 2010. Initially built for the Ardrossan-Brodick service, the ferry has subsequently been used as a relief vessel on most of Caledonian MacBrayne's major routes. The bow of the *Waverley* can be seen (to the left) as she lies at the North Pier. (John Peter)

wily and cunning 'operators', preying on rather foolish Highlanders, became a stock backcloth for much humorous Gaelic prose and verse in the later nineteenth century, though the theme had emerged much earlier.[59] The rustic who embarked on *bàta na smùid* (the steamship),[60] and was subsequently led astray in the city, is featured in such songs as Neil MacLeod's well-known 'Turas Dhòmhnaill do Ghlaschu' ('Donald's Trip to Glasgow').[61] There the 'innocent' is taken to a drinking-den by an attractive girl, has his pocket picked, fights back, and ends up in court facing imprisonment or a fine.

Nevertheless, Highlanders and Hebrideans soon became street-wise. By the 1860s, substantial numbers of Gaelic-speakers had become long-term residents of Glasgow, having been conveyed there by steamship. Many, like John MacInnes from Lismore, found work in the foundries and shipyards of Clydeside. MacInnes, an industrial blacksmith and metalworker, was employed by Robert Napier, and contributed to the building of Britain's first ironclad warships. MacInnes was so proud of these vessels that he composed Gaelic songs to celebrate their completion, among them a song in honour of the *Black Prince*, second only to the *Warrior* of 1860, and the first of her class to be built and completed on the Clyde in 1862.

As befits the ship's name and figurehead, a 'massive and beautiful' representation of the Prince,[62] MacAonghais personifies the *Black Prince*, and comments cleverly on the 'buttons' in its steel coat, i.e. its rivets, which, he claims, 'we sewed with the hammer'. He mentions how its frames had to be heated in a furnace before they could be bent into shape, and this was no

doubt his own particular contribution to the building process.

'*Saoil thu fhèin nach e tha làidir,*
Stàilinn tha na chòta,
'S na putain tha sìos mun cuairt air,
Dh'fhuaigh sinn leis an òrd iad.
H-uile aisinn tha na phearsa,
Sac do dh'each air còmhnard,
'S dh'fheumte 'm blàithteachadh san fhùirneis
Mun lùbadh iad òirleach.'

'Don't you think that he is a strong fellow,
With steel in his coat,
And the buttons that surround him down below,
We sewed them with the hammer.
Every rib that is in his body
Would be a burden for a horse on level ground,
And they had to be heated in the furnace
Before they would bend an inch.'[63]

By means of the steamship, Highlanders and Islanders were transported from what some would have regarded as the very 'fringes' of the United Kingdom, and many became an integral part of the 'Workshop of Empire', as Glasgow came to be known. The development of the Clyde, as waterway and dynamo of the industrial heartland, brought new opportunities on an unprecedented scale to the western seaboard of Scotland after 1800. These opportunities transformed the region.

A sunny panorama across Oban Bay captures the Craignure ferry *Isle of Mull* about to pass the German cruise ship *Arkona*. Oban receives numerous cruise calls in summer months, and so the bay is often full of activity. *(John Peter)*

The necessities and comforts of 'civilised life'

As tourists like Bowman were aware from the outset, the Hebrides began to experience social reconfiguration, if not transformation, as a consequence of steamship services and the power of accompanying market forces. It was a general – and seemingly irreversible – trend, and it was very welcome in many areas. The writer of the entry for the parish of Sleat, Skye, in the *New Statistical Account* commented tellingly as early as 1840: 'Steam-boats ply regularly, and facilities are afforded for the introduction of the comforts of civilized life'.[64] These 'comforts' were, no doubt, many and varied, and 'civilization' in the islands, as in previously less accessible parts of the mainland, was taking on a new meaning, thanks to the steamship.

Inevitably, there were gains and losses, as society adjusted to the new 'comforts', especially through trade. In 1842, the *Topographical and Historical Gazetteer* noted that:

'Except in the Outer or more Westerly Hebrides…the facilities of steam-navigation, and easy access to the grand emporium of Scottish manufactures on the Clyde, have already very much curtailed the range of the native manufacture.'[65]

Other writers, however, regarded the steamship as a means of extending the reach, if not the range, of 'native manufacture' and exportable goods. Its cargoes could also supplement 'local manufactures'. As early as 1837, the writer of the North Uist section of the *New Statistical Account* observed acutely and prophetically:

'Steam navigation, judiciously arranged and properly conducted, would in some degree supply the want of local manufactures, by affording facilities of export, and of communication with the south. No regular steam-boats are employed to ply in this quarter: and the failure of the attempts that have been made to establish them has arisen from the circumstances, that the boats were not well fitted for the kind of trade proper to the district. They should have been adapted to convey cattle, &c., instead of being splendidly fitted up

57 Meek, 2008, pp72-73.
58 Jones, 2006, p21.
59 Meek, 2003, pp152-9.
60 Meek, 2006.
61 *An Gaidheal*, 66 (1877), pp171-73.
62 Walker, 2001, p132, contains a photograph of the vessel and a caption describing its figurehead. The *Warrior* and the *Black Prince* were the last two Royal Navy vessels to carry figureheads.
63 MacAonghais, 1875, p47. It should be noted that the use of steel in constructing ships of this kind was relatively new, as was the use of iron.
64 New Statistical Account, Vol. 14, p322.
65 Topographical and Historical Gazetteer, Vol. 1, p762.

Built in 1846 as the *Mary Jane* for James Matheson, proprietor of Lewis, and quite probably the first iron-hulled steamship to sail to the Outer Hebrides, the *Mary Jane* was sold in 1851 to the Glasgow and Lochfine Steam Packet Company, taken over by Hutcheson's in 1857. She was remodelled in 1875, losing her fiddle bow and obtaining an aft deck saloon, and becoming *Glencoe*. *(A. Ernest Glen collection)*

for passengers. In conjunction with the projected plan of sending cattle and other produce from the West Highlands to the Liverpool and Glasgow markets, were a steam-boat of proper construction for the conveyance of cattle established, to ply during the season alternately, along the west side of Skye, with the Long Island coast, and the east side of Skye with the opposite part of the mainland, – no doubt can exist that the speculation would succeed, and would prove extensively beneficial to these remote quarters. The great variety of other raw produce that might be exported, and the goods of various kinds required for the overgrown population, would, in a short time, create a trade which must inevitably spur the industry, and promote the comfort of all classes of the inhabitants.'[66]

This passage is particularly illuminating in drawing attention to the failures of earlier steamship ventures to the Outer Hebrides, which the writer ascribes principally to the use of vessels which were ill-suited to the needs of the region, as they gave pre-eminence to passengers rather than cargo. To be effective, steamship services had to be two-way, not one-way, and vessels had to meet the needs of island communities, as islanders, certainly in North Uist, wanted to be part of the new world order which had been created by industrial developments.

The application of steamships to the cattle trade was specifically identified as a matter to be addressed with some urgency. In the first half of the nineteenth century, in fact, the Highlands and Islands lagged far behind the north-east and south-west of Scotland in the use of the steamship for this purpose[67] – a disparity which suggests that, in the first flush of the steamship era, the tendency to regard the Hebrides primarily as a tourist destination had retarded the economic growth of the area, compared with other regions. The trenchant observations of the North Uist contributor to the *New Statistical Account* furnished what could have been a blueprint – in effect, the rationale and broad route-map – for cargo-based shipping to and from the Hebrides in the course of the next hundred years, though the social instability of the period 1840-1850 was not conducive to immediate

and purposeful action. After 1870, however, when the challenge of the 'overgrown population' had been met by good means and bad, a new spirit of economic enterprise and self-confidence seemingly emerged in the Hebrides, and encouraged the steamship trade afresh, by means of suitable or purpose-built cargo vessels. An obvious and productive trading relationship between island farmers and Glasgow merchants was soon developed, and the aspirations of North Uist were fulfilled.

The foundations of this relationship were being laid by the 1840s, if not the 1830s. For the island of Lewis, James Matheson's steamers, among them the *Mary Jane*, facilitated imports as well as exports, and two-way trade was

David Hutcheson's tiny *Linnet*, built in 1866, was a superb example of mid nineteenth-century customised engineering. Equipped with twin screws, and resembling a floating tramcar with a telescopic funnel, she served on the Crinan Canal until 1929, conveying passengers between Ardrishaig and Crinan, and connecting with the larger steamers. *(Donald E. Meek collection)*

already significant by 1846. As William Mackay of Stornoway told the Napier Commission in 1883,

'Immediately after purchasing [Lewis], Sir James' attention was directed to opening steam communication with Glasgow. He offered a premium of £500 to any shipowner in Glasgow that would put on a steamer, but no one accepted the offer. He then took shares in a steamer named the *Falcon*, which then commenced to run between Stornoway and Ardrossan. Her career, however, was short, and she took fire and had to be scuttled. I may mention an incident which occurred at this time in connection with the burning of this vessel. The merchants by that time had begun to depend on getting their goods regularly by steamer, but when it so suddenly ceased to run, before they could order their supplies and get them brought by a sailing vessel, the town of Stornoway had run out of almost everything. There was not one pound of tea or sugar or tobacco or snuff in the place. After the *Falcon*, Sir James purchased the steamer *Mary Jane*, and it was put on in 1845 [*recte* 1846] to run between this town and Glasgow. This boat, however, became too small, and in conjunction with the Duke of Sutherland he got another vessel, called the *Marquis of Stafford*, which was stipulated to call at Locinvar [*sic*] on its way from Stornoway to Glasgow…

The inhabitants found in the south a ready market for their produce, and the prices of everything rose, particularly eggs. After the *Mary Jane* was put on I have heard the merchants say that it was such advantage to them that they could turn over their capital three times before their bills became due; whereas formerly, when they depended on sailing vessels, their bills often became due before their goods arrived.'[68]

The 'steamboat fire' evidently affected the town of Stornoway itself, and the commodities listed as imports were probably for refined palates rather than rustic consumption. Far from being 'luxury goods', the first recorded cargoes carried by steamship to the Hebrides and the West Highlands consisted mainly of 'large bulk', like the housing materials taken to St Kilda in 1834.

Contributors to the *New Statistical Account* from parishes in the Inner Hebrides and on the western mainland had become wholly familiar with the steamship by the time they wrote their articles. Oban was firmly established as a significant port by 1843:

'Owing to its centrical situation in the Highlands, its safe and commodious harbour, and good quays, it is visited almost daily in summer by steamers with passengers to and from Glasgow, Inverness, Iona, Staffa, and Skye.'[69]

The scribe for Morvern, like the scribe for Rothesay, reflected on the change from the appearance of the first steamship in the Sound of Mull in 1818, 'some of the old inhabitants expressing great surprise, that, during a long residence on the sea-coast, they had never seen another vessel of the same wonderful construction'. He recorded:

'In 1821, a steam-vessel, the Highlander, commenced plying regularly between Glasgow and Tobermory, calling at Lochalin as one of the intermediate ports. Recently an attempt has been made to perform this voyage in one day, with a degree of success that leads us to hope that it may yet, under better arrangements, be successful…During the winter months, the steam communication

From 1890 to 1905, the *Glencoe* served Islay from West Loch Tarbert, where she is seen in this picture. From 1905 until 1931, when she was withdrawn at the age of 85, she provided the Mallaig/Kyle-Portree service. *(A. Ernest Glen collection)*

with Tobermory is less frequent; sometimes it is entirely suspended; and consequently, during that period, a packet-boat plies between Lochalin and Oban.'[70]

Across the water in Mull, his counterpart set the steamship and its contribution to the parish of Kilninian and Kilmore firmly within the prevailing ethos of Improvement. According to him, the steamship had aided growth in population and seeming economic prosperity:

'There has been a decided change for the better, on this part of the country, since the preparation of the last Statistical Account; then, the writer thereof prophesied, "there seems to be little ground to hope for a speedy increase of its population or prosperity, but rather the reverse." By the census before noticed, this prediction will be seen not to have been realized; and the rentals of estates have been in some instances doubled, nay even almost tripled since then. Much of this is no doubt to be ascribed to steam navigation, and the facilities thereby afforded of intercourse with all parts of the low countries; and were the necessary lines of road made, and bridges built, low country capital and enterprise would find their way more readily than they have been doing into this district; the face of the country would undergo a thorough and beneficial change; and this portion of the empire, hitherto so much neglected, would assume and hold that position which the capabilities of its soil, sea coast, and climate so justly entitle it to.'

Such resounding rhetoric on the side of Improvement was intrinsically unrealistic. It overlooked the uncomfortable fact that the increase in the population of Mull and other islands of the Inner Hebrides had been caused and maintained by the harvesting of kelp, a labour-intensive industry which was a mainstay of early crofting communities. This industry expanded considerably during the period of the Napoleonic Wars when dried kelp was used as a substitute for potash in glass making. When the supply of potash was restored, the kelp industry fell into decline. As demand for kelp receded, the precarious life of the population faced ruin following the failure of the potato crop in 1846 (potatoes formed the workers' staple diet). For many in the islands, and particularly those at the sharp end of economic restructuring by impecunious landlords, the doubling and

66 New Statistical Account, Vol. 14, p81.
67 Haldane, 1952, pp217-9.
68 Napier Commission Report, p1091. Mackay's late evidence provides a much more buoyant picture of Matheson's early shipping enterprises than contemporary sources. John Munro Mackenzie, Matheson's Chamberlain, records (Mackenzie,

1994, p20, p43, p69) that the *Mary Jane* was running at a loss in 1851. This led to her sale in that year, as well as to arrangements with John Ramsay and his partners for services to Stornoway by the *Islay*.
69 New Statistical Account, Vol. 7, p532.
70 New Statistical Account, Vol. 7, p189.

The *Isle of Mull* gathers speed as she leaves Craignure, bound for Oban in June 2008. Lichen-covered rocks and machair (wild flower meadow) frame the scene. *(Bruce Peter)*

Above: A tranquil evening scene at Oban in May 2009 with the *Clansman* and the *Isle of Mull* at rest at the main ferry berths. *(Bruce Peter)*

Right: The Tobermory (Mull)–Kilchoan (Ardnamurchan) ferry *Loch Linnhe*, one of four 'Loch'-class vessels built in the mid-1980s for Caledonian MacBrayne's short duration routes, enters Tobermory Bay. *(John Peter)*

Below: Mallaig harbour in the mid-1980s offers a berth to the versatile *Pioneer*, operating to Armadale, Skye; originally built in 1974 to serve Islay, the *Pioneer* was later used successfully on various Firth of Clyde and Western Isles routes. Her chunky and purposeful appearance typified Caledonian MacBrayne's vessels of the 1970s. The Small Isles service vessel, *Lochmor* (1979), lies astern. *(Bruce Peter collection)*

Mallaig is the scene again, but this time with the *Lochmor* and *Iona* at the berth; built in 1970 to serve Islay, the vessel actually debuted on the Gourock-Dunoon service, but, as with the *Pioneer*, was widely used latterly on a number of key routes. As well as hosting two ferry services, Mallaig remains an important fishing port. *(John Peter)*

tripling of rent was far from being a welcome development. In 1846, bust followed boom and the now redundant kelp-labourers found themselves looking for steamships to rescue them from their grim circumstances.

Emigration

Unlike seasonal migration, emigration was usually one-way traffic. In the late 1840s, after the 1846 Potato Famine, removal of the 'surplus' population was strongly assisted by landlords in certain districts, and the relationship between landlords and shipowners must have guaranteed a steady stream of passengers. It is very telling that the steamships owned by the new generation of commercially-minded Highland and Hebridean landowners – James Matheson, the Duke of Sutherland and John Ramsay being chief among them – were particularly closely involved in moving emigrants from the Hebrides on the first leg of their outward journeys. Arrangements between Matheson and Ramsay for this purpose are revealed by the use of both Matheson's *Marquis of Stafford* and Ramsay's *Islay* in conveying 787 emigrants from Lewis to Troon in May and June 1851. The *Marquis of Stafford* called first at Loch Roag, where she took on board emigrants from Uig, and then sailed to Port of Ness, which she reached 'after a rather disagreeable passage…there being a heavy swell which brought on seasickness among the women and children and the appearance in the morning of the decks and fore hold was anything but agreeable.'[71]

The ability of the steamship to sail in conditions which would have been impossible for a sail-powered vessel helped to shorten the initial passage, but it was not infrequently at the price of immense discomfort, and even terror, for passengers. Fearing that smallpox would be transferred to their ship, the Uig people would not allow those from Ness to board, and the *Marquis of Stafford* made for Tolsta, where she loaded a further group of emigrants, and proceeded to Troon. The contingent from Ness, some 70 people, were then taken to Glasgow by Ramsay's *Islay*.[72] Matheson's *Mary Jane* (later to become David MacBrayne's celebrated and long-lived *Glencoe*, scrapped in 1931) was used to transport emigrants from other parts of the Hebrides, including Tiree. At least partly as a result of island-mainland linkages by steamship, the number of emigrant ships which sailed overseas directly from Hebridean harbours, such as Portree and Tobermory, appears to have declined sharply after 1850, in favour of departures from more southerly mainland ports, such as Campbeltown and Greenock.

The sad realities of the emigrant trade, assisted by steamships, were noted by contemporary observers. The Raasay House Weather Tables record the arrival of cargoes such as 'shoes for emigrants in a large package' on the *Duntroon Castle* in March 1852, and they note that emigrants from Raasay travelled on the *Islay* (May and June 1852), the *Cygnet* (June 1852) and the *Duntroon Castle* (July 1852). These emigrants were bound for Australia. Those who travelled in June and early July 1852 were almost certainly part

The *Caledonia*, ex *Stena Baltica*, was the first drive-through vessel in Clyde or Hebridean service. At first, she proved controversial due to her poor sea-keeping qualities but eventually found her niche on the relatively sheltered Oban-Craignure route. Here, she leaves Craignure in June 1987, her final season in Caledonian MacBrayne service. *(John Peter)*

of the large contingent who sailed from Greenock to Australia on the *Georgiana*. Others were to follow. On 6th June 1854, 'the *Chevalier* put into the bay at 4 pm and took on Board 129 Raasay People Emigrants to Australia'.[73] Well into the twentieth century, ships such as the *Hebrides* acted as tenders to emigrant vessels.

Raising a glass

Steamships had their own ways of alleviating the pain of parting from homeland and relatives, whether for a brief spell on the farms of the Lothians, or for permanent settlement in the Lowlands, North America or Australia. Alcohol had anaesthetic powers. From their earliest appearance in West Highland waters, steamships were associated with thick smoke and happy inebriation, and to a considerable extent they became the maritime equivalent of change-houses and inns on mainland roads, or, in the case of such grand vessels as the *United Kingdom* of 1826, banqueting halls and 'gin palaces' for the great and the good. Ailean Dall MacDougall, bard to MacDonell of Glengarry, paid tribute to the saloons of the *Ben Nevis* on her arrival in Lochaber waters in 1824:

> '*Seòmraichean geala gu h-ìosal*
> *Far an òlar fion na Spàinte.*'
> 'White-coloured saloons are below,
> where one can drink the wine of Spain.'[74]

Serious English travellers, intent on finding the spirit of Ossian rather than any other sort, took a less accommodating view. They resented the unromantic mayhem which they sometimes discovered on their first encounter with this unsteady, and unsteadying, generation of steam-driven vessels. On small, flush-decked vessels, it was impossible to avoid the swarms of inebriates attracted to, and commonly created by, the on-board facilities. Thus, when travelling on the west coast in 1825, J.E. Bowman was scandalised by the goings-on on the self-same *Ben Nevis*, which he wished to board at Oban for the journey to Fort William:

'It was nearly four o' clock when the *Ben Nevis* steamer appeared within the Sound of Kerrera, and when she stood under the pier at Oban, her deck was such a scene of tumult and disorder that we were at a loss to assign a cause. She was altogether so unsteady, that her wheels were lifted alternately out of the water. We, however, got on board, and with some difficulty made our way to the stern; where we learned she had a double complement of passengers (280 were on board) in consequence of the *Comet* being under repair at Glasgow. The captain was also extremely drunk; the heat and crowd both on deck and below, were intense, and some of the passengers were so much alarmed at their critical situation, that they got ashore and remained at Oban. They gave such an account of their voyage from Lochgilphead, that we determined, though reluctantly, not to go, and with some difficulty got again ashore.'[75]

Thanks to the steamship, Hebridean communities gradually developed a taste for new goods, including imported alcohol to supplement the products of local (and often illicit) stills. The steamship, however, was more than a new kind of portable drinks' cabinet; she was also a 'travelling mechanical island', with the power to transform the rock-solid Hebrides, which had stood firm in the face of hostile forces since the dawn of history.

The floating community

In shaping the lives of communities in the Highland and Islands by conveying emigrants, tourists, passengers, seasonal workers, ministers, landlords and many other people to and fro, the steamship itself formed, from its earliest days, a floating community of a deeply multivalent, cosmopolitan kind. Its principal characteristics were more than evident by 1850.

Of a much more heterogeneous variety than the local communities of the Highlands and Islands, the community on board the steamship had its roots to no small degree in a reformulation of 'external' (non-Gaelic) society to provide points of closer 'productive contact' between different

With the rugged mountains of Skye in the background, the *Pioneer* heads out of Mallaig bound for Armadale, Skye. *(Bruce Peter collection)*

classes, labouring, industrial and mercantile, in the wake of the Industrial Revolution. Tensions and contradictions and opposing processes were fully exemplified in what was, intrinsically, a vessel of social change, a conveyor of commodities, human, animal and material, with the capability (unlike the sailing-ship) to proceed against natural powers – and thus to shape the world, rather than be shaped by it, as the use of steamships in the emigrant context alone graphically underlines. The world was moving, and being moved, thanks to industrial forces, and it was also shrinking as steamships reached out to the ends of the Empire.

The shape of the 'travelling classes' too soon became evident, in a no less graphic display of contact and contradiction. On the earliest steamships, apparently, class distinctions were not rigidly observed, and, in any case, only the better-off could afford the passage. Gradually, however, as the

steamship became 'hybridised' and open to many kinds of traveller, class distinction on shore was even more rigidly demarcated at sea, largely because of the narrow confines of space. Yet, even as different classes were segregated, it remained possible to embrace the steamship as part of 'your' community, or as an extension or 'function' of that community, and to find your own 'micro-community' on board. Part of the fascination of the 'steamship experience' lay in trying to relate yourself and your community to the 'Other'. Negotiation was necessary, and worked powerfully in both directions.

The resulting uncomfortable compromise was achieved in different ways by different parties. There was much to embrace positively. The steamship immediately became a potential source of employment for men

The romantic grandeur of the steamship era is captured in the figurehead of a plaided Highlander carried proudly on the Campbeltown and Glasgow Company's *Davaar* (1885). Hutcheson and MacBrayne steamers, such as the *Clydesdale* (1870) and the *Claymore* (1881), carried a similar figurehead. *(A. Ernest Glen collection)*

A pig is lifted by rope and derrick on board a MacBrayne steamer at an unknown port. Vessels of the fleet typically transported a mix of passengers, livestock and general cargo. *(Donald E. Meek collection)*

MacBrayne's *Clansman* of 1870 at Greenock, displaying the ornate configuration typical of the Company's purpose-built Hebridean steamers. *(A. Ernest Glen collection)*

A stern view of MacBrayne's *Lovedale*, which was a second-hand purchase from the Great Western Railway. Built in 1867 as the *Great Western*, she operated initially on Channel and Irish Sea routes. Purchased in 1891 for Scottish West Coast service, she operated thereafter mainly to Stornoway. In comparison with MacBrayne's purpose-built tonnage, she was of plain appearance. *(A. Ernest Glen collection)*

from the Highlands and Islands, who readily became sailors, engineers, officers, Masters, and even owners, as fleets developed. Like the steamship herself, such workers became cultural hybrids, rubbing shoulders with men from the Lowlands while retaining their Gaelic cultural identity, but sometimes transferring their homes permanently to the Clyde or the principal seaport used by the ship.[76] For others, such employment was seasonal, and to this extent the steamship supplemented one of the very forms of industry to which she encouraged travel. The steamship also brought the potential for trade right to islanders' doorsteps, by encouraging barter and exchange at piers and other landing places, or even on board ship. In this way, she was a proponent of market forces, bringing monetary values to the islands, and pointing to much broader economic horizons, underpinned by different cultural values expressed in a different language, English. The steamship had the potential to change Gaelic culture.

It was thus possible for the steamship to act, in some respects, as the 'mirror-image community', a dangerous leviathan, a negative force, representing an alien and forbidding way of life, perhaps to be experienced fully in migration to the cities, or by a spine-tingling journey to the edge of the world. Once boarded, however, the steamship could function as a capsule of transformation or as a facilitator of conceptual change beyond the standard boundaries of society, leading to the reinforcement or reconfiguration of one's own identity or community or worldview. This inherent sense of 'difference', and the attempt to discover it or engage with it, encouraged economic development, including tourism.

One of the great appeals of the steamship, and especially the cargo-

carrying variety, lay in its capacity to grant ready access to 'other' communities which lay off the main track of 'human experience' (depending on one's starting-point) and off the timetable-dominated routes. Curiosity combined with economic determinism to encourage travel, especially for the middle classes, who were accommodated in the gracious saloons and cabins of the steamship, whose vantage points offered them new insights into the Hebrides and the west Highland mainland, and the lifestyles of their inhabitants. The same forces operated to change Hebrideans' views of 'other' mainlands across the sea, but, unlike cosseted tourists, they usually travelled in the steerage, on wooden benches with cold seas often spilling in through the chilly blast of the cowl vents in the forecastle, as the vessel shipped it green in heavy swells.

Out of this exchange, with the steamship at its very heart, there emerged, gradually, Hebridean communities which eventually became as diverse, multivalent and (ultimately) cosmopolitan as the steamship herself, representing many of its values, with a profound sense of the 'collective' significance of the steamship and her centrality to the maintenance of the now transformed (and ever-changing) community.

71 Devine, 1988, p219.
72 Devine, 1988, p219.
73 Raasay House Weather Tables, 1851-59.
74 Meek, 2006, pp48-49.
75 Bowman, 1986, p125.
76 The 1881 Census provides an illuminating snapshot of the *Dunara Castle*, then berthed at Tarbert, Harris, as a 'synthetic' floating community in terms of her crew, who were from different parts of Scotland and beyond. The following areas are represented: Mainland Argyll (3 – Master, Mate and Boatswain); Inner

Hebrides (8 – 7 seamen [3 from Tiree, 2 from Skye, 1 from Mull, 1 from Iona], 1 steward); Outer Hebrides (1 seaman); Oban (1 cook); Dunbartonshire (1 fireman, i.e. stoker); Renfrewshire (3 – 1 engineer and 2 stewards); Glasgow (3 – 1 fireman, 1 steward and 1 stewardess); Wigtownshire (1 engineer); Ayrshire (1 Clerk, namely William Donald); Ireland (2 firemen); Netherlands (1 winch driver). There were three passengers from Duirinish, Skye, one from North Uist, and a Free Church minister from Barvas, Lewis. See Mackay, 2006, pp56-7.

Chapter Three

Victorian Summer on the Clyde

The Highlands and Islands were not alone in undergoing profound change in the course of the nineteenth century. During the 1860s, Glasgow was reaching its zenith as an engineering and manufacturing powerhouse. The city's burgeoning wealth was reflected not only in its fine architecture, but also in the design of a number of outstanding saloon paddle steamers.

For Highlanders and Hebrideans, the steamship was a means of moving towards the industrial world of the Scottish Lowlands. For city-dwellers on the banks of the Clyde, however, who were already part of that industrial world, the steamship, and especially the saloon steamer, was a means of temporary escape from the squalor and grinding drudgery of ordinary working life. The brightly coloured liveries of the vessels offered an alluring alternative to the drab environment of factories, workshops and mines. The ships' on-board 'space' was differentiated from that of the city and even of the home by the sharply defined boundaries of the hull and cabins. As they cast off from the Broomielaw or from quays further 'doon the watter', the ships became small sea-borne worlds in their own right, 'floating

A relaxed observer surveys a deceptively tranquil scene at Mavisbank Quay, Glasgow, sometime in the 1870s. Hutcheson's saloon steamer *Chevalier* (1866) lies alongside the same owner's *Mountaineer* (1852), which has no saloon. The continuing significance of sail is indicated by the web of masts and yards up the river. *(A. Ernest Glen collection)*

communities' in which indulgences of various kinds could be countenanced, if not always appreciated by everyone on board. Here, men and women and children from 'single ends' could glimpse and even (at a push beyond class boundaries) briefly experience the 'posh house', laid out before them in fine furniture, curtains and drapery of various kinds in the First Class accommodation. They could participate in forms of group therapy as they discovered new and old 'buddies', deepened their bonds with family members, interacted with the facilities on board ship, and tasted food and drink, sometimes to excess, away from the stricter rules of everyday life. The steamship provided a 'release mechanism', emotional and psychological, as well as physical. The most obvious manifestation of emotional release was intoxication, which came to be called 'steaming', by association with such steamship-borne adventures and the apparently irrepressible urge to 'go to see the engines' (visit the bar). From the open upper decks of the steamer, those who were still steady on their feet and not addicted to 'engines' could gain a new perspective on land and landscape, a perspective which was normally blocked off by tenements, factories,

churches, shops and steeples. In short, the saloon steamer became a capsule of liberation and transformation, the latter being achieved in different ways, many undoubtedly beneficial, but others much less commendable. To some extent, therefore, the Clyde saloon steamer was the precursor of the massive ferries and cruise ships of our own time, attempting to cash in on the consumer boom of a particular era, and to entertain the consumers with the fling and bling appropriate to their generation and social class.

The saloon steamer was primarily a product of the Clyde, but the design came to be adopted throughout Britain. Its development was stimulated by the need to provide more and better-covered accommodation on board ship. The first generation of Clyde excursion steamers had been flush-decked, much like the old *Comet*, usually providing covered accommodation only below the weather deck, with some deckhouses above. On the saloon steamer, the saloon commonly ran along the weather deck from a position forward of the sponsons to the stern of the ship, and was surmounted by a promenade deck. On the grander ships, the saloon was full-width. Later in the nineteenth century, the promenade deck was extended forward and aft,

33

forming a shelter over the fore and aft deck. Eventually, the open sides of the foredeck were plated in, thus extending the reach of the deck saloon, and producing what became the standard design for the final phase of paddle-ship building in the United Kingdom.

As the saloon steamer developed, so too did restrictions on access to its various 'posh' lounges and cabins. In effect, the saloon steamer came to replicate the class distinctions that were more than evident in Glasgow and in other industrial cities by the mid-century. She became a reflection of the city, mirroring its social structure, while retaining a sturdy independence by virtue of being sea-borne. First Class and Steerage areas were demarcated; the 'top hats' were to be distinguished from the 'bunnets' in the saloons assigned to each, and a place had to be given to those who occupied, or

world in which she had been created, and in which she had to operate. As on *terra firma*, the 'upwardly mobile' tried their best to rule the immobile, much to the resentment of the latter.

The acquistion of capital to fund the building of saloon steamers also reflected the risk-taking ethos of the time, and the somewhat ruthless 'double standard' of Clyde shipowners and shipbuilders. Clyde-built steamers had already gained an international reputation for speed and manoeurability in shallow waters when the American Civil War broke out. At a time when many groups in Scotland supported the anti-slavery cause, the venture capitalists of the Clyde, with an eye on the main chance, conveniently sided with the slaving-owning Confederates of the Southern States. Confederate sympathisers were willing to purchase Clyde steamers

Leaving a splendid wake as she heads downstream, while showing her ornate stern scrollwork to advantage, David MacBrayne's *Iona* epitomises the power and elegance of the finest post-1850 paddle steamers of the Clyde. *(A. Ernest Glen)*

aspired to occupy, a middle station. Inevitably, the seeds of potential conflict were sown. Unsurprisingly, the saloon steamer witnessed 'pugellistic encounters' between First Class travellers and those in steerage, between the usually (but not invariably) more sober 'upper class' and the frequently (or recklessly) inebriated 'lower class'. These 'rammies' occurred on board ship and also (commonly) on pier heads. Such encounters had their day-to-day equivalents on dry land, as managers and workers clashed over wages, and 'lock-outs' were arranged by owners and managers who would not countenance their workers' insubordination. Paradoxically, therefore, the saloon steamer, while helping to act as a safety-valve at one level, fomented tensions at another. In all of this, the steamer reflected the uneasy industrial

for generous sums for use as blockade-runners, which would allow them to export cotton. Selling their ships as soon as an offer came, perhaps at the very outset of a ship's career or even when it was still on the stocks, the Clyde venturers were able to amass wealth which aided the rapid advancement of vessels of this type. Suitably stripped of their furnishings and filled to capacity (or more) with appropriate munitions for the Confederates, the ships would leave Scottish shores at full speed in cover of darkness, with minimal on-board illumination, bound for the broad Atlantic and, if fortune favoured them, a safe haven in Confederate ports such as Wilmington, Alabama. As numerous vessels ran aground, sank or exploded at sea, these canny Clyde steamer owners were careful to get their money before the ships set off.[77]

This extremely dangerous cloak-and-dagger operation enabled steamer owners frequently to replace existing tonnage with new and improved vessels, embodying the latest technical advances and improvements in passenger comfort. The building of some of the finest vessels ever to grace the Clyde was financed in this way, and the foundations of major companies were laid. Hutcheson's first *Iona*, completed in 1855 by Messrs J. & G. Thomson (Govan) for service between Glasgow and Ardrishaig, was regarded as being the finest Clyde steamer of her era, but was sold to America already in 1862; sailing surreptitiously from the Clyde under cover of darkness, she collided with a larger steamer, and foundered off Gourock. A second, improved, *Iona* followed from Thomson's Govan yard in 1863.

After only one Clyde season, she too was sold for American blockade running (she foundered in a storm while *en route* across the Atlantic, however). Prior to the sale, her passenger saloons were carefully dismantled for re-use on Hutcheson's third *Iona*, already under construction at Thomson's Govan yard; she was completed in 1864. Her machinery was similar to her previous namesakes (but with navy-type horizontal boilers, rather than the vertical 'haystack' variety then generally favoured for Clyde steamers). *The Glasgow Herald* observed that:

'As in the last *Iona*, the great feature of the present boat consists in the introduction of spacious decks saloons…The cabin saloon…is elegantly decorated in white and gold, is provided with cushioned seats of the most luxurious description and is fitted all round with

Pulling alongside at Greenock, the *Iona* displays the slim lines of her canoe bow and her fine ornamentation. *(A. Ernest Glen)*

Whereas existing steamers of the Clyde fleets offered only limited sheltered accommodation, the second *Iona* exemplified the developing principles of the saloon steamer, with spacious and luxuriously furnished deck saloons enclosing nearly all of Main Deck and expansive outdoor promenades on the deck above – a most significant innovation in making the steamer more attractive to tourists and pleasure seekers even in typically Scottish West Coast drizzle. Thus, the advent of a new generation of the saloon steamers, of which *Iona* was the first large example, transformed the comfort of travel.

plate glass windows, which slide up and down like those of a railway carriage. At the extreme end next to the stern, a small space is partitioned off, and most tastefully and commodiously fitted up as a ladies' retiring room. Beneath this saloon is the First Class cabin, a spacious apartment, admirably lighted and ventilated and affording all the comfort of a well-furnished dining room. On the forward part of the deck is a second saloon…comfortably fitted up, and affording equally with the other the advantages of shelter from foul

77 Graham, 2008.

Well-doing Glaswegians enjoy a day trip on the *Ivanhoe* in about 1908. *(A. Ernest Glen)*

weather, abundant light, and perfect ventilation.'[78]

Being designed to carry large numbers in relative comfort, the *Iona* attracted an enthusiastic following and occasionally became so crowded that 'steerage' passengers invaded her First Class accommodation, as one correspondent to *The Glasgow Herald* observed:

'All the First Class passengers were crushed by this excursionist party. Ladies were rather rudely pushed about, and in many cases had their beautiful dresses destroyed by the tobacco spittles which were squirted about in all directions… Having taken tickets for Dunoon, I had my children collected in readiness to disembark them there as soon as we reached the pier, but keeping at a reasonable distance for

fear of my young charges getting into danger. No sooner had the *Iona* made fast to the quay, than we were carried by the tremendous pressure of the excursionists…completely off our feet and, but for the merciful hand of Providence, some of my children would have been trampled on and crushed to death…but the shrieks of women and children behind us told too plainly of the dreadful crushing and disorder in getting to the gangways. But the scene at Dunoon quay when the excursionists were getting on board the *Iona* about five o'clock on her return trip to Glasgow, baffles description. During the day a large proportion of the excursionists had become intoxicated, the result of which was that, as the hour approached when the steamer was expected, many were quarrelling and fighting and bleeding faces and torn clothes were almost universal. At the entrance to the pier, many refused to pay the penny of dues, and

78 Glasgow Herald, 20th June 1864.

36

Above: Full Astern! The *Iona* reverses away from Tarbert Pier, and threshes the sea with her paddles. *(A. Ernest Glen collection)*

Right: Seen here off Greenock, the **Marquis of Bute** of 1868 demonstrates the very different experience of travelling on a steamer with an open main deck, rather than enclosed saloons. The vessel joined the Glasgow & South Western Railway's fleet in 1891. *(A. Ernest Glen collection)*

Below: The flagship of the MacBrayne fleet, the *Columba*, was significantly larger than the *Iona*, and had an extensive saloon. The steamer is seen here at Ardrishaig. *(A. Ernest Glen)*

MacBrayne's famous *Columba* passes the Water's Neb, opposite John Brown & Co's Clydebank shipyard, during her latter career in the mid-1920s. *(A. Ernest Gle*

tremendous fighting ensued… In a state of madness a number of fellows got on the quay, which was crowded with about 1,000 people. The drunken brutes attempted to force a passage for themselves by knocking down all before them. Women, with infants in their arms, were mercilessly knocked down and trampled over; husbands and fathers, protecting their wives and children, were likewise knocked down and abused, and probably not a few seriously injured.'[79]

This correspondence was followed some days later by an editorial in which the problems caused by accommodating tourists and travellers in First Class and crowds of riotous excursionists elsewhere on the same, relatively small vessel were seen as having the potential to cause national embarrassment:

'Travellers who are paying handsomely for their transit to and from the Highlands have good reason to complain if the vessel is inundated with a swarm of excursionists or others who pay a shilling or eight pence to sail on the *Iona* to or from a place like Dunoon. The

disgraceful scene described by the correspondent is the natural consequence of the present arrangement. Such spectacles must give the English and other strangers travelling by the steamers concerned a most humiliating idea of Glasgow life and Glasgow morality… The plain fact is, that before they reach their destination, great numbers are drunk and riotous, and pour themselves, like a horde of Goths, over the quiet watering place where the steamer stops, filling the roads, shores and quays with brawling, fighting and every kind of drunken excess.'[80]

Behaviour of this kind was specific to the Glasgow (Broomielaw)-Dunoon-Rothesay route; after disgorging at these popular resorts, the *Iona* would probably have continued half-empty for the remainder of her passage to Ardrishaig. Traffic on this route was seasonal and did not justify the employment of so capacious a vessel as the *Iona* during the winter months when Hutcheson's smaller steamer *Mountaineer* met the obligations of the Royal Mail contract.

For 12 seasons, the *Iona* had a monopoly on the Glasgow-Ardrishaig

route – indeed she remained the most commodious, attractively appointed and weatherproof Clyde steamer in operation throughout the period. Eventually, in 1877, a new rival appeared, splendidly named the *Lord of the Isles*. Her owners, the Glasgow & Inveraray Steamboat Company, were a newly established subsidiary business of the Lochgoil and Lochlong Steamboat Company; trading since 1825, this connected Glasgow with Inveraray and Lochgoilhead. Built by D. & W. Henderson & Co, the *Lord of the Isles* was developed from the *Iona*'s design. Unfortunately, her construction was delayed by an acrimonious labour dispute which came to affect all of the Clyde yards. When workers in Partick and Govan began agitating for pay rises, the yard owners joined forces to lock out all employees, irrespective of whether they had taken part in industrial action. The owners' strategy was to cause the workers such hardship that they would think twice about making pay demands in future. Although the

workers' initial strike had only involved around 3,000 men, the lock-out affected 25,000, meaning that shipbuilding work effectively ground to a halt. In consequence, progress to complete the *Lord of the Isles* was slow and, in the meantime, relations between her owners and builders deteriorated to the extent that legal arbitration was required to compensate for the owners' missing a month of the lucrative summer season. Of far greater consequence in the long term was the sad legacy of the cruel treatment of Clyde shipyard workers by their employers – the summer-long lock-out being only one of several infamous incidents of callous brutality towards Glasgow's labouring classes whose lives were all too often dangerous, poverty-stricken, unhealthy and short.

When the *Lord of the Isles* actually entered service, she was not fully finished as her desperate owners had lost patience (after her inaugural season, she was returned to her builder for proper completion).

79 Glasgow Herald, 31st August 1864.
80 Glasgow Herald, 13th September 1864.

saloon. Between these staircases is a well-lighted and comfortably furnished smoking room, from the windows of which a good view is obtainable of the engines. Further aft, and on either side of the boat, are ladies' and gentlemen's lavatories, the mountings of the wash hand basins being silver, and everything else *en suite*. The saloon is a magnificent apartment nearly 80 feet long, lofty, and lighted by continuous plate glass windows hung with crimson drapery. The ceiling both of this and of the dining saloon below is artistically stencilled in light slate-blue upon a rich ground of ribbed gold, and being panelled with boldly-mounted girders, also painted blue, has a wonderfully light and agreeable effect. The seats are placed at right angles to the windows, as in a Pullman car, and are upholstered in crimson silk velvet. From the stern windows a fine view is obtainable, and the saloon being adorned with several large mirrors, has an air of space even out of proportion with its undoubted roominess. But the dining saloon is the great feature of the *Columba*. Situated below the main saloon, and of the same dimensions, it is decorated in the most lavish and artistic manner. The panels are polished wood – teak, maple, mahogany and rosewood being the materials used. Some of the panels are painted to represent inlaying in pattern and the capitals of the pillars and moulding of the cornice are heavily coated with gold. The pillars are of teak, the upper part being white, with gold flutings. Great taste has been shown in the choice of the carpets and the upholstery, the chairs being covered with a rich, old-fashioned dark canary-coloured velvet. At the stern end of the saloon, advantage has been taken of the narrowing and shelving character of the boat above the helm to arrange a conservatory, a fine lot of rare plants being disposed in front of the mirror which closes in the view.'[81]

Nonetheless, she was a beautifully designed vessel. *The Glasgow Herald* observed that it was 'scarcely possible to conceive of a more handsome or better equipped steamer', her First Class saloon being 'elegant in taste and luxurious in furnishing.' One innovation for tourists was the promotion of circular excursions with horse-drawn coach travel to Loch Awe, from which they returned to Glasgow via the Caledonian Railway. The following year, tours to Loch Eck were introduced, involving coach travel from Dunoon, Kilmun and Blairmore and a trip on the new Loch Eck steamer *Fairy Queen*.

The great acclaim of the *Lord of the Isles* caused Hutcheson's *Iona* to suffer a loss of traffic. Even although Hutcheson invested heavily to keep the *Iona* in pristine condition and mechanically up to date (new boilers were fitted and her saloons were refurbished in 1875), she was perceived by upwardly mobile travellers to be an ageing vessel in comparison with her new rival.

To maintain lead position, a response was required from the Hutcheson fleet, and it came in 1878 in the shape of the *Columba*, the most famous Clyde paddle steamer of all time. The moving force in her creation was the former junior partner in the Hutchesons' company, namely David MacBrayne, who had gradually assumed leadership, and who was soon to become a household name in Scotland and far beyond. MacBrayne thus made his presence felt from the outset, in magisterial, though traditional, style. The *Columba* was essentially an improved version of the *Iona*, but 50 feet longer, impressively measuring just over 300 feet. Built of steel by J. & G. Thomson, Clydebank, she was equipped with massive oscillating engines which drove her through the water at over 18 knots. She was placed on the premiere Glasgow-Ardrishaig route. The *Oban Times* commented favourably on the *Columba*'s luxurious appointments:

'Descending from the Promenade Deck – which is 220 feet long and the whole width of the vessel – two staircases lead to the aft

Buchanan Steamers' *Elaine* dated from 1867 and operated between Glasgow and Rothesay until 1899 when she was sold for scrap. Here, she is pictured off Greenock. (A. *Ernest Glen collection*)

First Class catering on the *Columba* followed the very latest trends in hospitality provision in the grandest hotels on *terra firma*, rather than being arranged and operated like a naval wardroom as was hitherto standard practice on passenger ships of all sizes:

'Mr Turner, the steward, who now undertakes the purveying of both the *Iona* and *Columba*, has effected a revolution in the art of dining on board ship by the use of round instead of long, straight tables, and by serving diners at all hours instead of at one stated time. By this means, a little party of tourists may dine at their own table without interference from others, and at any time they may choose. The steward's pantry and scullery, leading off the dining saloon, are fitted up with all the latest improvements, one of the most novel of which is a counter warmed by steam, on which there is room for ten or fifteen dishes…

The saloon for steerage passengers is plainly though substantially furnished, and below is a refreshment bar, with semi-circular counter, silver-plated rail, decanters and glasses all complete. Forward of this again is the fore-cabin very comfortably upholstered. Bathrooms, pursers' cabins, and store-rooms are closely adjacent, and their fittings serve to show how thoroughly the demands of passengers and officials have been anticipated.'[82]

The *Lord of the Isles* and *Columba* were the largest and finest Clyde steamers of their era and, as they sailed in parallel from Rothesay towards the Kyles of Bute, it was inevitable that their captains would be tempted to race one and other towards the narrows beyond Colintraive. In the 1880s, racing by Clyde steamers was commonplace and, while it was acknowledged to be potentially dangerous, the authorities usually turned a blind eye. The reason was that it was regarded as an exciting sport by enough of the travelling public and rival steamers owners, officers and

steamers on the stretch from Rothesay Bay to Colintraive, Kyles of Bute. Both steamers left Rothesay Bay at the same time, the *Lord of the Isles* having, if anything, the advantage of about her own length of a lead. It was evident to the crowd on the pier as well as to the passengers on both steamers that a trial of speed was about to be made. As Ardbeg Point was reached, the *Columba*, on the outside berth, forged ahead and crept up on the stern of the *Lord of the Isles*, the clouds of smoke emitted from the funnels gradually changed to flame and showing that steam was well upon both steamers. At the entrance to the Kyles, it was evident to those on board both vessels that the *Columba* was slowly but surely making way, and when fairly into the Kyles she passed the *Lord of the Isles*, winning, so to speak, a stern race by two boat lengths. Approaching Colintraive, the *Columba* slowed in order to take the pier, and the *Lord of the Isles* passed on, her crew and passengers maintaining a suggestive silence, whilst the *Columba*'s passengers cheered vociferously.'[83]

A forest of funnels and masts at Bowling Harbour; there, steamers were laid up in large numbers during the quiet winter season. In the foreground is MacBrayne's *Gael* with *Mountaineer, Fusilier, Grenadier* and *Lord of the Isles* behind, as well as five North British Railway steamers plus four Clyde Navigation Trust hoppers. *(A. Ernest Glen collection)*

crews to make it worth the risk and slight expense of wasted coal. Besides, this was relatively cheap and plentiful, as was the labour needed to man the stokeholds. Several steamer captains were admired for their prowess in competition and there was good money to be made by arriving first at a crowded pier and boarding as many as possible ahead of a steamer belonging to a competing operator. (In the late-1880s, racing for piers came to an end when a signalling system was introduced to force vessels to berth in an orderly sequence.) The Glasgow River Bailie Court could reprimand captains, imposing fines or week-long prison sentences but, in spite of occasional collisions, steamer racing remained a common occurrence on the Firth of Clyde. In September 1888, *The Glasgow Herald* reported on a particularly exciting contest between the *Lord of the Isles* and the *Columba*, from which the younger steamer emerged victorious:

'Yesterday, a fair trial of speed took place between the crack river

For the Lochgoil and Lochlong Steamboat Company, the obvious solution to the threat posed by the magnificent *Columba* was to order a new *Lord of the Isles* of improved design. This vessel was built by D&W Henderson and delivered in 1891. Her larger dimensions and full-width deck saloons successfully emulated the *Columba*'s feeling of spaciousness but although the second *Lord of the Isles* was both popular and long-lived, the *Columba*'s regally ornate design helped her retain a loyal following and ultimately she survived the longer of the two in commercial service.

First Class catering aboard such fine Clyde saloon steamers as these was of a very high standard. An early-1890s menu from the *Columba*'s Dining Saloon shows that for dinner, costing 2/6, passengers could order soup, cold salmon and cucumber, roast beef, roast mutton, roast lamb with mint sauce, boiled mutton with caper sauce, chicken, green peas, mixed vegetables and cheese salad. The drinks list was extensive and included five

81 Paterson, 1972, pp111-112.
82 Paterson, 1972, pp112-113.
83 Glasgow Herald, 21st September 1888.

Above: The original *Lord of the Isles* approaches Rothesay Pier in the latter 1880s. *(A. Ernest Glen collection)*

Right: A busy scene at Rothesay Pier during the 1904 Glasgow Fair holiday with the *Lady of the Isles*, ex *Lord of the Isles* (I), loading and unloading the multitudes. During a period of service on the Thames, the steamer was fitted with telescopic funnels, as shown here. *(A. Ernest Glen collection)*

Below: Captain Alexander Williamson's *Sultan* and the Lochgoil & Lochlong Company's *Chancellor* racing in the Firth of Clyde circa 1890; shortly thereafter, both vessels were acquired by the Glasgow & South Western Railway. The *Chancellor*'s deck saloons provided a far higher level of comfort and protection than was available on the *Sultan*. *(A. Ernest Glen collection)*

different kinds of champagne as well as a special *Columba* blended whisky only available on the vessel. After dinner cigars were available.

While the First Class accommodation of the *Lord of the Isles* and the *Columba* set very high standards for comfort and service, much of the remainder of the Clyde fleet sailing from Broomielaw in central Glasgow remained comparatively downmarket. Moreover, the upper river was fetid as, at that time, Glasgow lacked provision for sewerage treatment and so raw excrement, as well as industrial waste, was discharged, causing a sickening stench to hang over the consequently blackened water. As one English visitor described it in a letter to *The Glasgow Herald*,

'It is nothing better than the foulest sewer…and it is astonishing that the effluvia constantly emitted have not been the cause of some serious epidemic… You have a city of palaces, magnificent streets, well paved and thoroughly clean, but your main artery, which should be as pure as possible, is a continuous stream of reeking filth and noxious vapours…'[84]

Meanwhile, newspapers frequently commented disapprovingly on

confess that I have never seen on any river in Europe or America such disgraceful scenes as I have witnessed on board the…boats which run daily on out…river. A week or two ago the writer went with a party…who were most anxious to see the beauties of the romantic scenery of our highland lochs, of which they have heard so much. The weather was splendid, the boat was comfortably full at both ends, and everything looked as if we were going to have a good time of it without anything happening to distract our attention. We had just got as far as Govan, the river was low, the water was black as ink, and the smell was – well, such as no one who had a nose would think of asking his lady love or anyone else to hasten with him to Kelvin Grove to inhale the perfume, certainly not of 'Araby the blest'. We had not yet got clear of the sweet smelling Kelvin ere many of our female passengers began to overhaul their bags and baskets in search of the irrepressible black bottle, which having found, they pulled out the cork using their teeth for a screw, then applying the neck of the bottle to their mouths, they took a long, hearty pull of the contents,

The impressive second *Lord of the Isles* at speed in the Firth of Clyde. By this point, her promenade deck had been extended forward to the bow, thus increasing her deck accommodation. *(A. Ernest Glen collection)*

examples of drunkenness on board steamers from the Broomielaw as even a handful of inebriates could potentially spoil the atmosphere of a cruise. The Sunday steamers, in particular, were notorious as refuges for habitual drinkers, whose reliable patronage was welcomed by steamer operators as their sacrificing health and dignity made a substantial contribution to the ships' profitability. As one correspondent to *The Glasgow Herald* observed, sailing from Glasgow, it was seemingly impossible to enjoy:

'A good day's sail without being compelled to witness the continuous…profane and obscene language that is so freely bandied about, and so familiar to the ears of the natives of the 'Second City'. It is too bad that strangers who come here to enjoy a few weeks' holiday…should have their pleasures marred by the senseless, ignorant conduct of a number of Glasgow rowdies…I am free to

handed it to their neighbour who followed suit… The above process continued all the way down, and by the time we reached Greenock the horse play was in full swing – dancing and singing, swearing and tumbling about, screaming of women and children, who could not get out of the way quick enough, was truly pitiful to witness. We left the boat at Greenock and came home by train, glad to escape.'[85]

Such scenes led the morally-minded to support the Temperance Movement, which in Glasgow became a powerful social and political force in the latter decades of the nineteenth century. Moreover, deeply entrenched class distinctions meant that the expanding and prosperous *haute bourgeoisie* sought to distance themselves from the *hoi polloi* who formed the majority of excursionists on the steamers from Broomielaw. To cater specifically for this relatively wealthy and discerning market, a syndicate was

84 Paterson, 1972, p180.
85 Paterson, 1972, pp201-202.

The graceful *Ivanhoe* leaving Millport in the livery of the Caledonian Steam Packet Company, by whom she was operated from 1897 onwards. *(A. Ernest Glen collection)*

formed in 1879 to finance a new steamer operator, the Frith of Clyde Steam Packet Company Ltd. This was backed by the well-known Glasgow ship owners Alexander Allan, owner of the Allan Line, George Smith and Captain James Brown of the City Line and the Clyde steamer operator Captain James Williamson.

Williamson was one of three sons of the well-known and admired Clyde steamer owner Captain Alexander Williamson. Each of his three sons – James, John and Alexander (jnr) – went on to become a leading operator of Clyde steamers, thereby making the Williamson family the most influential dynasty involved in the provision of Clyde services from the mid-nineteenth century until the inter-war era.

In 1880, a new steamer named the *Ivanhoe* was launched from D. & W. Henderson's shipyard at Partick to operate daily excursions from Helensburgh via Greenock, Dunoon and Wemyss Bay to Rothesay and Arran piers – an inspired itinerary, both enabling passengers to board at rail-connected piers on both banks of the Clyde and giving an attractive day's cruising through the most scenic sections of the Firth.

Externally and within, the *Ivanhoe* was a magnificent vessel – her livery introducing yacht yellow funnels while her hull was in black and adorned with a profusion of gilt lining and ornament. Captain Williamson was her senior master and he ensured that crew discipline was strict and service First Class. The *Ivanhoe* was elegantly appointed – an unusual feature of her dining room being grape vines trained up the walls and across the ceiling.

In promoting the benefits of temperance cruising, the *Ivanhoe*'s owners were typically forthright:

Safety and Comfort on board the 'Ivanhoe'
During the Fair Holidays
As this STEAMER DOES NOT SAIL TO OR FROM
GLASGOW, PASSENGERS may rely on having a PLEASANT SAIL
without the Ordinary Rabble common on board Clyde steamers
during the Glasgow Fair

From the outset, the *Ivanhoe* proved popular with 'respectable' citizens who flocked to her safe in the knowledge that they would enjoy a day's sail free from drinkers. Additionally, her cleanliness, polite crew and generous itinerary guaranteed her success. (Even on a saloon steamer, however, the

Clyde estuary could be chilly and so entrepreneurs in Brodick began to sell hipflasks of whisky to her passengers to warm them up; these became known as 'Ivanhoe flasks'.) Once a new generation of railway-owned saloon steamers appeared in the 1890s, emulating the *Ivanhoe*'s upmarket style while providing bar facilities, her profitability declined. Eventually, in 1897 the Frith of Clyde Steam Packet Company capitulated, chartering their steamer to the Caledonian Steam Packet Company, who operated her with renewed success as a licensed vessel.

The saloon steamer and her less grand contemporaries reflected the norms of their era, and also the hallmarks of their urban environment and clientele, at every level. Their designs, internal and external, represented the top line of aspiration in their day, but their class divisions, the ill-feeling between the 'temperate' traveller and the 'intemperate', the struggles between well-to-do passengers and the 'rabble', and the on-board live musical entertainment which boomed loud across the Clyde, mirrored city life. Ships helped to shape Glasgow and the Clyde, but, equally, Glasgow and the Clyde shaped ships, not only as hulls and superstructures, but also as 'floating communities'. Further adaptation of ships, services, communities and facilities was to be caused by the advent of the railways.

A stern quarter view of the *Ivanhoe* in her original Firth of Clyde Steam Packet Company livery. *(A. Ernest Glen collection)*

Above: A busy scene at the Broomielaw with the Lochgoil & Lochlong Company's *Chancellor* setting sail with a good load of passengers, several of whom are sheltering beneath umbrellas. *(A. Ernest Glen collection)*

Right: The Broomielaw again, this time with Buchanan Steamers' *Undine* nearest the camera. *(A. Ernest Glen collection)*

Below: The Lochgoil & Lochlong Company's *Edinburgh Castle* at Lochgoilhead. *(A. Ernest Glen collection)*

Below right: A deck scene on the *Edinburgh Castle* - a steamer instantly recognisable on account of her very large paddle boxes. *(A. Ernest Glen collection)*

Chapter Four

Railway Steamers and Rail-connected Services

The first railway to reach the Clyde Coast was the Glasgow, Paisley & Greenock in March 1841, followed by the Glasgow, Paisley and Ayr in August 1843. These developments immediately challenged the steamers from the Broomielaw for passenger traffic. Going by rail from Glasgow to Greenock reduced the overall journey time to Dunoon and Rothesay by an hour and thus the era of combined rail and steamer journeys began.[86] Furthermore, by taking the train to the coast and joining a steamer there, better-off passengers could avoid having to sail through the industrial pollution and untreated sewerage in the upper river – and also evade the hoards of heavy drinkers who took excursions *en masse* from the Broomielaw.

For a complexity of reasons, initial efforts to provide rail-connected steamer services with through-ticketing were unsuccessful. The first to attempt this was the Glasgow, Paisley and Greenock Railway. This opened in 1841, connecting Bridge Street station – located immediately to the south of the Clyde where the running in lines to Glasgow Central are today – with Paisley, Langbank and Greenock. To get from train to ship, passengers had to make their way through the alleys of the poorest part of Greenock to reach Customhouse Quay, where steamers called *en route* from Glasgow to destinations in the lower firth. Carrying heavy luggage in torrential rain would have made this connection most unpleasant. Besides, combined rail and steamer travel was relatively expensive in comparison with taking a steamer direct from the Broomielaw.

The railway entered into an agreement with the Bute Steam Packet Company, whose steamers *Isle of Bute* and *Maid of Bute* it acquired in 1844, before adding a further three vessels to their fleet. A lack of experience on the part of the railway's management meant that losses were incurred and so the steamers were sold back to private owners in 1846.

The Caledonian Railway absorbed the Glasgow, Paisley & Greenock in

Fathers, mothers and children, showing a splendid range of late Victorian fashion which concedes little to warm weather, board a steamer at Craigendoran Pier. On the left, the ship's officers are talking to a gentleman with top hat and stylish walking cane. *(A. Ernest Glen collection)*

1851 and, by the 1860s it had attracted away a large proportion of the steamers' passengers between Glasgow and Greenock, leaving mainly Glasgow's poorer citizens, for whom time was less a factor than cost, to sail all the way from the city centre.[87] The challenge for the railways was to find a suitable location for a combined station and pier so as to attract a larger proportion of travellers continuing to Dunoon, Rothesay and other destinations in the lower firth.

By 1865, the Caledonian and the Greenock & Ayrshire (later Glasgow & South Western) railways had rival proposals for lines to Gourock, which was separated from Greenock by a hilly projection of the Renfrewshire Plateau, meaning that it would be necessary to bore a 1.2 mile long tunnel. Parliament favoured the Caledonian's proposal but, pending the accumulation of sufficient funding to proceed, the project was allowed temporarily to lapse.[88]

In May 1865, the Wemyss Bay Junction Railway was opened. Owned by a separate company, this had joint running powers over the Caledonian's line to Greenock, from which it deviated at Port Glasgow and continued via the Spango Valley and Inverkip to a new station and steamer pier at Wemyss Bay. In contrast to the Caledonian's station in Greenock, this facility offered a direct transfer from train to ship and was the closest departure point for Rothesay, the Clyde's most popular resort. Unlike many Scottish railways, which were primarily dedicated to the carriage of freight, the Greenock & Wemyss Bay was planned from the outset for passenger traffic. The directors were three prominent local landowners, James Scott of Kelly, James

Lamont of Knockdow and Alexander Struthers Findlay of Castle Toward; the Caledonian Railway provided £35,000 of the project's £180,000 budget and was required to work the line for 45 per cent of the receipts.

The Wemyss Bay Railway Company had no authority to run steamers in connection with its rail services and so a separate Act was obtained in early 1864 to enable the Wemyss Bay Steamboat Company to be formed.[89] They ordered three new ships, two from Messers Caird & Company of Greenock and a third, smaller vessel from Messrs Wingate, their intention being to inaugurate a network of routes reaching as far as Ardrishaig. One vessel being built at Caird's shipyard was sold to agents of the American confederacy before completion and so a replacement was then ordered. The first to be delivered was the Caird-built *Kyles* and the second was the *Largs* from Wingate. The *Bute* followed somewhat belatedly, as Caird required to begin afresh following the sale of the previous hull to America. This meant that services from Wemyss Bay were inaugurated with only two steamers, rather than the three initially intended.

Yet again, mismanagement undid what should have been a recipe for success as the *Kyles* and *Bute* proved embarrassingly slow and unreliable. In order to bring early morning Glasgow-bound commuters to Wemyss Bay in time for the 08.10 train, the steamers lay overnight in Lamlash and Tighnabruaich respectively. During the day, they made return crossings to Rothesay and Millport before returning commuters to Lamlash and Tighnabruaich in the evening. Scheduling was tight and, unfortunately, the vessels soon proved to have insufficient reserves of speed. This meant that

86 MacIntosh, 2009, p2.
87 MacIntosh, 2009, p2.
88 MacIntosh, 2009, pp2-3.
89 MacIntosh, 2009, p4.

travellers frequently suffered delays of over an hour and, as the rail connection could not be broken, their late running delayed the trains as well with knock-on effects on other services sharing the route between Glasgow, Paisley and Greenock. The Wemyss Bay Steamboat Company's acquisition of further steamers could have eased matters, but they decided to use these additional vessels between Broomielaw and Firth piers, rather than to provide a more reliable service from Wemyss Bay. No wonder the service failed to prosper and, in early 1869, the Wemyss Bay Steamboat Company went into liquidation, the *Kyles* and *Bute* being sold for use on the Thames.[90]

To ensure that steamer services were properly maintained, the Wemyss Bay Railway Company entered into an agreement with Captain James Gillies and his son-in-law Captain Alexander Campbell (who lived close to Wemyss Bay in Skelmorlie) to take over the steamer service. This meant that the railway company was dependent on two operators over whose affairs they had little control – the Caledonian running trains and Gillies & Campbell operating steamers. As in today's privatised rail industry, this fragmentation was a recipe for legal disputes between the three. Gillies & Campbell felt that both the Caledonian and Wemyss Bay Railway companies were squeezing them unfairly in terms of the percentages each received from the sale of through-tickets. The Wemyss Bay Railway, meanwhile, argued that they were being unfairly squeezed by the Caledonian, which appeared to be using their powerful position to advantage. In 1879, their new Central Station was opened in Glasgow's city centre, but departures to Wemyss Bay were not transferred there and instead continued to operate from the old Bridge Street station, south of the Clyde.[91] Meanwhile, the Caledonian were planning to build a rail extension to Gourock with a steamer terminal and to develop their own network of services. This could explain why they did relatively little to encourage travel via Wemyss Bay.

On the Clyde's North Bank, the North British Railway Company was also becoming involved in steamer operation. The NBR first gained a foothold in the Clyde steamer market through a process of railway consolidation in the 1860s. The Glasgow, Dumbarton and Helensburgh Railway had first opened in 1858 and merged with the Edinburgh & Glasgow Railway Company in 1862. Less than three years later in July 1865 this joint company passed to North British ownership. The following year, a steamer service was inaugurated from Helensburgh by their newly established subsidiary, the North British Steam Packet Company, using the steamers *Meg Merrilies* and *Dandie Dinmont*. These sister ships were purpose-built for the Company by Messers A. & J. Inglis. Beginning a North British tradition of naming steamers after characters in Sir Walter Scott's romantic novels, they operated to the Kyles of Bute and Ardrishaig via Rothesay. Most unfortunately, the *Dandie Dinmont* suffered mechanical breakdowns, necessitating the chartering of replacement vessels to cover her schedule while extensive and costly repairs were carried out. Worse still, the NBR's Chairman and some directors were found to have criminally mismanaged the railway's affairs to such an extent that the Company was effectively bankrupt. Consequently, retrenchment was inevitable and so the *Meg Merrilies* was withdrawn after only one season. She was sold overseas for service on the Bosphorus from Constantinople, while the *Dandie Dinmont* was switched to established North British routes on the Forth and Tay before returning to the Clyde in 1869 to serve Dunoon and the Holy Loch.[92] Yet again, a railway company had failed to seize the initiative from the various private steamer owners operating from the Broomielaw – but

they had at least gained a foothold.

The opening of a substantial new steamer terminal at Craigendoran in 1882 first established the North British as the leading operator of steamers from the Firth of Clyde's North Bank. By then, the Company's affairs were in better order and their steamer services were effectively managed by Robert Darling. A second *Meg Merrilies* was introduced in 1883, but saw only brief service before being returned to her builder, Barclay, Curle & Company, due to her failure to meet the contracted speed requirement. After rebuilding work to save weight, they, in turn, sold her to the Clyde excursion operator Captain Robert Campbell of Kilmun, of whom more later. The North British Railway replaced this steamer in 1884 when Barclay, Curle & Co delivered the *Jeanie Deans*. As the builder's reputation was at stake, they ensured that she was a notably fast vessel which attained an impressive 17.5 knots on trials.[93] Initially, her fleetmate was the *Guy Mannering*, formerly the Gillies & Campbell Wemyss Bay steamer *Sheila*, built in 1877 by Caird & Co and also famed for her speed. Soon, more fine vessels were added to the resurgent North British Clyde fleet – the neat little saloon steamer *Diana Vernon* of 1885, again a Barclay, Curle product, and the outstandingly successful and long-lived *Lucy Ashton* of 1888, built by T.B. Seath & Co of Rutherglen with machinery by Hutson & Corbett. Intended for a short-duration 'ferry' service to the Holy Loch, the *Lucy Ashton* was neither particularly speedy nor ornately appointed inboard, but she was solid, reliable and of very attractive appearance. In comparison with the biggest and fastest Clyde vessels of her era, she was economical and no doubt this enabled her to enjoy a career spanning over 50 years on the Firth.

The North British Railway's steamer services from Craigendoran enjoyed a boost when in 1886 the Company opened a new underground line through central Glasgow from High Street via Queen Street Low Level and Charing Cross to Great Western Road (now Anniesland). This enabled faster services to Craigendoran and Helensburgh than were possible on the NBR's existing northerly route via Maryhill.

At Wemyss Bay, meanwhile, Captain Alexander Campbell's Wemyss Bay Steamboat Company had taken delivery from Blackwood & Gordon in 1886 of a magnificent new steamer, the *Victoria*. Unlike the North British fleet's moderately sized vessels, this steamer, while likewise intended mainly for rail-connected ferry operation, was of similar layout, propulsion and outward appearance to the stately excursion ship *Ivanhoe*. In describing the *Victoria*'s very commodious and opulently appointed interiors, *The Glasgow Herald* noted a fresh innovation:

> 'The steamer is fitted throughout with electric lighting by Messers Bennet & Co, Glasgow, and is the first in the river fleet fitted with this luxury, it is sure to be a great attraction for evening trips. The upholstery work... is of the most pleasing and complete description. The principal saloon is all finished in solid hardwood, polished walnut, and plane tree, richly done with blue velvet... In every respect the *Victoria* will fully maintain the high standard of beauty and comfort of a Clyde passenger steamer.'[94]

The *Victoria* was highly suited to meeting the requirements of special charterers – for example, to carry spectators during yacht regattas. The Wemyss Bay Junction Railway, however, was most keen that Campbell should use her exclusively on regular rail-connected services from Wemyss Bay to Rothesay, Port Bannatyne, Innellan, Largs and Millport. As the railway took a substantial percentage of revenue from this arrangement it

90 MacIntosh, 2009, p5.
91 MacIntosh, 2009, p7.
92 Duckworth and Langmuir, 1972, pp52-53.
93 Duckworth and Langmuir, 1972, p54.
94 Glasgow Herald, 31st May 1886.

Above: Three Gillies & Campbell Wemyss Bay Steamboat Company paddle steamers - the *Largs*, *Argyle* and *Cumbrae* - lie at Millport. *(A. Ernest Glen collection)*

Right: The Wemyss Bay Steamboat Company's flagship *Victoria*, delivered in 1886. *(A. Ernest Glen collection)*

Below: Robert Campbell's steamers *Benmore* and *Meg Merrilees* at the Broomielaw, both bound for Kilmun, in 1885. Note the distinctive windmill-type destination indicator behind the latter vessel's funnel, with the various piers painted on fingers attached to a central cog. *(A. Ernest Glen collection)*

Below right: The *Benmore* at the Broomielaw; Robert Campbell's white-funnelled steamers were popular with Glasgow's multitudes on account of their reasonable prices and relatively high level of service. *(A. Ernest Glen collection)*

The *Meg Merrilees* in the Caledonian Steam Packet Company's stylish livery of dark blue, pink, white and buff yellow off Greenock. *(A. Ernest Glen collection)*

was not surprising that, whenever possible, Campbell sought more lucrative charter work for the *Victoria*, meaning that her advertised scheduled service could not be relied upon to take place on a daily basis and frequently she was replaced by older, less attractively appointed members of Campbell's fleet. Passengers complained and this strained relations between Campbell and the Wemyss Bay Junction and Caledonian Railways. This situation gave the Caledonian an impetus to develop a steamer fleet of their own so as to control directly the development and operation of a Clyde estuarial shipping service.

By the late-1880s, Glasgow was reaching its zenith as a great industrial city. To celebrate its wealth and prowess in 1888 a great International Exhibition was held in Kelvingrove Park. There, Glasgow's engineering achievements were displayed in a series of substantial iron-framed pavilions with ornate facades in a fascinatingly eclectic variety of colonial styles. The exhibition was actually the first of three such events which defined the city's 'golden era' in the quarter-century prior to the outbreak of the First World War (other such exhibitions were held in 1901 and 1911). Over five and a half million visitors visited the 1888 International Exhibition and the Clyde's rail and steamer services enjoyed record-breaking business. With many visitors visiting Scotland from overseas, the vessels had an unusually cosmopolitan atmosphere, carrying as they did significant numbers of 'colourful peculiar foreigners' who were 'a source of fascination to locals.'[95]

Also pictured off Greenock, the Caledonian Steam Packet company's other pioneering steamer, the *Madge Wildfire*, lays down a thick cloud of coal smoke. *(A. Ernest Glen collection)*

The *Madge Wildfire* later in her Caledonian Steam Packet Company career and by now sporting an additional deck saloon, forward of her paddle boxes. *(A. Ernest Glen collection)*

The lead-up to the exhibition gave Scottish businesses increased confidence to invest in new infrastructure. In 1889, the Caledonian Railway opened their Gourock extension, where they inaugurated a new steamer pier. In anticipation of this, they entered negotiations with a number of independent steamer owners to begin regular services from there. The request received a mixed response; some owners ignored it altogether, while David MacBrayne simply offered to add an extra call at Gourock by their existing steamers *en route* to Ardrishaig. None of the operators were prepared to offer the Caledonian the network of regular rail-connected services their directors felt were necessary to make their Gourock extension viable.

With site works underway at Gourock's harbour front, the inevitability of rail-connected steamer services being introduced from there was a challenge in particular to the Kilmun and Holy Loch steamer service operated from Glasgow by Peter and Alexander Campbell. They were the inheritors of the business hitherto run by their recently deceased father, Captain Robert Campbell. This had been founded in 1854 by his uncles, Alexander and John Campbell from Roseneath, both of whom were steamer captains in the 1830s. The first steamer they owned outright was the *Duchess of Argyle*, to which they assigned Robert Campbell as captain. He succeeded his uncles as owner of the business, and then entered into partnership in 1871 with Glasgow coal merchants Hugh Keith & Co to expand it. Unfortunately, in 1884, the Keith & Campbell steamer operation went bankrupt and their seven-strong fleet was sold to another prominent Clyde operator, Captain William Buchanan.

Buchanan's firm had been founded in 1853 when, with his business partner, Captain Alexander Williamson, he purchased the steamer *Eagle* from the shipbuilders William Denny & Bros of Dumbarton for service between the Broomielaw and Rothesay. In 1862, Williamson and Buchanan sold her to American interests as a civil war blockade-runner and thereafter dissolved their partnership, each owner subsequently developing an independent steamer business.

From the mid-nineteenth century onward, the photographic record of the vista downriver from Glasgow Bridge almost invariably shows a paddle steamer with funnels painted in Captain William Buchanan's livery of black with a white band.[96]

Buchanan's steamers became synonymous with the Glasgow-Rothesay/Kyles of Bute service. Meanwhile, vessels belonging to Captain Alexander Williamson, with the same funnel colours, also utilised the Broomielaw berths, and served the same routes. Popularly known as the 'Turkish Fleet', Williamson's steamers initially carried names such as *Sultan*, *Sultana* and *Viceroy*, while the Williamson house flag, sporting a yellow star and crescent on a blue background, was reminiscent of the Turkish national flag. The imperial grandeur implicit in Buchanan's eagle symbolism, in tune with British aspirations in the high Victorian era, was thus complemented by a touch of 'orientalism' in the Williamson fleet, in keeping with another dimension of Victorian grandeur, namely its concern with the 'mysterious', 'luxurious' East. Both symbols say much about the ethos of Glasgow and its maritime aspirations in the mid-nineteenth century. During the ensuing 20 years, Buchanan's fleet expanded rapidly through the purchase of mainly second-hand vessels from other faltering private owners, including those belonging to Robert Campbell.

95 Kinchin, 1988, p49.
96 *Glasgow Victoriana: Classic Photographs by Thomas Annan*, Ayr, undated, p37.

Above: The Caledonian Steam Packet Company's impressive flagship *Galatea* makes a stirring sight at speed in the Firth of Clyde in her 1890s heyday. Greedy on coal, her career on the Clyde was relatively short. *(A. Ernest Glen collection)*

Right: The *Galatea*'s engine room. *(A. Ernest Glen collection)*

Below: The *Caledonia* was the CSP's first new delivery in June 1889 and a very successful member of the fleet, remaining in service until 1933. Here, she is seen off Gourock after her 1903 rebuilding, when her bridge was re-located forward of her funnel. The forward windows in her deck saloon are boarded over to protect the glass from breakage during winter service. *(A. Ernest Glen collection)*

Below right: The splendid CSP Arran steamer *Duchess of Hamilton* at Gourock in April 1908. *(A. Ernest Glen)*

Having sold his existing vessels to Buchanan to pay off his company's debts, Campbell planned, at the earliest opportunity, to raise sufficient capital to re-enter the steamer business. Naively, Buchanan failed to insist on a clause in the take-over contract forbidding Campbell from competing directly with his vessels, unwisely believing that a 'gentlemen's agreement' would be sufficient. As Campbell was well connected he quickly accumulated sufficient finance to buy from the North British Railway their unsuccessful *Meg Merrilies*, plus a new steamer built by Messers S. McKnight & Co of Ayr which he named *Madge Wildfire*. These initiatives understandably caused Buchanan considerable irritation as he believed that, in purchasing Campbell's ships, he had bought the goodwill to serve the Kilmun and Holy Loch route without competition from the previous operator. Yet, as Campbell's steamers were popular with the travelling public, he quickly won back much of the trade to the Holy Loch from Buchanan.

Following Campbell's death in 1888, his sons Peter and Alexander decided that, with Gourock Pier nearing completion, their best course of action would be to sell the business to the Caledonian Railway. Already the brothers had a profitable excursion operation on the Bristol Channel using their steamer *Waverley* and it was there that they decided to focus their business interests. Indeed, during subsequent decades, they built up a magnificent fleet and a great reputation in South-West England, notably in the Bristol Channel.

The travelling public deeply regretted the Campbells' departure from the Clyde for they were regarded as being among the best steamer operators with regard to comfort, punctuality and reasonable fares. In comparison, Scotland's railway companies were viewed with suspicion due to their political clout, reputation for sharp practice and often steep ticket prices. Indeed, many felt that the railways should be prevented by law from running their own steamer services, an activity viewed by large numbers as being outwith their remit and expertise in any case.[97]

In March 1889, a parliamentary committee was convened to consider the implications of the Caledonian Railway's desire to operate steamers on the Clyde. The railway argued that, as over half a million pounds had been invested in the construction of Gourock Pier, it was natural that they would wish to ensure that an appropriately intensive service was provided to offset their considerable investment in the facility. Furthermore, they argued that the majority of Clyde steamers were obsolescent and that their proposed operations would use only fast, clean and well-appointed steamers. The following day, objections were heard, predictably enough from existing steamer operators. The third day of evidence proved most embarrassing for the Caledonian Railway when it was revealed that not only had they pre-empted the committee's outcome by purchasing the *Meg Merrilies* and *Madge Wildfire*, but they had also placed orders for two further steamers without parliamentary sanction. This caused the committee to conclude that the Caledonian Railway should be refused permission.

With Gourock Pier due to open only two months thereafter, the Caledonian Railway's directors were in a most awkward situation and so they decided that the best solution in the circumstances would be to establish a separate company to run steamers from Gourock and Wemyss Bay. Such a move would avoid any need for parliamentary approval, and so on 7th May 1889 the Caledonian Steam Packet Company was established, the Marquis of Breadalbane being appointed Chairman and Captain James Williamson, co-owner of the *Ivanhoe*, being named Company Secretary. Thus, through an awkward combination of circumstances, what was to become the largest and most enduring Clyde steamer operator was launched.

The *Meg Merrilies* was probably the first steamer to wear the Caledonian Steam Packet Company's outstandingly elegant livery of a sea-green underbody, white boot topping, a midnight blue hull with two thin gold strakes, the saloon deck and sponsons being pale pink with white paddle boxes, deckhouses in varnished teak and a buff yellow funnel. In addition, the paddle boxes were generously adorned with gilded ornamentation, the overall effect being that the vessel resembled a large private yacht. Of course, her crew was smartly uniformed so as to reinforce this impression. Hitherto, Clyde steamers had been painted mainly in black, often with dark brown deckhouses and perhaps some red paint on their funnels. The Caledonian Steam Packet Company's very refined livery signalled style and sophistication to upwardly mobile passengers – and a very different kind of travel experience from the mainly ageing and crowded vessels sailing from Broomielaw.

The Caledonian Railway's Gourock extension was opened on 1st June 1889, the first train being driven by the Company's famed locomotive superintendent Dugald Drummond, who had designed the 4-4-0 express locomotive type used on the route. Large crowds turned out to spectate and residents whose homes backed on to the line side waved towels and bed linen from their windows as the inaugural train passed by. Before the railway opened, however, the *Meg Merrilies* had called at Gourock Pier on a trial basis while *en route* from Glasgow to Kilmun. The timetabling of 26 trains a day in each direction from Glasgow Central called for an intensive steamer service to the popular resorts of Dunoon and Rothesay and, as the Caledonian Steam Packet Company's own new buildings were not ready on time, they chartered the *Ivanhoe* to supplement their own vessels from Gourock.[98]

The new CSP steamers, named *Caledonia* and *Galatea*, were ordered respectively from marine engine builders Rankin & Blackmore, who subcontracted hull construction to John Reid & Co, and Caird & Co. The *Caledonia*'s innovative compound machinery and twin forced-draught boilers promised better fuel economy and increased power output than typical of existing vessels. In addition, she boasted extensive enclosed passenger accommodation for both First and Third classes and very elegant internal appointments. Notwithstanding her relatively large top hamper and the fact that her boilers were considerably heavier than the less sophisticated 'haystack' variety installed in the majority of steamers of her era, she achieved nearly 17 knots on trials.[99]

The *Galatea*, which the CSP intended as their flagship, was also technically forward-looking, being fitted with the first twin-crank compound engine on a Clyde steamer. Not only did this give her a 17.36-knot trials speed, but also avoided the distinctive jolting motion which characterised paddle steamers with single crank machinery, such as the *Caledonia*. She was fitted with no less than four forced-draught boilers which gave her both a high speed and a large consumption of coal. In terms of layout and outward appearance, the *Galatea* somewhat resembled the *Ivanhoe* and she was widely regarded as being among the finest steamers of her day. Unfortunately, her machinery and paddles were located too far forward, meaning that the drag caused by her hull's aft body reduced their effectiveness and so, as her engines consequently required to be worked hard to maintain schedule, the *Galatea* was a disappointment in terms of fuel economy. Indeed, her operational costs ensured that her Clyde career lasted

97 Paterson, 1969, pp38-39.
98 MacArthur, 1971, pp14-17.
99 MacArthur, 1971, p16.

Elegant, speedy and superbly appointed inboard, the *Duchess of Hamilton* was a great success for the CSP on their Ardrossan-Brodick route. In the manner of Thames steamers of the same era, her promenade deck was carried all the way forward to the bow above her forward mooring deck. Here, she is seen operating under charter to carry spectators of a yacht race. *(A. Ernest Glen collection)*

only 17 years, whereas the *Caledonia* survived for no less than 44 years in the CSP fleet.[100]

Not only did Gourock Pier host the CSP's four handsome steamers, but most of the wider Clyde fleet called there too on their way between Broomielaw and destinations on the Firth. Rather than travelling downriver by steamer from Glasgow, increasing numbers of passengers now preferred to take the train to Gourock and sail onward from there. On Glasgow Fair Saturday 1889, *The Glasgow Herald* described the rush of passengers to the coast from Central Station:

'Nothing could have surpassed the genial, exhilarating atmosphere of the morning... At the Central Railway Station the passenger traffic throughout the day was heavier than on any previous Fair Saturday. Gourock alone was the destination of several thousand passengers... The *Cobra* train for Gourock [operating in connection with the day sailing for Belfast] was sent off in two portions, each of 16 carriages, and every compartment was quite filled... Next came the *Columba* train, also despatched in two portions. The *Lord of the Isles* passengers filled one long train of carriages. The nine o'clock train to Gourock was run in two portions, as were the ten o'clock, the 10.23 and the 11.35. Some idea may thus be formed of the enormous number of passengers who journeyed on Saturday over the Caledonian Gourock line...'[101]

In 1890, the Caledonian Railway expanded their reach to Ardrossan Harbour through the completion of the Lanarkshire and Ayrshire Railway which branched off their Glasgow-Kilmarnock route at Lugton and reached Ardrossan via Kilwinning. The Caledonian had intended this line primarily to carry lucrative coal traffic from Lanarkshire's mining areas for export to Ireland. A secondary role was to carry boat trains connecting with steamers from Ardrossan to Belfast. For the Caledonian's directors, the chance to run a steamer service to Arran was also an attractive proposition.

Hitherto, the Glasgow & South Western Railway had solely operated passenger traffic to Ardrossan, with Captain William Buchanan's steamers making the onward connection to Arran. The CSP therefore decided to build a vessel to capture the bulk of the Arran trade from Buchanan, and so, in the autumn of 1889, they placed an order with William Denny & Bros of Dumbarton. By May 1890, their new vessel, named the *Duchess of Hamilton*, was completed. In order to conceal from the Glasgow and South Western Railway their intention to base her at Ardrossan, during construction, the CSP's directors allowed a rumour to spread that she was for operation in Australia.

While Dunoon and Rothesay were developed with villas for wealthy Glaswegians and numerous pubs, guesthouses and entertainments for visitors arriving *en masse* by steamer, Arran remained largely unchanged until the final decades of the nineteenth century. The 1881 census revealed that of the island's population of 4,700, no fewer than 2,880 were Gaelic speakers. The reason was that the Duke of Hamilton, who owned the island, did little to encourage tourism and so the limited numbers of visitors who did visit were required to put up with rather run down cottages. No doubt, accommodation of this kind – coupled with Arran's mountainous scenery and lush vegetation – greatly appealed to romantic visions of the picturesque for those who really sought temporarily to retreat altogether from the grime and grind of Glasgow. Once the Caledonian Railway's service appeared, Arran became a very popular destination, especially for the prosperous middle classes to take family holidays in tranquil surroundings with relatively clean and secluded beaches and bays in which children could paddle safely.

With her promenade deck carried forward to the bow, the new CSP steamer *Duchess of Hamilton* more closely resembled steamers subsequently built by Denny for the Thames than any Clyde vessel of her period. Inboard, her First Class accommodation was magnificently appointed, as *The Glasgow Herald* observed:

'The saloon…is of walnut with mahogany pilasters, enriched with hand painted gilt panels. The ceiling is very pretty, the colours being cream and gold. Spring-stuffed settees, affording a most luxurious seat, are placed athwartships in the saloon. There are also a writing and a reading table, while the heating is effected by means of a very handsome stove. The floor is laid with carpets and carpet runners; the curtains and spring blinds, in

The *Duchess of Hamilton*'s sumptuous First Class dining saloon - the height of late-Victorian shipboard sophistication. *(Jim MacIntosh collection)*

terracotta and tan, harmonise well with the general decorations. At the aft end is a sliding door, having a stained glass panel with a portrait of the *Duchess of Hamilton*, admits to the quarter deck. The dining saloon is underneath… The cushions are old gold frieze velvet, and the curtains in the ports are in blue and tan silk damask. The table covers are in silk tapestry, woven especially to the size of the table, and having gold borders all round.'[102]

Not only was the *Duchess of Hamilton* luxurious but she was also speedy, attaining 18.1 knots on trials and, in an impromptu race, overtaking MacBrayne's *Columba* during a special trip for invited guests. The Caledonian Railway's Arran Express train, which brought passengers from Glasgow Central, was formed of new bogie carriages and the total journey time from Glasgow via Ardrossan to Brodick was scheduled to take only 90 minutes. For First Class passengers, the *Duchess of Hamilton* offered

added refinements:

'Not the least attractive feature in connection with the Caledonian Company's phenomenally cheap and efficient steam packet service is the sea water bathing arrangements on board their steamer *Duchess of Hamilton*, plying between Ardrossan and the isle of Arran. Those of the cabin passengers who care to indulge in *saline ablutions* in a comfortably equipped bathroom on the passage are at liberty to do so, without either charge for the accommodation or towels etc, and during the warmest portion of this summer the luxury was so popular as to render the demand far greater than the supply. The bath is operative only while the boat is in motion.'[103]

No doubt the provision of baths was highly popular with tourists who had travelled from afar to reach Ardrossan and wished to have a good wash before reaching their holiday destination. In addition, the facility probably reflected the fashionability at that time of the Hydropathic Movement, whose followers believed that bathing in cold water bestowed benefits to health. Several large spa hotels were built in rural Scotland in the late Victorian years and, no doubt, the *Duchess of Hamilton*'s First Class passengers would have been the same clientele as were attracted to recuperate in these facilities. The link between 'health tourism', railways and steamships is demonstrated vividly in an article written in 1895 by a visitor to the 'hydropathic establishment' at Shandon, near Helensburgh:

'My stay in Glasgow was limited, and, having only a few weeks to spare, I thought they could not be spent better than in one of the hydropathic establishments in the north of Scotland. After some cogitation, the spot selected was Shandon, near Helensburgh. It was a place of which I had never heard before, but there was something romantic in this very ignorance which made me all the more desirous to visit it. If not agreeable, I was not bound to stay there more than a week, thus I argued and thus I consoled myself. Accordingly, having sent a telegram to Shandon to secure rooms, I took the train from Glasgow to Craigendoran Pier. The journey lasted less than two hours, and, being through very variegated scenery, was most enjoyable. At Craigendoran a steamer was waiting for us to convey us to our temporary home. I got on board in company with a noble band of tourists – young, old and middle-aged – looking at one another with an eye of interest, for were they not going to be fellow-sojourners with the same object – the pursuit of pleasure or the search for health?…

The days passed away pleasantly enough; excursions were planned; we visited Rothesay; we took steamer to Garelochead, and walked from there to Whistlefield. From the top of a hill at the latter place we got a splendid view of three lochs – Loch Long, Loch Goil, and Gareloch. We took steamer from Helensburgh, and sailed up Loch Long. Landing at Arrochar, we took the coach to Tarbert, and sailed down Loch Lomond, the Queen of the Scottish lakes…

In conclusion, I may mention that the banks and braes of bonnie Scotland team with lovely spots, and that the insane desire to rush off to the Continent is due to the fact of these places being a sealed book to the British tourist. Paterfamilias with a large family, or the struggling professional man with a slender purse, cannot spend their holiday better than in the North, inhaling the healthy ozone-laden atmosphere of the heather-clad hills.'[104]

100 MacArthur, 1971, p17.
101 Glasgow Herald, 15th July 1889.
102 Glasgow Herald, 30th May 1890.
103 The Railway Engineer, September 1896.
104 The Queen, July 1895, p187.

A stern-quarter view of the **Duchess of Hamilton** at speed off Dunoon. *(A. Ernest Glen collection)*

Next, the Caledonian Steam Packet Company turned their attention to the expansion of steamer services from Wemyss Bay. The Wemyss Bay Railway Company's litigious owners had so irritated the Caledonian Railway's management that in August 1889 they mounted a take-over. Shortly thereafter, the rail service to Wemyss Bay was switched to depart from Glasgow Central rather than Bridge Street.

Meanwhile, the CSP ordered two new steamers from John Reid & Co to a design similar to their existing *Caledonia*, the plan being that these vessels, to be named the *Marchioness of Breadalbane* and the *Marchioness of Bute*, would take over services from Wemyss Bay from Gillies & Campbell's Wemyss Bay Steamboat Company. When Captain Alexander Campbell discovered what was afoot, in April 1890 he suddenly announced the withdrawal of the entire fleet from Wemyss Bay. Perhaps his intention was to coerce the Caledonian directors into buying his vessels to augment their own new buildings. They refused to negotiate, however, and so the Wemyss Bay Steamboat Company's steamers were sold elsewhere. Their flagship *Victoria*, for example, left the Clyde for further service on Belfast Lough.

The *Victoria*'s somewhat chequered subsequent career illustrates the lengths to which private steamer owners went in order to turn a profit in the face of railway competition. Having passed through various hands, endured a serious fire and operated for a spell on the Thames, in 1897 the *Victoria* returned to the Clyde having been acquired by Andrew Dawson Reid, a dynamic and resourceful operator of excursion steamers. He established a new subsidiary, The Clyde Steamers Ltd, to operate her from the Broomielaw with Sunday sailings while the crews of the other steamers based there had their rest day. When the Dunoon Commissioners discovered that Reid was planning to break the Sabbath by landing Sunday excursionists

there, they enacted a new bye-law to prevent this from happening. Dunoon Pier was fitted with robust iron gates which were to be closed on Sundays to prevent steamer passengers from entering the town. This did not deter Reid who firstly wrote a letter of objection to the Dunoon Commissioners, then announced that the *Victoria* would in any case call at Dunoon on her inaugural cruise on Sunday 9th May. To prevent disorder and consequent negative publicity, she would operate as a dry ship on that day. With over 600 mostly young male Glaswegians on board, the *Victoria* departed the Broomielaw in fine weather. Large crowds gathered ashore to watch her progress towards Dunoon where, due to a strong wind, her master decided not to risk taking her alongside. On the return leg of her cruise, she symbolically landed over 20 passengers there, but as the gates were locked, they got no further than the landward end of the pier. Subsequent Sunday sailings followed a similar pattern but, come the Glasgow Fair, the *Victoria*'s owners decided to take more robust action. Dunoon was crowded with Glaswegian holidaymakers and as many as 12,000 came to spectate when the *Victoria* approached the pier on 18th July. Graeme Hunter, a colleague of Reid's, announced his intention to break down the pier gates and take full responsibility for the consequences of doing so. Thus, when the *Victoria* docked, he led 100 male passengers ashore to carry out this task. The *West Coast Times* records that:

'The quiet little watering place of Dunoon on the Clyde, was the scene on a recent Sunday of an occurrence which brings into sharp contrast the advanced spirit of the age and the conservatism of the ancient Scotch element. The Burgh Commissioners had resolved to prevent the landing of excursionists from Glasgow by the Sunday pleasure steamer *Victoria*, popularly known as the Sunday breaker, and with that intention had closed the pier gates. There were upwards of 1000 passengers on board, and the intention to call at Dunoon and land passengers had been extensively advertised. The commissioners had a large body of police present, and great crowds were present to see the fun. As the *Victoria* touched the pier deafening cheers were raised and handkerchiefs and hats were wildly waved ashore. The passengers, who were mostly men, landed, headed by Graeme Hunter, who is known as the 'boss union smasher' and advanced towards the new gates erected at the head of the pier. Outside the gates a strong force of Argyleshire constabulary were formed in line. Hunter advanced, and in a loud voice warned the police officer in command to withstand at his peril the landing of the passengers. The police officer replied that he would keep the peace at all hazards, and refuse to open the gates. Hunter, who is a powerful man, then rushed at the barricade with all his force, backed by the male passengers in a solid phalanx. The gate resisted the first assault. The crowd outside then attacked the police, and a conflict ensued, there being a great number of individual wrestling bouts. The police were badly hustled and swept aside by the mob, who immediately attacked the gates, pulling at them, while the passengers inside pushed and battered with feet and shoulders. Reinforcements were sent for, but ere they could arrive the gates were reduced to fragments and the crowd poured along the pier. No arrests were made and no serious injuries were inflicted. The victory of the Sabbath breakers was celebrated by a popular demonstration, and it was decided to present a testimonial to the Manager of the Sunday Steamer Company for the success 'in securing what is looked upon by a majority of the West of Scotland residents and English tourists as the most important improvement in the steamer service to the Clyde watering places.' Sunday excursions 'doon the watter' will no doubt be regarded as one more step on the downward path.'[105]

The Caledonian Railway's successes with their Steam Packet Company at Gourock, Ardrossan and Wemyss Bay had a devastating effect on their rival, the Glasgow & South Western Railway and the steamer owners who collaborated with them to provide through services from Glasgow to Firth of Clyde piers. To make matters worse for Captain William Buchanan in particular, the CSP quickly decided to make their Arran route from Ardrossan a year-round operation and so they ordered an additional steamer of more robust construction specifically to work the route during winter months while, in summer, she would provide additional sailings as necessary from Gourock and Wemyss Bay. The *Marchioness of Lorne* was delivered from Russell & Co in June 1891 and, although slightly slower than her fleet mates, her sturdy build and fine appointments guaranteed her success. The combined effect of the CSP's *Duchess of Hamilton* in summer and the *Marchioness of Lorne* in winter was to capture over three quarters of traffic to Arran, leaving Captain Buchanan's *Scotia* running nearly empty at all but the busiest times. To maintain a service, the Glasgow & South Western's directors felt obliged to compensate him for his consequent losses.

The Glasgow & South Western decided that their best option was to follow the Caledonian's lead and establish their own steamer fleet. In seeking parliamentary approval, they learned from the Caledonian's directors' mistakes two years previously and so their bill was carefully worded. Nonetheless, the parliamentary committee hearing involved similar arguments from the remaining independent steamer owners who now were alarmed by the pace of CSP expansion and feared that the development of a Glasgow & South Western fleet would drive them out of business. Their joint petition stated:

'There is a keen open competition…on the Clyde, and the result is beneficial…in keeping fares at the very lowest figure, and providing cheap and convenient transit for the working classes and the general population…This the private owners could not continue to maintain unless they received a fair proportion of the traffic to and from the coast by train.'[106]

James Caldwell MP expanded on this point, stating that he had,

'Made a careful study of the bill from the point of view of the working classes… The mass of the people of Glasgow were much indebted to the river steamers for the health and enjoyment they had obtained through their means… [If the railways were allowed to gain a monopoly] the working classes would lose the benefit of the cheap fares and consequently would not be able to enjoy the sea breezes…'[107]

The Caledonian Steam Packet Company's *Marchioness of Bute,* delivered in 1890 by J. Reid & Co is seen off Dunoon. *(A. Ernest Glen collection)*

Gourock Pier in the 1890s with a winter-boarded *Marchioness of Lorne* raising steam. The station and pier buildings are in the then-fashionable Arts and Crafts style, which the Caledonian Railway thought a suitable aesthetic for station buildings in suburban and seaside locations. *(A. Ernest Glen collection)*

Caldwell observed that combined rail and steamer services were the preferred mode of travel of the middle and upper classes, who wanted to commute to Glasgow from their coastal villas in comfort and as quickly as possible. Thereafter, John Wilson MP, a renowned supporter of the Temperance Movement, objected on similar grounds to the potential further decline of steamer services from the Broomielaw in the face of competition from expansive railway fleets. Other speakers followed suit in protesting on the working classes' behalf – though none had actually deigned to ask them what their preference was. A letter in *The Glasgow Herald*, signed 'A Working Man' stated,

> 'I object to those gentlemen posing as the only guardians of working class interests… It seems, so far as I am able to judge from the evidence, that their objections are solely in their own interests… I am surprised to find a temperance reformer like Mr Wilson, who is so earnest in his desire to remove all temptations to drinking out of the way, opposing what is undeniably a step in that direction. Surely Mr Wilson knows that when a man embarks on board the steamer at the Broomielaw, he embarks on board a floating public house, and that if he is going, say, the length of Rothesay, that temptation is in his way for 3 hours; whereas if he goes by rail and boat, that temptation is reduced to a minimum.'[108]

The Glasgow & South Western Railway received influential support from the Greenock Harbour Trust and from the Duke of Hamilton, owner of Arran, who hoped to benefit from the enhanced services the Glasgow & South Western might bring to the island's piers. Moreover, it was obvious to the parliamentary committee that the railway was at a severe disadvantage given the strength of the Caledonian and their expansive CSP steamer fleet.

Consequently, in July 1891 the Glasgow & South Western received permission to establish a steamer fleet of their own and immediately the company began to buy up second-hand vessels. Captain Buchanan's Arran steamer *Scotia* was the first, followed by the Lochgoil & Lochlong Company's *Chancellor* and the entire Williamson fleet, comprising the *Viceroy*, *Sultan*, *Sultana* and *Marquis of Bute*. One of Williamson's sons, Alexander, was appointed as Marine Superintendent of the new G&SWR steamer fleet.

Its vessels were ageing, however, the *Sultan* being the most elderly, having been constructed as long ago as 1861, while the *Chancellor* and *Scotia* dated only from 1880. None offered anything more than the most perfunctory accommodation for their hardy passengers. To compete effectively with the Caledonian Steam Packet Company, it would be necessary to build anew and on a lavish scale. The G&SWR therefore instituted a substantial new building programme, immediately placing orders for three steamers for delivery in 1892. Not surprisingly, priority was given to procuring a suitably grand competitor to take on the CSP's *Duchess of Hamilton* on the Ardrossan-Brodick route, for which an order was placed with J. & G. Thomson of Clydebank.

A second, smaller steamer was ordered to serve Rothesay, for the design of which the G&SWR looked to P&A Campbell's Bristol Channel vessel *Lorna Doone* for inspiration. They therefore entrusted the design of their own new buildings to her naval architect, Robert Morton of Morton & Williamson. The Rothesay steamer was ordered from David Rowan & Sons. Next, a third vessel, similar to this, was commissioned from the same builder and they subcontracted the building of both hulls to Napier, Shanks & Bell of Yoker, who had previously built the *Lorna Doone*.

105 West Coast Times, 29th September 1897.
106 Glasgow Herald, 30th June 1891.
107 Glasgow Herald, 30th June 1891.
108 Glasgow Herald, 8th July 1891.

58

Above: The Glasgow & South Western Railway's *Sultan*, inherited with the Williamson fleet and showing the primitive standard of accommodation in comparison with the Caledonian Steam Packet Company's saloon steamers. *(A. Ernest Glen collection)*

Right: The Glasgow & South Western Railway's *Princes Pier* at Gourock was designed in the Italianate manner as a rival to the Caledonian Railway's pier only a short distance to the west. The G&SWR's *Viceroy* and the North British steamer *Lady Clare* are alongside. *(A. Ernest Glen collection)*

Below: Pictured gliding through Rothesay Bay, the elegant G&SWR steamer *Neptune* of 1892 commenced the railway's fight-back against the Caledonian and their expansive fleet of saloon steamers on the lower Clyde. *(A. Ernest Glen collection)*

Below right: A stern-quarter view of the *Neptune*, leaving Craigmore Pier and next bound for Rothesay. *(A. Ernest Glen collection)*

Above: In original condition, the Glasgow & South Western Railway's flagship *Glen Sannox* is seen at speed in the Firth of Clyde. The steamer was fast but coal-hungry - so much so that, when she was requisitioned for First World War naval service, the Admiralty quickly rejected her and she was returned to the Clyde. *(A. Ernest Glen collection)*

Right: The G&SWR paddle steamer *Mercury* at speed off Gourock in April 1908. *(A. Ernest Glen)*

Below: The *Duchess of Hamilton* and *Glen Sannox* were great rival saloon steamers on the Arran run in the1890s-1900s period. Here, both lie offshore at Whiting Bay on excursion sailings between their main commuter runs to Ardrossan while their passengers are tendered ashore to enjoy strolling on the beach and paddling, circa 1892. *(A. Ernest Glen collection)*

Below right: A bow-on view of the *Glen Sannox*, entering Ayr harbour and emphasising her sleek hull lines. *(A. Ernest Glen collection)*

The Glasgow & South Western Railway's *Juno*, built in 1898 and mainly stationed at Ayr. *(A. Ernest Glen collection)*

The first of the new G&SWR steamers to be completed was the Rothesay steamer *Neptune*. As the G&SWR felt particularly exposed to CSP competition from *Duchess of Hamilton* on the Arran run, upon delivery in April 1892 they placed the *Neptune* in service between Ardrossan and Brodick, pending the completion of the route's larger, dedicated vessel. The *Neptune* was inevitably finely appointed, as *The Glasgow Herald*'s correspondent observed:

> 'The decoration of the saloon is in the best possible taste. The seats, which are on the railway carriage principle, have sprung cushions covered with the finest moquette; on the floor are pretty Brussels carpet runners; and dainty damask curtains adorn the windows. The First Class dining saloon, which is seated for seventy and is situated below the general saloon, is furnished pretty much in the style of the drawing room. The ceiling and sides are beautifully decorated, and the floors laid with tastefully designed carpets and runners. On each side of the central passage are handsome mahogany tables while right round the saloon run velvet-cushioned seats.'[109]

The *Neptune* was fitted with a twin-crank compound engine and two Navy boilers and proved capable of 18 knots, making her one of the fastest examples of her type and size. In April, she entered service between Ardrossan and Brodick, replacing the *Scotia*. At the same time, the G&SWR's train service from Glasgow St Enoch to Ardrossan was accelerated to 45 minutes non-stop and the steamer was scheduled to take 40 minutes onward to Brodick, similar to the CSP's *Duchess of Hamilton*. There was thus cut-throat competition between the CSP and G&SWR vessels, as a cautionary letter published in *The Glasgow Herald* on 14th May records:

> 'Now that the coasting season has fairly commenced, and with the great competition that exists this season... the travelling public

should take a lesson in time and be carefully on their guard as to safety. It may be gratifying... that on Monday morning the steamer belonging to A left Brodick Pier three minutes later than the steamer belonging to B and, notwithstanding this, A arrived at exactly the same time at Ardrossan as B... but it is to be considered, on the other hand, that both steamers were running side by side with each other nearly all the way to Ardrossan at a high pressure of steam, having each a large complement of passengers, whose lives, I think, were somewhat endangered should anything have taken place...'[110]

The correspondent was right; only one week later, the *Neptune*'s reversing gear failed on entering Ardrossan and she crashed into the Caledonian pier, severely denting her stern, but without serious injury to her passengers. Most embarrassingly for the G&SWR, until a substitute vessel could be brought to Ardrossan, their passengers were transferred to the rival *Duchess of Hamilton*.

In June 1892, the G&SWR's purpose-built Arran steamer *Glen Sannox* was completed by J. & G. Thomson. Costing no less than £30,000 (a third more than *Neptune*), she was a magnificent vessel with very powerful compound machinery supplied with steam by one navy and one double-ended boiler. Inboard, she was as lavish as her CSP rival, but her speed of over 19 knots made her the Clyde's fastest steamer yet seen. Externally, she was gracefully proportioned and majestic in equal measure, her light grey hull and white upper works being capped by two lofty and well-raked red funnels with black tops.

The rail service from Glasgow to Ardrossan was further speeded up and the G&SWR now claimed an overall journey time from Glasgow to Brodick by train and steamer of between 80 and 90 minutes. Between her morning and evening rail-connected sailings, the *Glen Sannox* offered excursions to Ailsa Craig, round Arran and to Campbeltown Loch (but not to Campbeltown itself as this was out of bounds to G&SWR vessels).

Even during such excursions, no opportunity was missed to show the G&SWR flagship's superiority to any CSP steamer whose captain was daring enough to challenge. As Alan J.S. Paterson records:

The Caledonian Steam Packet Company's 1895-delivered *Duchess of Rothesay* off Corrie. *(A. Ernest Glen collection)*

A specially arranged North British Railway publicity photograph featuring their entire steamer fleet gathered at Craigendoran Pier. In the foreground are the **Dandie Dinmont, Waverley, Kenilworth** and **Lucy Ashton** while, behind, the **Jeanie Deans** lies offshore. *(A. Ernest Glen collection)*

'The Caledonian steamer *Duchess of Rothesay* was on an excursion trip round the Island of Arran. Her last call for passengers was at Millport, from which she was making her way across the channel for the Garroch Head. When she was about half-way from Cumbrae the South Western steamer *Glen Sannox* was seen evidently lying in wait, and as the *Duchess* came near the former made a circuit and came up on the rear of the *Duchess* on the south side. From this point to the north end of Arran, near Loch Ranza, there was a keenly contested race. On board the *Duchess* every pound of steam was forced into action, with the result that the hull of the vessel quivered from stem to stern because of the tremendous pressure on the machinery. Excess steam was blown off with a deafening noise, and the passengers, who by the way were railed off from the wings of the steamer by ropes, and who had come out to enjoy a pleasant excursion sail, were compelled for half an hour to endure an experience of excitement which I can best describe as like what sitting on the edge of a volcanic crater would be that was every moment liable to have an eruption...'[111]

The third member of the G&SWR's new fleet was the *Neptune*'s sister *Mercury* and she operated with the *Neptune* and older second-hand fleet members from Greenock Princes Pier. Two further slightly smaller steamers, the *Minerva* and the *Glen Rosa*, both J. & G. Thomson products, joined the fleet in 1893 and, three years later, a further pair of new buildings, the *Jupiter* and the *Juno* were added and these too were constructed in Clydebank, the former by J. & G. Thomson and the latter by Clydebank Shipbuilding and Engineering. The *Juno* had actually been

ordered by a South Coast steamer operator, who ran out of money while she was under construction, thus enabling the G&SWR to step in and purchase her. As she was heavily built, she was well suited for operation in the more exposed waters of the lower Firth.

The CSP and North British fleets meanwhile also acquired further steamers during the boom years of the latter 1890s. The former introduced the J. & G. Thomson-built *Duchess of Rothesay* in 1895 while the latter acquired no less than five additional steamers between 1895 and 1899 – the *Redgauntlet*, built by Barclay, Curle & Co being followed into service from Craigendoran by the *Dandie Dinmont* (II), the *Talisman*, the *Kenilworth* and the *Waverley*, all of which were delivered by A. & J. Inglis Ltd.

The *Waverley*, in particular, was an outstanding vessel. Unlike the *Kenilworth* and *Talisman*, which were, like all existing NBR steamers, built for rail-connected ferry work, the *Waverley* was the Company's first vessel intended equally to handle excursion traffic. Substantially longer, broader – and therefore with more commodious saloons – than her most recent fleet mates, she was one of the most elegant and modern-looking on the Clyde. Due to there being shallow water off Craigendoran, as with all existing NBR steamers, she was however fitted with a haystack boiler, this being lighter than the more modern (but relatively heavy) horizontal Navy-type. Even so, her two-cylinder compound engine enabled her to reach nearly 20 knots on trials, placing her in the same speed category as the G&SWR's *Jupiter* and *Juno* – but, with only one boiler, the *Waverley* was a more economical ship to operate than the G&SWR's flagship. With *Waverley*'s delivery in 1899, the Clyde paddle steamer arguably reached its apotheosis.

109 Glasgow Herald, 1st April 1892.
110 Glasgow Herald, 14th May 1892.
111 Paterson, 1969, p124.

Above: A busy scene at Rothesay pier circa 1895 with the North British steamer *Redgauntlet*, MacBrayne's *Columba*, the Glasgow & Inveraray Steamboat Company's *Lord of the Isles* and the Caledonian Steam Packet's *Marchioness of Bute* all loading and unloading passengers. *(A. Ernest Glen collection)*

Right: The Glasgow & South Western Railway's *Mars* at Greenock. *(A. Ernest Glen)*

Below: The *Waverley* of 1899 speeds out of Rothesay Bay in the 1936-38 period, passing the inbound *Queen Empress*. The *Waverley* was, for her time, a very modern and effective paddle steamer, but the technology was soon to be largely superseded on the Clyde by steam turbine propulsion. *(A. Ernest Glen)*

Chapter Five

Hebridean Steamers in the Railway Age

Scotland's great Railway Age was a mainland-based, and pre-eminently central and southern, affair. Given the ruggedly indented nature of the coastline north of the Firth of Clyde, to say nothing of the immense challenges presented to track-laying through hills, mountains and valleys north of Stirling, it is not surprising that the progress and impact of rail were much less evident in the Highlands and Hebrides than in the Scottish Lowlands. The lines which 'linked the lochs' took longer to link the ports which came to be synonymous with steamship services to the Hebrides. The Callander & Oban Railway reached Oban only in June 1880, while the Fort William branch of the West Highland Railway did not complete 'the Mallaig extension' until 1901.[112] Likewise, the celebrated 'Kyle Line' did not reach Kyle of Lochalsh until 1897, although the railway had arrived at Strome Ferry more than 20 years previously.

In certain cases, the coming of railway lines served simply to invigorate developments which were already well under way, thanks to the steamships. Oban, for example, was a thriving seaport by 1865, and had assumed much of its present-day character. Alexander Smith, who chronicled his well-known 'Summer in Skye' in that year, travelled north via Oban, and described what he saw:

'All kinds of people, and all kinds of sounds are there. From the next street the tones of the bagpipe come on the ear; tipsy porters abuse each other in Gaelic. Round the corner the mail comes rattling

Campbeltown pier is busy, as the gangway is pulled clear, and the Clyde and Campbeltown Company's *Davaar* prepares to leave. The *Duchess of Argyll* in the background also makes ready. (*A. Ernest Glen collection*)

from Fort William, the passengers clustering on its roof; from the pier the bell of the departing steamer urges passengers to make haste; and passengers who have lost their luggage rush about, shout, gesticulate and not infrequently come into fierce personal collision with one of the tipsy porters aforesaid. A more hurried, nervous, frenzied place than Oban, during the summer and autumn months, it is difficult to conceive. People seldom stay there more than one night. The old familiar faces are the resident population. The tourist no more thinks of spending a week in Oban than he thinks of spending a week in a railway station. When he arrives his first question is after a bedroom; his second, as to the hour at which the steamer from the south is expected.

And the steamer, be it said, does not always arrive at a reasonable hour. She may be detained some time in Greenock; in dirty weather she may be 'on' the Mull of Cantyre all night, buffeted by the big Atlantic there; so that he must be a bold man, or a gifted man with second sight, who ventures anything but a vague guess as to the hour of her arrival in Oban… Heavily the hours creep on; and at last the *Clansman* does steam in with wet decks, thoroughly washed by the Atlantic brine last night – and her hundred and fifty passengers, two-thirds of whom are sea-sick.'[113]

Thankfully, given the severe discomforts of rounding the Mull of Kintyre, the creation of railheads at strategic ports on the west and north-west coast offered a means of shortening voyages to and from the islands. As Smith indicates, the principal West Highland steamship services sailed from and to Glasgow. This continued to be the case in certain circumstances,

A painting from the turn of the twentieth century catches the colour and majesty of the *Claymore*. *(Family of Emma Beaton, courtesy of Alasdair Munro)*

particularly with cargo vessels, until 1976. However, given ready conveyance by rail and the prospect of decent accommodation at the railhead, travellers had greater choice in the matter of routes, and they could begin or end their voyages at Oban, Mallaig or Kyle, thus avoiding the dreaded 'Mull'. In due time, Oban became the principal terminal for the Inner Hebrides, while Mallaig became the terminal for Skye and the Outer Hebrides, until it was replaced eventually by Ullapool in the 1970s. The principal harbours were remodelled by infilling and land reclamation, and also deepened, to facilitate their new roles.

As passenger numbers grew, hotel accommodation at the railheads had to be increased. Once again, it was often a case of augmenting the initial impetus given by the steamship. In 1864, Alexander Brown, a banker and steamboat agent and one of the principal shareholders in David MacBrayne's original company, built the Columba Hotel in Oban, hot on the heels of the Kings Arms (1855) and the Great Western (1863). As Charles Hunter further records, 'Around 1880 the Station Hotel and the new Royal in Argyll Square were built, convenient for the railway station.' Thereafter, an

This stern-quarter view of MacBrayne's stately *Claymore* (1881), reckoned by many to be the best-looking West Highland steamship of her time, shows her as she lies in dock in Glasgow. *(A. Ernest Glen collection)*

attempt was made to build a Hydropathic at Oban, but money ran out in 1882.[114] Steamships and steam-hauled trains combined with other forms of transport to make Oban an essential interchange for servicing the west coast and the Inner Hebrides.

Steamship services came to be more closely linked to train arrivals and departures at the railheads, thus creating at least the embryo of today's transport network. The benefits of 'joined-up transport' of this kind were evident in the North Lorn and Lochaber districts, as John Thomas relates:

'An express service was provided by MacBrayne's steamer *Iona* between Oban and Fort William. The steamer left Fort William at 9.30am and arrived at Oban at 12.30 to connect with the 12.45 train departure for the south. The return sailing was at 1pm, conveying passengers who had arrived by train at 12.28, and regaining Fort William at 4.30. The steamer called at Port Appin, Ballachulish and Corran Ferry in each direction. Railway and steamer combined thus gave a vastly improved service to North Lorn and Lochaber.'[115]

The managers of the Callander and Oban Railway were also alive to the value of linking their train timetables to those of the little steamers that served sea-lochs, such as Loch Etive, and landlocked ones such as Loch Awe. As the use of the celebrated *Iona* on the Crinan-Oban-Fort William route indicates, business was brisk all round. 'The rail-coach-steamer trips were fully booked day after day.'[116] In the first flush of the Railway Age in the West Highlands, as elsewhere, ships increased in size and splendour, and in the quality of on-board facilities. The 'glory days' of the Hebridean steamship lay, in round terms, within the 50 years from 1860 to 1910. Their 'high'

112 The completion of the railway to Fort William enabled passengers and goods traffic to reach the town by rail, rather than by steamer from Oban.
113 Smith, n.d., pp69-70.
114 Hunter, 1993, p43.
115 Thomas, 1991, p77.
116 Thomas, 1991, p77.

Above: MacBrayne's *Grenadier*, which was destroyed by fire at Oban's North Pier in 1927, prepares to embark passengers at Iona. The ship carries her original (thin) funnels. *(A. Ernest Glen collection)*

Right: The *Davaar* had a very narrow escape when she ran aground in Belfast Lough in 1895. This picture shows how serious the incident was. *(A. Ernest Glen collection)*

Below: Seen off Inverkip in the Firth of Clyde, the *Islay* (III), formerly the *Princess Louise* (1872), was acquired by David MacBrayne in 1890. She served Islay until 1902, when she went aground in dense fog on a rock near Sheep Island, Port Ellen. *(A. Ernest Glen collection)*

Below right: The *Lochiel* (II) was built for MacBrayne's by Scott's of Bowling in 1908. Here, she is seen on builder's trials. She was requistioned for war service in 1917, and blown up in the Bristol Channel in 1918. *(A. Ernest Glen collection)*

noon was represented by such fine vessels as David Hutcheson's *Clansman* (built in 1870 as successor to the earlier *Clansman* which Alexander Smith had observed in Oban in 1865) and David MacBrayne's *Claymore* (1881).[117] Both ships had clipper bows adorned with finely wrought figureheads of plaided, sword-bearing Highlanders, well-raked masts and single funnels. The last representative of this class of elegant West Highland steamers, with more than a touch of residual Victorian grandeur, emerged in the Edwardian era in the form of David Hope MacBrayne's magnificent *Chieftain* (1907).[118]

No significant new shipping companies were formed by the railways which served the seaports of the West Highlands, perhaps an indication of the relatively low numbers of tourists and other passengers in the area, compared with the Clyde. Circumstances conducive to profitable competition did not exist, and railway companies had no desire whatsoever to complicate their lives by managing ships. The Dingwall & Skye Railway, however, faced a severe challenge when the track reached Strome Ferry, and a shipping connection had to be provided for Skye and the Outer Isles. David Hutcheson, whose steamers used Kyle and Mallaig, resolutely refused to let his vessels make a detour to Strome Ferry to meet the railhead. With great reluctance, the railway was compelled to purchase four ships – the *Oscar*, *Jura*, *Carham* and *Ferret* – which operated at a loss. This undertaking included an important service to Stornoway, which handled fish traffic. It was not easy to sustain, and was sometimes supplemented by through-ticketing arrangements with Hutcheson, via Portree and the *Clansman*.

The Highland Railway, however, came to the rescue by taking ownership of the vessels – a move which it was later to regret, not least because it became embroiled in an immensely embarrassing 'hijack' in 1880, following the dispatch of its steamship *Ferret* to Greenock for lay-up prior to sale. The Highland Railway, clutching at the prospect of any potential wad of notes, accepted a charter for the use of the vessel as a yacht in the Mediterranean – strange in itself, but even stranger when the individual making the charter suddenly vanished, along with the ship. The Railway's management watched and waited with amazement as the *Ferret* was sighted passing through the Straits of Gibraltar and then calling at Malta. Changes of name added ever-increasing depth to the mystery, as did a doubling back into the Atlantic and a deep-sea voyage via Cape Verde to Santos, Brazil, and yet another voyage, this time with a cargo of coffee intended for Marseilles – which travelled via Cape Town. Eventually, having to leave Cape Town in a hurry because the coffee could not be sold, the ship arrived in Melbourne, Australia. There she was seized, and the swindlers fled. The ship was then sold by the Highland Railway agent to the Australian Shipping Company for £8,000, giving her another lease of life 'Down Under', thus adding the final chapter to the most colourful set of adventures ever to befall a West Highland steamship. The fraudsters were eventually brought to book in Melbourne, but acquitted of defrauding the Highland Railway. To add insult to injury, the charter fee was never paid, and members of the crew successfully brought a case for unpaid wages against the Railway. Mercifully, David MacBrayne stepped into the breach in 1880 with his *Lochiel*, and showed the railway operators how to run a proper steamship service.[119]

As if this catalogue of tribulation was not enough, the departure of the infamous *Ferret* succeeded in creating even more trouble for the Dingwall & Skye and the larger Highland Railway. Railway companies in the Highlands, as in the Lowlands, were profit-driven and highly competitive at heart, and a railway company would normally involve itself in shipping only when it

sensed an opportunity to snatch trade from a rival. This happened in 1881, when the Highland Railway, having withdrawn the *Ferret* from the Stornoway service, still taxed shippers, through the Railway Clearing House, with the costs of carriage from Stornoway to Strome. Despite demands, rebates were not forthcoming, and protests about charges and facilities at Strome continued. John Anderson of the Callander & Oban Railway saw his chance, and placed three steamships on the Stornoway-Oban service to haul the fish to his own port and railway line. He succeeded in 'virtually absorbing the whole of the important fish traffic of the western seaboard'. The Highland Railway fought back, but, while regaining some of its former trade, it had to concede much to Oban. By skilful networking with the promoters of fisheries, especially during the winter herring season on the west coast, Anderson helped to make Oban a prosperous fishing port. Fishery companies based at Oban later became a threat – if only temporary – to the conveyance of mail by other companies interested in general cargo and passengers. The railways thus brought an element of competition into an otherwise rather relaxed trading sector.[120]

With the advent of railways, it was possible to move break-bulk cargo more easily to Oban, Mallaig, Kyle of Lochalsh and Fort William, for onward shipment to the Hebrides. The exporting of goods from the islands was likewise facilitated, and the range of potential markets was enhanced. Glasgow, nevertheless, remained the principal port for the shipment of large quantities of heavy cargo to the Hebrides, although smaller cargoes were dispatched to and from the railhead ports. The real challenge after 1850 was to provide adequate numbers of cargo ships to handle island products, as horizons expanded and market opportunities increased. The pressure on existing steamship capacity as early as 1865 is indicated by Alexander Smith's description of the *Clansman*, as she left Oban on the inward run to Glasgow, having reached as far north as Stornoway and called at numerous West Highland harbours on the way south:

'The *Clansman* had received a quantity of cargo at Tobermory, at Loch Aline a flock of sheep were driven on board, goods were taken in plentifully at other places in the Sound at which we touched, and when we had received all the stuffs waiting for us at Oban, the vessel was heavily laden. The entire steerage deck was a bellowing and bleating mass of black cattle and sheep, each 'parcel' divided from the other by temporary barriers. The space amidships was a chaos of barrels and trunks and bales of one kind or another, and amongst these the steerage passengers were forced to dispose themselves. Great piles of wooden boxes containing herring were laid along the cabin deck, so that if a man were disposed to walk about it behoved him to take care of his footsteps.'[121]

From 1860 onwards the need to increase capacity to transport cargo from the islands to the mainland produced several island-led initiatives for the creation of new steamship companies. Some, such as McCallum & Orme, became household names, alongside that of David MacBrayne, and lasted into the mid-twentieth century. As a consequence of such progress, the need for piers, jetties and warehouses began to be articulated much more urgently, and to greater effect, than it had been before 1850.

Fisheries, fish and other exports

As Smith's description of the *Clansman*'s cargo indicates, and as subsequent rivalries confirm, fish, and especially herring, formed an

117 This was a period of significant development in merchant shipping in Britain more generally. See Harvie, 2008, pp94-96.
118 Robins and Meek, 2006, pp85-90.
119 Thomas, 1990, pp72-75.
120 Thomas, 1991, pp87-91.
121 Smith, undated, p490.

The plain but elegant lines of the *Mountaineer* (III) are evident in this photograph taken at Gourock. She was built in 1910 for services from Oban, but she also served Loch Goil. *(A. Ernest Glen collection)*

important component of Hebridean exports from at least the 1860s. Fishery societies – based on the principle of developing an indigenous industry in the Highlands and Islands, rather than encouraging people to leave the region for employment in the Lowlands – had been established in the area after 1760, and they played a very significant part in developing cargo-ship services and harbour facilities in the West Highlands and the Hebrides.

The British Fisheries Society, founded in 1786, was instrumental in creating several of the ports which were to be used by ships of all kinds in the course of the next two centuries, among them principally Tobermory and Ullapool. James Maxwell of Tobermory, writing to the Society's Secretary in 1790, foresaw that 'when any of the People of Substance, who have taken lots at Tobermory, shall have built their Houses, and be otherwise prepared for attempting the Fishing Business, they will chuse to follow it in the manner practised from the Towns of the Firth of Clyde; that is, by means of larger vessels, fit to navigate a Sea agitated by frequent storms…'[122]

The nature of Hebridean trade before the advent of steam is well depicted by Dr Jean Dunlop in her summary of vessels which utilised Tobermory in 1792:

'All the ships clearing out of Tobermory were involved in coastal trade, their cargoes wool, kelp (1,369 tons), salt and fish. One ship – the *Ardgour* of Tobermory (26 tons), owned by Donald Carmichael – left for Glasgow carrying fifteen tons of lead from the mines at Strontian. The largest ship recorded that year was the *William* of Rothesay (81 tons) taking ninety-one tons of kelp to Liverpool. Of the thirty-three vessels checking in, fourteen were open fishing boats. The cargoes included corn, oats and oatmeal, wines (1,066 gallons), spirits (1,035 gallons), salt and 153 barrels of herring in late August and September. The *Grace* of Tobermory (25 tons), owned by Hector Cameron, had a crew of three and arrived with a cargo of mixed goods from Oban. The greatest event of 1792 was when George Wilson, her master, brought in the *Clementina* of Maryport from Memel with a cargo of fir timber, part of which was landed at Tobermory and part of which went to Oban.'[123]

In 1797, the opening of the Crinan Canal, with its benefits for ship traffic, was being anticipated by the Society. It would, said the Society, 'occasion many vessels to pass through the sound of Mull and of course to call at Tobermory that would otherwise hold further out to sea'.[124]

Ships using Tobermory in those years were, of course, wind-powered. As the British Fisheries Society remained in operation until 1893, it must have conveyed its produce by steamship. There is, however, no record of a Hebridean fishery which owned its own steam vessel until the creation of the Great West of Scotland Fishery, a limited liability company with shareholders, incorporated in Glasgow on 14th April 1857. In 1861, the company maintained stations in Harris and in Skye, at Stein, Glendale, Roag and Tarskavaig, and also at Fraserburgh. It was put into the hands of a liquidator in January 1861, and was finally wound up on 3rd March 1863.[125]

The Fishery owned a screw-driven steamship, the *Islesman*, built in 1858, which was destined to become the harbinger of a new cargo-carrying era for the Hebrides. Company accounts for 1860-61 show that the *Islesman* was being well used, and that she had the potential to bring significant income to the Fishery. Her revenues, however, were evidently not sufficient to

122 Dunlop, 1978, p85.
123 Dunlop, 1978, p85.
124 Dunlop, 1978, pp85-86.
125 National Abstract of Statistics, BT2/15517.

Above: Captain John McCallum's flagship *Hebrides* (1898), designed by G. L. Watson, shows her good lines as she powers purposefully past the Water's Neb on the Clyde. A sailor can be seen on the rigging of the foremast, presumably adjusting the block and tackle of the derrick. The *Hebrides* and the *Dunara Castle* (right) conveyed cargo and passengers from Glasgow to the Outer Hebrides, but are best remembered for their summer sailings to St Kilda, which were maintained until 1939. *(A. Ernest Glen)*

Right: Few Hebridean steamers were more famous than the *Dunara Castle*, built for Martin Orme in 1875. The 'Dunara', as she was affectionately known, inaugurated summer-season steamship services to St Kilda in 1877, and was the very last passenger steamship to leave Village Bay when the island was evacuated in 1930. Along with the *Hebrides*, she became part of the combined McCallum and Orme fleet in 1929, and joined MacBrayne's in 1947, shortly before she was scrapped in 1948. *(Linda Gowans collection)*

Below: David Hope MacBrayne's ornate and elaborately appointed 'cruise yacht' *Chieftain*, built in 1907, represented the high point of the Hebridean steamer in the Edwardian era. *(A. Ernest Glen)*

Below right: David MacBrayne's *Sheila* (1904) undertook the Stornoway service from Mallaig and Kyle of Lochalsh (her location in this picture), until she was wrecked south of the entrance to Loch Torridon on New Year's Day, 1927. *(A. Ernest Glen collection)*

offset other costs. A catalogue of difficulties, misfortunes and expenses had been incurred by 1860 – at least one sinking in a harbour, hull damage at Bunessan, and an incident involving another steamer, the paddle vessel *Lapwing*, in a fog off Kintyre in 1859, with the loss of the latter.[126] These incidents probably hastened her dispatch from the ailing company. Bought by William Lang and managed by a former employee of Thomson & McConnell, Martin Orme, who had previously managed her for the Fishery, the *Islesman* was lengthened in 1861. Thus rejuvenated and apparently none the worse for her various scrapes, she continued to serve the Hebrides until 1868, conveying passengers as well as freight.[127] William Donald, who joined the *Islesman* as clerk and traffic manager in 1860, wrote in 1913:

> 'The *Islesman* was the first steamer to give direct steam communication to Colonsay, West of Mull, Tiree, Coll, Barra, South and North Uist, West of Skye, Canna, St Kilda, Badcal, Lochinver, Terera [*recte* Tanera], Ullapool and Altbea. Messrs Hutchison's steamers called at intervals at Lochmaddy, Ullapool and Lochinver.'[128]

The *Islesman* succeeded the *Queen* and *Chieftain*, becoming the third in a line of Hebridean vessels owned by Martin Orme and his partners. Within the Orme confederation, the *Islesman* was herself superseded by the *Dunvegan Castle* (1868-1875), the *Talisman* (1871-1874), the *Dunara Castle* (1875-1948), and the *Aros Castle* (later renamed the *Handa*, in MacBrayne ownership) (1878-1886).[129] Orme's vessels were essentially cargo-boats which carried a small number of passengers, and the pattern of their acquisition shows that the 1870s were a crucial period in the development of steam-powered cargo services to the Hebrides.

The cargo vessels of Martin Orme (like those of John McCallum) were decidedly plain and workmanlike, with straight stems and minimal ornamentation, but they had extremely robust iron hulls. The *Dunara Castle* was 73 years old when she was formally incorporated into the MacBrayne fleet, and her consort, the comparatively youthful *Hebrides*, a mere 50. Such survival was aided by the nature of the role and the schedule. Cargo vessels were not bound to strict timetables of the kind that had to synchronise, if possible, with developing train connections at railheads such as Strome Ferry, Kyle of Lochalsh, Mallaig and Oban. Steam propulsion also tended to last longer in dedicated cargo ships than in passenger vessels, at least in the Hebrides.

Island investment

The 1870s produced further shipping companies whose chief interest lay in cargo, and whose shareholders were resident principally in the Hebrides. The Western Isles Steam Packet Company was incorporated on 11th February 1873, 'for conveyance of goods in ships or boats between Glasgow and the West Highlands'. It aimed to raise capital of £20,000, offering 4,000 shares at £5.00 each. Its registered office was at 133, West George Street, Glasgow, and its secretary was James Steward. The company's Memorandum of Association had seven subscribers, all resident in Glasgow: John McIntyre, Wine Merchant; Archibald McPherson, Wine

and Spirit Merchant; Thomas Roy, Grocer and Wine Merchant; John Walker, Merchant; W.C. Gow, Seaman; Ronald McIntyre, Wine and Spirit Merchant; and Archibald Colquhoun, Ships Broker.

Surviving company papers provide a full list of the company's shareholders. Of the 51 shareholders listed, 30 (some 60%) were located in the Highlands and Islands. Of these, 16 were in South Uist, 7 were in Barra, 2 were in Skye, and 4 were in the Strontian and Salen area. The Glasgow and Paisley area provided 18 shareholders.[130] It is noticeable that the shareholders consisted mainly of merchants and farmers, and that the two largest shareholders, who were in the wine and spirit trade, were based in Glasgow. It is quite possible that John McIntyre and Archibald McPherson, the principal shareholders, were themselves of Highland extraction. Overall, the shareholding of the Western Isles Steam Packet Company provides a graphic demonstration of the concern of Highlanders, and pre-eminently islanders in the Outer Hebrides, to take practical steps to finance a new steamship service for the region. The strong South Uist representation suggests considerable unease in that district with regard to existing steamship services, and similar sentiments were also manifest in Barra.

The value of the Western Isles Steam Packet Company to the islands is indicated by the cargo conveyed by its first steamship, the *St Clair of the Isles*, when she arrived at the Broomielaw in November, 1873: 70 head of cattle, 2 horses, 2 'fine Highland bulls', 83 tons of cheese, dried fish, lobsters, wool, and 87 passengers from Barra and Uist.[131] The significant number of cattle on board shows that, after a slow start, the steamship was regarded by now as a thoroughly viable alternative to the traditional drove roads and the previously essential ferrying of cattle from the islands to the mainland in smacks and gabbarts.[132] As anticipated by the *New Statistical Account* in 1837, the steamship offered a direct route from the Outer Hebrides to Glasgow, and was in every way much more convenient than earlier methods, particularly for the transporting of fat cattle.

Trade was so brisk that a second vessel was launched on 10th December 1873. The new screw-driven *Lady Ambrosine* was engaged in the conveyance of large cargoes to Tiree and other islands by March 1874. The Western Isles Steam Packet Company could now offer a service to both the Inner Hebrides and the Outer Hebrides, the former provided by the *Lady Ambrosine*, and the latter by the *St Clair of the Isles*. The company covered all of the areas represented by its Highland and Hebridean shareholders, and added numerous other ports *en route*.[133]

The future looked bright, but the optimism was short-lived. The Western Isles Steam Packet Company failed to obtain sufficient shareholding capital to guarantee its viability, and in 1875 its ships were sold. Fortunately for the islands, the *Lady Ambrosine* was bought by her Master, Captain John McCallum, a native of Crinan, Argyll, who had formed his own company (presumably with other partners) by 1876, and had built a second vessel, the *St Clair*. In 1881, following the sinking of the *St Clair*, McCallum launched another purpose-built vessel, the *Hebridean*, which provided the backbone of his company.[134] In a manner resembling the

126 National Abstract of Statistics, BT2/15517, which records that the company spent £124-1-7 in defending the action raised by the owners of the *Lapwing*. See also Duckworth and Langmuir, 1987, p20.

127 Duckworth and Langmuir, 1987, p127.

128 Oban Times, 22nd December 1923.

129 Oban Times, 22nd December 1923.

130 National Abstract of Statistics, BT2/481.

131 Robson, 2005, p484.

132 Haldane, 1952, p219, notes that 'by about 1880 transport of cattle by steamer to the railheads at Strome Ferry and Oban had almost entirely superseded the old methods.'

133 Duckworth and Langmuir, 1987, pp123-4.

134 Robins and Meek, 2006, pp60-61.

strategy of the Western Isles Steam Packet Company and its dependence on wine and spirit merchants as principal subscribers, McCallum evidently secured the long-term goodwill and major share investment of Glasgow businessmen, in this case the family of Hugh Campbell Young and William Young. They supported the company after McCallum's untimely and tragic death by drowning when at St Helier, Jersey, while serving as Mate on his own *Hebridean* in the summer of 1902.[135] The *Hebrides*, a larger version of the *Hebridean* and very similar in size and design to Orme's *Dunara Castle*, was launched in 1898. Alongside the *Dunara Castle*, she was destined to serve the Hebrides primarily as a cargo vessel until the mid-twentieth century.

The importance of the companies of both Martin Orme and John McCallum in shaping and maintaining life and society in the Hebrides for almost a century cannot be overestimated. Their ships became at least as well known as those of David MacBrayne, and, arguably, fulfilled an even more significant role by conveying cargo from the Clyde to St Kilda, and from the islands to the mainland, along an inter-island spinal route, with spurs, as 'inducement' required, to many 'remote' bays and townships. Before they amalgamated in 1929 to become McCallum, Orme and Company Limited, John McCallum and Martin Orme and their partners regarded one another as 'friendly rivals', acting 'in conference'. Their ongoing trade continued to be furnished mainly by large bulk cargoes on the outward journey, and by the output of smaller, island-based industries, such as cattle-rearing, fishing and distilling, on the inward. Alongside cargo, their ships carried small complements of tourists and passengers – and also importantly the mail.

Postal services

The first steam-driven cargo vessels, and particularly those of Martin Orme, played a very significant part in bringing postal services to the Hebrides, thus transforming the nature of communication between the islands and the mainland. William Donald, the Ayrshire-born clerk or purser on the *Islesman* and later the *Dunara Castle*, provided a vivid overview of the contribution made by the vessels on which he sailed:

'[Before these services] a sailing smack conveyed the mails between Dunvegan and Lochmaddy, which was very irregular in stormy weather or in calm weather. Postal facilities barely existed at this period, and postage stamps were not always procurable. I became the carrier of the most part of the letters from the Isles to the south and from isle to isle, and a great many letters were sent with me from Glasgow and Greenock to the Isles. Much of my time and attention was taken up with this work, many of the letters requiring to have stamps affixed by me. The people at places would come and push their letters to me without any ceremony, as if I were an animated letter pillar-box for their convenience. On occasions the steamer would be hailed to stop by a boat, and having stopped a letter or two would be handed on board. Traffic having grown to the Outer Islands, the calls in Sutherland and Ross were given up in 1866, and the route afterwards was leaving Glasgow and Greenock every Thursday for Colonsay, Iona, Bunessan, etc., as at present. This was continued until the opening of the Callander and Oban Railway, when the route was changed to include Oban and Tobermory, after Colonsay and again returning via Oban, etc. Mailbags were shipped and landed at Oban. This route was continued until the end of 1886, when a subsidy was granted to a Fishery Company to run a steamer

three times a week with mails from Oban to Coll, Tiree, Barra and Lochboisdale. This intrusion caused the *Dunara Castle* to revert to the former route via Oban and Bunessan. The earliest sealed mailbags were from Greenock to Bunessan and Iona. In course of time, Post Offices were established along the route and mailbags were sent from Greenock to Colonsay, Iona, Bunessan, Tiree, Coll, Barra, Lochboisdale, Lochmaddy, Rodel, Tarbert, Dunvegan and Canna. Intermediate bags were also carried entailing much attention. This would be in operation, I think, in 1875. The government refused to grant a subsidy for the work, saying that it could not afford any. However, the government ultimately proposed to pay 2s 6d per 100 letters.

When the Agrarian Agitation forced the attention of the government to the Islands, they were prepared to spend lavishly for the performance of work that had been carried out to a great extent by me for years. The present service of steamers from Oban and Portree to the Outer Isles and Tiree, Coll and Oban, costs about 8s. per annum per head of the population in the districts served. I consider that I have a claim on the government for unrecognised postal work done during my itinerary of 16,000,000 miles in 53 years among the Isles.'[136]

As 'proper' steamship services were established, the latter-day fishery companies were evidently seen to be somewhat predatory, snatching resources and subsidies which ought to have been bestowed upon the 'settled and developed' network. Through the earlier labours of William Donald and others like him on board the Orme steamships, the foundations had been laid for the carriage of the Royal Mail, and they felt that they themselves should have been awarded the first formal contracts.

In the event, McCallum and Orme were favoured with only a restricted mail contract, underpinned by a subsidy of £250 each from 1898, allowing them to take the mail to St Kilda, Soay and Colonsay, which were not served by David MacBrayne, who acquired most of the contracts.[137] When questioned by the Napier Commission in 1883, the Rev. John MacKay, minister of St Kilda, was able to report that Orme's *Dunara Castle* and McCallum's *Hebridean* allowed islanders to have as many as six mails in the year, with three calls each by these steamers in the summer season.[138]

St Kilda sailings

It is remarkable that St Kilda's potential as a steamship destination, even for tourists, had not been exploited more fully before 1870. One of the reasons was undoubtedly the small passenger and industrial significance of the 'lonely' island, relative to its distance from the mainland. Another was the challenge posed by bad weather. When a regular steamship service to St Kilda was eventually established, it operated only in the summer season, from May to August. Developments in marine engineering, and the improvement of overall design, facilitated matters. The first steamers to reach the island were the larger of the paddle-driven vessels, all of them over 100 tons. However, as paddles tended to come out of the water when a ship heeled over, propeller-driven vessels were more effective in rough seas. The most successful and reliable St Kilda steamships, in service after 1875, were all propeller-driven.

Financial considerations were important too. In March 1874, the Western Isles Steam Packet Company intimated that 'the proprietors are projecting a special trip to St Kilda, in June', depending on applications. Despite interest by Highlanders in north Skye and tourists from the

135 Marine Register of Deaths, No. 84322. See also Oban Times, 21st June 1902.
136 Oban Times, 22nd December 1923.
137 National Abstract of Statistics, AF48/28.
138 Napier Commission Report, p865.

mainland cities, sufficient passengers did not enlist, and the proposed voyage by their paddle steamer, *St Clair of the Isles*, was cancelled. Clearly, a possible revenue-based enterprise had failed.[139]

Then, three years later, Martin Orme stepped in purposefully with the screw-driven *Dunara Castle*, and John McCallum followed in his wake. The reason for such eventually speedy and relatively strong commitment to St Kilda probably lies as much in philanthropy – and the generosity of such benefactors as the Young family, who supported both the McCallum and the Orme ventures – as it does in technical advance.[140] From at least 1879 McCallum's *St Clair* – not to be confused with the *St Clair of the Isles*, which was sold in 1875 – partnered the *Dunara Castle* on regular summer-season voyages to St Kilda. The *St Clair* was usually commanded by Captain John McCallum. From 1881 the service was provided by the *Hebridean*, commanded initially by John's brother, Captain Archibald McCallum, but frequently thereafter by John himself, who was also content to sail as Mate or 'Extra Master' as required. From 1898 the *Hebrides* became the main McCallum vessel serving St Kilda, alongside Orme's *Dunara Castle*, and the *Hebridean* was assigned to summer charters as far away as Bristol and the Channel Islands.[141]

St Kilda offered 'delightful scenery', but the St Kildans were apparently a different matter. To the external eye, intent on finding difference, St Kildan society was in a state of 'primitivism', represented by a peculiar and out-of-date people. At the same time, the unkempt human menagerie there was worth viewing for its own sake, as it affirmed the progress of those who considered themselves 'civilised' compared with the rest of mankind. By challenging external standards of 'civilisation', however, the St Kildans made the sightseers uncomfortable, and provoked them into producing a stream of (often) disparaging writing in books and newspapers.[142]

Commercial tourism, bringing condescending external observers as well as 'mainland goods', was to become a key factor in the exposure of St Kilda to the outside world, as also happened in many other 'remote' regions of the globe influenced by steamships. It precipitated a change from subsistence and self-sufficiency to increasing dependence on a seasonal, cash-based economy, relying on the pockets of strangers from a very different part of 'civilisation'. The Rev. John MacKay, minister of St Kilda, informed the Napier Commission in 1883 that 'When the steamers come here, they leave a good deal of money among the people', some of it through purchase of island produce.[143] The steamer tourists, said Mackay, 'generally buy a sheep here', and Donald MacDonald affirmed that 'we have sold a little cloth [i.e. tweed] to them', and that he had seen 'one cow sold to the steamer'.[144] The steamer also brought 'a few bolls of meal', in addition to what was normally supplied to islanders.

The speed with which the cash-based economy permeated the community is illustrated by an account of the arrival of the steamship *St Clair* in early August 1880, three years after the first visit by the *Dunara Castle*. It is summarised as follows by Michael Robson:

'On board [the *St Clair*] was 'an excursion party of twenty-five ladies and gentlemen who were anxious to visit this now famous island'. She approached at 8am on Monday 8 August, fired a gun to announce her presence, and anchored close in two hours later; John Mackay [the Free Church minister] naturally welcomed the party ashore. Purchases were made, the islanders offering stockings, socks, homespun clothes, seabirds' eggs and 'wild fowl' at prices 'about twice the value of them'. Not deterred, the tourists bought over sixty pairs of stockings and socks and about fifty yards of cloth. Presumably some acquired eggs and specimens. Leaving in the late evening the ship was back in Greenock by Wednesday afternoon, and as usual everybody thanked the captain, John McCallum in this instance, and his purser for looking after them so well.'[145]

Five years later, in the autumn of 1885, the *Hebridean*, with Captain John McCallum, 'managing owner' of the company, acting as Mate and probably Extra Master, had to make a 'mercy dash' to St Kilda with essential supplies for the island. This became a highly controversial sailing, because it raised issues about whether the alleged plight of the St Kildans after a major storm in September had been exaggerated. At the centre of the 'call-out' was the Free Church minister, John MacKay, who was later accused by a journalist who had travelled on board the *Hebridean* of having overstated the case. MacKay, in turn, accused the journalist of not having sufficient familiarity with the levels of islanders' supplies. MacKay claimed that the storm had destroyed the St Kildans' crops of corn, barley and potatoes. The trip was arranged in a philanthropic spirit by Sir William Collins, the Glasgow publisher, and the Rev. Dr Robert Rainy, of the Free Church of Scotland, with the support of the Highland and Agriculture Society of Scotland. At the heart of this debate lay crucial matters, including a growing sense of isolation in St Kilda, its increasing dependence on the mainland when crops failed or were damaged, and the question of what constituted grounds for activating the 'steamer lifeline' to the mainland.[146]

Reshaping Hebridean society

From 1850 onwards, the steamship continued to reshape the demography and material culture of the wider Hebrides, as well as St Kilda. Travelling in July 1938, Robert Atkinson found the ageing *Dunara Castle*,

'[a] well-known figure in the Isles…unloading second-hand furniture and sectional buildings at Tarbert [Harris]. She had just come in and her cruise passengers were streaming ashore, 'free for one glorious week from cares, creditors and carping critics', as the cruise literature had it. Lashed on deck were a motor lorry and a dogcart; the only visible concession to cruising was the marking for shuffle-board on the tiny afterdeck.'[147]

The presence of the 'motor lorry' alongside the 'dogcart' is particularly telling as an indicator of changing conventions for local transport. The arrival of 'second-hand furniture' and the forerunners of 'kit houses' suggest the emergence of another facet of 'steamer dependency syndrome', namely the potential decline of local crafts, or their inability to meet demand without back-up from the mainland.

Dependency moved progressively from the 'agrarian' to the 'domestic', from the byre and the workshop to the barn and the kitchen. Gradually smaller 'essentials', including pre-eminently food for humans and animals, assumed greater significance as part of the regular cargo conveyed from the mainland to the islands. Writing in Gaelic in 1933, the Rev. Donald Lamont, a native of Tiree, commented trenchantly on changing social patterns in his native island. In particular, he noted that, when the population of Tiree numbered around 5,000 (in the mid-nineteenth century),

'*cha robh unnsa de'n bhiadh a bha 'gam beathachadh air a thoirt a steach do'n eilean…ach an diugh, ged nach 'eil ann ach mu ochd ceud duine, tha a' chuid-mhór de bhiadh an eilein air a thoirt á Glaschu leis an Dunara.*'

'not an ounce of the food that sustained them was imported to the island…but today, when it has only about eight hundred inhabitants, most of the island's food is brought from Glasgow by the *Dunara*.'[148]

He noted further:

'*Cha robh muinntir na Gàidhealtachd riamh cho comhfhurtachail is a tha iad an diugh, ach cha robh iad riamh cho gann de chloinn – sgoilean 'gan dùnadh a chionn nach eil clann ann a theid annta. Chan e a mhàin gu bheil Tiriodh agus eilean I agus àitean eile anns a' Ghàidhealtachd a' faotainn am bìdh á Glaschu, ach tha iad a' faotainn na cloinne as. Cuiridh iad litir do Ghovan a dh'iarraidh pàisde mar a chuireas iad litir gu*'

MacPhàrlain Shearer a dh'iarraidh poca mine, is thig am pàisde agus am poca mine air an Dunara còmhla.'

'The people of the Highlands [and Islands] were never as comfortable as they are today, but they were never as short of children – schools being closed because there are no children to go to them. Not only do Tiree and Iona and other places in the Highlands get their food from Glasgow, but they [also] get their children from there. They will send a letter to Govan asking for a child in just the same way as they will send a letter to MacFarlane Shearer [a merchant in Greenock] to ask for a sack of meal, and the child and the sack of meal will come together on the *Dunara*.' [149]

Lamont's sharp pen brought to the surface the ironies of declining self-sufficiency, as dependency syndrome came to embrace the acquisition of 'human commodities'. City children dispatched to Hebridean islands often were either abandoned by their parents or orphaned. Four years later, Iain F. Anderson, seeing the world with a somewhat more romantic and artistic eye, painted a graphic word-picture of the cargo waiting by the Glasgow dockside for shipment on board the *Hebrides*:

'Beside each of the long walls of the shed are heaps of miscellaneous cargo. In one large heap, beside which we stand for a moment, we can recognise bags of cement, boxes of groceries, a bedstead, three rolls of barbed wire, a piano in a case, several bundles of wood, a hut in sections, three bags of sugar, a plough gaudy in its brilliant crimson and yellow paint, two tins of a well-known brand of lamp oil, a kitchen range and a case of tinned fruit; and this is only one heap of many covering the floor. As each lorry or motor is unloaded its contents are placed in the part of the shed appropriate to its destination. 'Pooltiel, Bill,' shouts a carter to the shed foreman. 'Over there, Bob,' the foreman replies, pointing to an already heterogeneous heap of cargo for that little community.' [150]

'Steaming' in the Isles

Alcoholic beverages continued to be offered on board steamships, but were stewarded much more effectively by means of bars as the nineteenth century progressed. These 'floating bars' were very attractive to island-based passengers. John MacLean, a Tiree bard from Balephuil and latterly (1878) resident in Manitoba, composed a humorous song on his neighbour, Calum MacArthur, who evidently sailed to Glasgow on Martin Orme's *Dunara Castle* or the *Islesman*:

'*Nuair thàinig an oidhche, cha robh suim do na dh'fhàg sinn;*
Chuir an dram às ar cuimhn' iad is sinn cruinn anns a' chàbin.
Cò nach òladh na fhuair e, 's daoin'-uaisle ga phàigheadh?
Nuair a dh'iarradh a-suas sinn, bha is' an Cluaidh aig a h-àite
Gar cur a-mach.'

'When night came, we did not give a hoot for those we had left behind;
the dram erased them from our memory when we were gathered in the cabin.
Who would not drink what he had received, when gentlemen were paying it?
When we were summoned on deck, she was in the Clyde at her place,
disembarking us.' [151]

Later MacArthur allegedly sought refuge from the Glasgow hordes through the good offices of his friends, who took him to a heavenly 'snug' on board another ship:

'*Thug iad mi chàbin a' Chlansman, 's shuidh mo shamhladh ceart làimh rium:*
S math gum fòghnadh e dhaoine an dèidh an saoghal seo fhàgail,
Mar àite math.'

'They took me to the cabin of the *Clansman*, and my very double sat beside me; it would well suffice people after they had left this world as a good place.' [152]

It was not necessary, of course, to go as far as Glasgow to savour such delights. The steamship brought them to 'dry' islands such as Tiree, and doubtless played a part in encouraging a desire for licensed hotels and public houses. John T. Reid, who travelled to the island on the new McCallum steamship, *St Clair*, in 1876, observed at Scarinish Harbour:

'…The Temperance Hotel – the only hotel in the island, and but seldom patronized; so those who want spirits find in the steamboat a house "licensed to retail spirits, porter and all", and drouthy customers have thus a special interest in the steamboat sailings.' [153]

When Ada Goodrich Freer visited Tiree in 1894, the 'drouthy customers' were much in evidence as soon as the MacBrayne vessel, *Fingal*, arrived at the same harbour. Noting that two ferry-boats which were already 'apparently quite full of people were boarding our little vessel', she wrote:

'Later we learnt that there were other reasons besides the desire to meet friends, to get the mails, to fetch the cargo, why some of the islanders greet MacBrayne with such eagerness…' [154]

Going ashore from the *Fingal*, she shared a ferry-boat with 'the men who had so mysteriously come on board and who now came out of the deck-cabin wiping their mouths and smelling of whisky.' The ships, it would seem, were a very well-known source of alcohol for the hitherto licence-free island. When asked by the Napier Commission in 1883 how a person who required it might obtain a 'stimulant' under such straitened circumstances, Hugh Macdiarmid, the local factor, replied, 'Well, there are ways and means always – by having it in the house, they will get it from the steamers.' [155]

Tourists to St Kilda too made the most of what the steamer offered, as the evidence gathered by the Napier Commission also indicates. In response to the question, 'When the steamers come here do they do any mischief by the sale of liquors or in any other way?' the Rev. John Mckay, minister of St Kilda, replied:

'I don't think it. Some of these passengers are very loose in their

139 Robson, 2005, pp484-5.
140 See Meek 2010 for some further discussion of philanthropy in maintaining West Highland shipping.
141 Robins and Meek, 2006, p56, pp60-61.
142 This is well covered in Robson, 2005, which does St Kilda a great service by providing a very full and reliable digest of attitudes to the island. See also Robins and Meek, 2006, p76 for a particularly derogatory (but not untypical) account of the St Kilda 'natives'.
143 Napier Commission Report, p866.
144 Napier Commission Report, p871.
145 Robson, 2005, p568.
146 Robson, 2005, pp597-600.
147 Atkinson, 1949, p215.
148 Murchison, 1960, p56.
149 Murchison, 1960, p57.
150 Anderson, 1937, pp5-6.
151 Cameron, 1932, pp231-33.
152 Cameron, 1932, p233.
153 Cooper, 2002, p161.
154 Cooper, 2002, pp217-18.
155 Napier Commission Report, p2162.

character, and some of them are drunk when they come ashore, but the people avoid them as far as they can.'[156]

Clearly, there were two sides to the St Kilda story, and the islanders must have marvelled at the primitive practices of the 'menagerie' who had arrived by steamship to enjoy their own much more civilised ways.

It is a telling comment on the social power of the steamship that the Gaelic word for 'vapour', namely *smùid*, had begun to assume the meaning of 'steam' and also 'drunken spree' (as happened with 'steam' in Scots and Scottish English) by the 1870s. Highland people, like their Lowland counterparts, were extending the semantic range of their vocabulary to accommodate the derangement created by the steamship's wares. The resulting idioms, whether 'steamin'' in Scots, or '*a' gabhail smùid*' in Gaelic, have outlasted the steamships despite the durability of the latter.[157]

The pressure that the steamship exerted on the actual use of Gaelic, as well as its semantics, is no less evident, particularly in the Highlands' and Islands' principal towns, where the main piers were usually located. Commercial hubs of this kind were liable to become hubs of anglicisation. The writer of the section on Portree, Skye, for the *New Statistical Account* noted:

> 'The language generally spoken in the parish is Gaelic. From the facility of intercourse with the low country, by means of steam navigation and Parliamentary roads, the people have acquired a taste for the English language, and are desirous to learn it.'[158]

Steamships, with their various forms of pressure, steam and otherwise, were thus indigenised, physically and metaphorically, in the Highlands and Islands, and became part of normal Hebridean experience. Their tall funnels, exhaling what Walt Whitman memorably called 'dusky and undulating, long pennants of smoke',[159] helped to redefine not only the deeper recesses of human emotions and aspirations, but also the sea-riven landscape and island life itself.

Puffers, schooners and luggers

As these miscellaneous 'necessities of life' ('necessities', that is, in the 1930s, though not in the 1830s) increasingly filled the holds of the steamships, larger bulk cargoes were transported by smaller vessels, most notably steam lighters or 'puffers' (a catch-all and misleading designation, applicable only to the first generation of such vessels). The 'puffer', with her snub nose, tub-shaped hull and capacious hold capable of carrying about 100 tons of cargo, originated on the Forth & Clyde Canal, when steam power was applied to canal lighters in the 1850s.[160] No better indicator could be found of the pervasive influence of the Industrial Revolution in Scotland than the regular arrival of these avowedly Lowland 'canal boats' in Hebridean harbours. Given their ungainly configuration, and the vulnerable expanse of hatches across a hold occupying three-quarters of the hull, it is not surprising that wreckings were common in adverse conditions; what is much more surprising is that so many of these ships reached the islands unscathed, and that they commonly discharged their cargo successfully on sandy beaches surrounded by treacherous waters. This called for navigation and seamanship of the highest order, to avoid strandings and even worse mishaps. Well into the 1950s, steam-powered puffers carried coal to Tiree and other islands in May and June in response to the call of the local township 'Coal Club' for their annual shipment from the Ayrshire coalfields. By utilising the services of the puffer, it was easier for Tiree people to obtain coal fuel direct from Irvine and Troon, than to continue their earlier nineteenth-century practice of crossing to the Ross of Mull to cut peat, and bring it home in small boats.

In the 1950s the puffer's arrival filled the township with bustle, as horses and carts, and a motley assortment of Fordson and Ferguson tractors, driven by crofters, headed for the shore, and lined up to take a trailer of coal

This splendid view, looking across the Sound of Iona towards the Ross of Mull on a glorious day in the late 1950s, catches two contrasting sides of Hebridean life. J. & J. Hay's hard-worked and rust-stained puffer *Kaffir*, beached on the shore, unloads coal into a trailer pulled by a 'Little Grey Fergie', while MacBrayne's magnificent *King George V* (1926), at anchor in the sound, transfers her round-Mull day-trippers to a ferry-boat, which will bring them to the 'Sacred Isle'. *(A. Ernest Glen)*

to each home. The puffer herself, usually one of J. & J. Hay's vessels with tribal names such as *Serb*, *Dane*, *Anzac*, *Lascar* or *Spartan*[161], looked and sounded splendid when high and dry on the sand, with rust-streaks adding an extra dash of colour to her red and black hull. For a couple of days and nights, she was a veritable hive of activity, with a hissing steam winch, loud voices shouting orders, a squeaky derrick being 'slewed' by rope and tackle,

and the rumble of coal tumbling out of bucket after bucket into carts, as clouds of dust and wisps of smoke drifted skywards over the tall funnel and varnished wheelhouse. Set in the context of white sands and rugged shorelines surrounded by deep blue-green sea on a low tide, this was an unforgettable scene, nowadays impossible to replicate but indelibly etched in memory. As the ship lightened, she had to be pulled further up the shore by means of a winch and mooring rope. Puffers sometimes took sand back to the mainland, but, having discharged their cargo, normally sailed light-ship homewards through the Crinan Canal, their red auxiliary sails occasionally helping them along in the summer breeze.

Puffers were very useful little vessels, and several were owned by island industrialists, such as White Horse Distillers of Islay, with two successive vessels named *Pibroch*, and the slate-quarry owners in Luing and Easdale,

with the *Sylph* and the *Rachel*.[162] As late as the 1920s, however, topsail schooners, like the *Mary Stewart* of Tiree,[163] or large smacks or luggers, such as the *Mary & Effie* of Lismore,[164] still operated alongside puffers by offering 'low-cost competition'.[165] Doubtless representing the conventions of pre-puffer days, the *Mary & Effie* too discharged her cargo on the beach, but, being a deep-keeled vessel, she had to be held upright on the ebb by enormous wooden 'legs'. The 'flat' bottom of the puffer was both a happy convenience and a labour-saving advantage, dispensing with the need for 'legs', piers and ferries, and also for harbours with relatively deep water at all states of the tide.

Ferries, piers, harbours and storage

Suitable piers and harbours, or the lack thereof, assumed greater significance as the larger steamships became a standard part of Highland and Hebridean life. Tiree and Coll, for example, did not have deep-water piers until the early and mid-twentieth century respectively, and both were dependent on 'ferries' which conveyed passengers between the large steamship and the harbour. This was not uncommon in other parts of the Hebrides and the mainland; latterly shipping companies owned a fleet of small boats which were deployed wherever required. A particularly vivid glimpse of the challenges prevailing in the early 1870s in the Morvern area is provided by a diary written by Gertrude Susan Astley and her sister, Constance Charlotte Astley, when visiting Ardtornish House as the guests of Gertrude Craig Sellar. The Astley sisters had taken the Orme steamship, *Talisman*, from Greenock via Oban, and required to disembark at Loch Aline. They wrote as follows in the entry for Friday 4th October 1872:

'A bitterly cold morning; the prospect is not cheering. The *Talisman* does not, will not & cannot call at any place between Oban & Queenish, a place in Mull many miles north of Ardtornish. At Oban things look still more dreary. It is blowing a gale down the Sound & no boat could get to Loch Aline. A smack is starting for Mull with letters but she does not look inviting & as they find that even if they go in her to Mull they will not be able to get across that night, they determine to remain in the *Talisman*. They persuade the captain to fly a signal & keep close to the shore as they pass Loch Aline & are a little comforted by hearing that a boat is coming off to the steamer from Tobermory in which boat if all else fails the benighted pair may be landed at Tobermory. They receive an immense amount of advice & sympathy from a compassionate fellow passenger but G[ertrude] is unable to spend the awful moment passing Loch Aline on deck & retires below. C[onstance] betakes herself to the bridge; there is the Bay, the cliffs, the woods, the house! The signal is waved; not a human being in sight. C wildly thinks of asking them to ring the dinner bell and to request all steerage passengers to utter a simultaneous shout. – The signal is hauled down & hope is extinct.'[166]

The sisters were able to land at Tobermory, and then to proceed to Loch Aline in a small, open sailing-boat. By 12th November, they were making the return journey, but this time they embarked on the *Talisman* at Loch Aline:

'…at last about 6pm the black sea-serpent-like monster steams slowly to the mouth of Loch Aline. The fatal moment has arrived. GC, maid & boxes get into the boat (not the red boat) & are rowed away Gertrude faithful to the last watching them from the shore. As soon as they get on board their melancholy thoughts are much aggravated by finding the whole steamer crammed with steerage passengers, cows, sheep, horses etc. The upper deck is so covered with luggage that they cannot get from one side to the other & the last straw is added when they find that the deck cabins are both taken. They spend about an hour at Craignure taking in three boatloads of sheep. By the time they reach Oban, about 9pm all hope of catching the early train from Greenock next morning is gone, so they console themselves with the prospect of seeing Mr Sellar.'[167]

The expectations of the social class represented by the Astleys are sharply reflected in these extracts; the human ('steerage'), animal and material 'clutter' on the *Talisman*, which was principally a cargo-boat, was something of a nuisance in their eyes.

So too was the mode of 'ferrying' passengers to and from the ship. Argyll was, however, fortunate in having good bays and harbours, even if it often lacked piers. Overall it appears to have been significantly better-provided with these facilities than the north of mainland Scotland, which was seen by some as being disadvantaged by its lack of steamship services compared with

other parts of the Highlands and Islands. When examined by the Napier Commission in 1883 with regard to rent levels, the Rev. Thomson Mackay, parish minister of Tongue, responded:

'I have been a minister in Argyleshire [*sic*] for half a year, in the island of Ulva, and I was a student missionary in the island of Tyree, and also assistant to the late Rev. John Macleod of Morven, and I consider that the rents of the crofters in Argyllshire are much higher than the rents of the crofters in the Reay country. But the Argyllshire men on the other hand have steamboat communication, and can send their produce direct to the market; any produce in the shape of eggs and dairy produce they can send to the best markets in the south. We have no steamboat communication in the north.'[168]

He continued:

Two of Hay's puffers, *Boer* and *Chindit*, in the foreground, and two of Ross & Marshall's puffers, in the background, occupy berths at Ardrossan, along with two Ballantrae-registered fishing-boats. *(A. Ernest Glen)*

'I wished to say that this north country is very badly off for steamboat communication, and for want of piers. I do not mean a harbour of refuge as some delegate stated yesterday, but piers at which a small steamer could land and discharge goods – piers at which fishing boats could be securely moored. I think there is traffic enough to keep a small boat going, say for Strome Ferry to Thurso, right round the coast.'[169]

Mackay went on to suggest suitable places for piers, or for the development of existing facilities, at Melness, and at the tidal ferry at Tongue. Without such conveniences, crofters were having to carry meal many miles by land. His points were later corroborated by H. Morrison from Bettyhill:

'In regard to steamboat communication I may say that I had a correspondence with Mr McBrayne, and Messrs Langlands, and both parties said there were no proper landing places on this coast and that it would not pay to send steamers round, or to add to their present routes.'[170]

The issue here is 'landing places', not piers, which may well mean that good harbours did not exist in any profusion, or that existing piers were not fit for the purpose. It is fascinating to note that Matthew Langlands' Liverpool-based company, which was probably better known for its Hebridean cruise vessels at the end of the nineteenth century, was considered a viable operator alongside David MacBrayne.[171] Shipowners were indeed alive to these challenges, as well as to the unexploited potential around the coast. From the early twentieth century, new jetties and piers were high on the list of desiderata of Martin Orme & Company, who petitioned county councils for appropriate action, but had to contend with somewhat wary civil servants in the Scottish Office who were suspicious of the company's motivation.[172]

Although circumstances were appreciably better in the Hebrides than in the north of mainland Scotland, St Kilda, to the far west of Lewis, lacked a pier, and Donald MacDonald, speaking before the Napier Commission in 1883, affirmed why it would help the island: 'If you saw some of the days when we have to land here you would understand then what need we have of it'.[173] Similar problems sometimes appeared in the Inner Hebrides. John Macpherson of Glendale, Skye, stated to the Commission, in response to the question of whether there was 'a good place' in the district for landing goods:

'There is a good place down at the store-house; but there are none calling, for the want of a pier. There is a road to it, and I believe if there was a pier they would come oftener.'[174]

A small boat had to be used to put goods on board the larger vessel. According to another witness, Alexander Ross, however, there was no appropriate or convenient storehouse at Glendale, and 'the goods have to be placed on the shore in tarpaulins, and I have never heard of a penny worth being stolen of these goods during that time.'[175] The district depended on steamers to relieve poverty, 'and you may know that when the steamers are coming twice a week they are bringing plenty to eat, but there is no store-house in the place.'[176]

In parts of Skye where there were piers, however, the steamers actually created challenges and threats to livelihood, especially if fishermen used the coastline or the facilities. The Rev. Donald MacKinnon of Broadford reported to the Napier Commission that:

'If [the fishermen] come with a take of herrings, the steamer cannot get near the pier...'[177]

Here the problem seems to be that there was only one pier, and the fishermen and the steamships were in competition, if not in conflict, over its use. Two piers were needed. The steamship also had another 'down' side, as Finlay McInnes, also at Broadford, stated to the Commission:

'Another thing is troubling us very much, and is touching our township very much, namely, that the steamer which passes up and down has often taken away our nets, and we got nothing like compensation for them. The steamer is not coming at a set time, neither is she taking the same course when she comes.'[178]

This marks the emergence of a range of conflicts and power-struggles between transport and local industry, which, ever since, have been part of island life. Sometimes too the steamship could bring, or was believed to bring, very unpalatable 'arrivals' to island piers, including colds and fevers (which were particularly evident in St Kilda). Living in isolation, islanders often lacked immunity to infections commonly found in mainland Scotland. The writer of the section for the parish of Killean and Kilchenzie in Kintyre in the *New Statistical Account* chose to lay blame on the steamship and their 'undesirable' passengers for the deteriorating health of the area:

'Typhous fever and other epidemic diseases are becoming prevalent, which, it is believed, have been introduced into the parish by Irish vagrants who are conveyed by steam-boats to Campbelton [*sic*], and itinerate through the parish, begging their way from house to house.'[179]

Yet, if the steamships by their presence could sometimes be a menace, it was far worse to live without them. As the demand for piers and 'landing places' indicates, steamships were seen by the early 1880s as essential and central to the maintenance of 'normal' life in the Highlands and Islands, and the region required miniature 'commercial hubs', with stores and holding areas, in purpose and principle not unlike the docks and warehouses of the Clyde. The absence of steamships, and any accompanying lack of appropriate facilities to encourage them, created a sense of 'deprivation'. Clearly, they had the power to change not only the economy of island societies, but also the conventions of these societies, by influencing construction and building patterns and by altering people's means of subsistence. More subtly, they initiated, and then had to sustain, a major shift in the priorities of communities, and in their self-perception.

Even by the 1880s, steamships all but controlled island life, its 'essentials' and its corporate rhythms. Through their arrival at island piers, where they would be met by shippers or other members of the community, or, in the case of puffers, by 'beaching' in the summer season, steamships created 'events' for local communities. They provided a new source of conviviality too, not least by offering ready access to alcohol, which was quaffed generously by tourists or passengers on the voyage and by 'natives' when the ship arrived at a Hebridean harbour, or by hardy puffermen in need of some comfort in the face of considerable hardship. For most of the twentieth century, this was the pattern that continued with little variation.

156 Napier Commission Report, p865.
157 Meek, 2006.
158 New Statistical Account, Vol. 14, p226.
159 Harvie, 2008, p1.
160 The finest account of the early development of the 'puffer', often erroneously termed 'the Clyde puffer' rather than 'the Forth and Clyde puffer', is Bowman, 1983. For a very useful overview of 'puffers' and their role down to modern times, see Paterson 1996.
161 Paterson, 1996.
162 We are most grateful to Ms Christine MacKay, Luing, for drawing the 'slate lighters' to our attention.
163 The *Mary Stewart* was built at Ardrossan in 1868 by Barclay's yard, and was owned originally by Stewart & Co., her first Master being A. Stewart. Her subsequent owners included A. Shaw (from 1876) and James Foster of Carnlough, manager of the Carnlough Lime Company, who sold her to Donald MacLean, *Dòmhnall Og*, Scarinish, Tiree, in 1908. We are grateful to N. Burden, Bristol, for this information. The *Mary Stewart* was 'laid up' in Scarinish harbour in the early 1930s, and gradually decayed. Parts of her keel and frame, which have assumed the status of revered relics, are still visible. See Simper, 1974, p75.
164 The *Mary & Effie* belonged to the MacFadyen family of Lismore, who also had close connections with Tiree. Simper, 1974, p48, notes: 'The *Mary & Effie* traded as far north as Orkney and south to Ireland, but most of her work was done in the

Western Isles and mainland lochs. She occasionally delighted the MacFadyens by sailing at ten knots. In 1928 a Kelvin engine was fitted and after this the ketch was kept mostly to the inner islands and lochs until finally the puffers took over the trade.'
165 This paralleled the continuing use of sailing-ships alongside steamers in the greater oceans. See Harvie, 2008, p95.
166 Gaskell, 1968, p189.
167 Gaskell, 1968, p196.
168 Napier Commission Report, pp1635-6.
169 Napier Commission Report, p1640.
170 Napier Commission Report, p1655.
171 Robins, 2008, pp20-21.
172 National Abstract of Statistics, AF 42/7522.
173 Napier Commission Report, p871.
174 Napier Commission Report, p382.
175 Napier Commission Report, pp392-393.
176 Napier Commission Report, pp392-393
177 Napier Commission Report, p251.
178 Napier Commission Report, p264.
179 New Statistical Account, Vol. 7, p379.

Chapter Six

Fin de Siècle on the Clyde

The 1900s represented a high-water mark for Glasgow's importance as an industrial, mercantile and cultural powerhouse. The era began with the staging of the 1901 International Exhibition in Kelvingrove Park, the largest such event yet attempted in Britain and aiming to illustrate the development of science, industry and art during the previous century. The architect James Miller, who designed the exhibition's layout and many of its pavilions, was among Glasgow's most versatile and imaginative. He spread the Exhibition's pavilions over 73 acres of Kelvingrove Park and its environs. A substantial new Art Galleries was constructed as the Exhibition's permanent legacy (nowadays the Kelvingrove Museum). The Industrial Hall, designed by Miller, was vast in scale and ornately decorated in a free mix of Spanish Moorish and Oriental design styles. Elsewhere, the exhibition's architecture pointed forward from Victorian eclecticism to the Arts and Crafts Movement and to the emerging 'jugend' style of the new century. As well as showcasing manufactured goods, there was an ambitious cultural programme in the Concert Hall, in which international star performers of the classical music scene and orchestras were presented.

The exhibits and attractions, plus the many cafes, restaurants and live music, reflected a growing leisure culture, also exemplified in Glasgow's growing numbers of variety theatres and dance halls – and in the increasingly ambitious catering and programmes of entertainment to be enjoyed on the Clyde's finest saloon steamers. Indeed, the excursion steamer operator Andrew Dawson Reid, still anxious to prove the respectability of his Sunday cruises from Broomielaw, was bold enough to hire the Berlin Philharmonisches Blas-Orchester, conducted by Herr Moser, to perform a 'Grand Al Fresco Sacred concert' on board the *Duchess of York* (formerly the North British steamer *Jeanie Deans* of 1884) during a June cruise to the Kyles of Bute. The sight of the steamer paddling through the Kyles while the orchestra played pieces by Mendelssohn, Stainer and Sullivan must have been one of the most astonishing spectacles of the era, but it demonstrated the ambition of Clyde steamer operators at that time. During the International Exhibition, Scotland experienced warm and sunny summer weather and so steamer loadings rose to an all time high.

The forward-looking spirit of the era was reflected in the development of new and more efficient forms of marine propulsion than conventional steam expansion engines – namely, steam turbine and diesel power. The Clyde's shipbuilders and steamer operators were at the forefront of commercial applications for these developments.

The most modern existing vessels, such as the North British Railway's *Waverley* and the G&SWR's *Juno* and *Jupiter*, capable of speeds in the 18.5-19.5-knot range, marked the ultimate development of the Clyde paddle steamer, powered by a triple-expansion engine. The *Glen Sannox* demonstrated that, to go any faster, such machinery became very fuel-hungry and so, for the next stage in steamer development, an entirely different approach to propulsion would be required. Triple-expansion engines were large, heavy and labour-intensive installations and, as they occupied the majority of a steamer's mid-body up to Promenade Deck level, they significantly reduced the amount of the hull's volume available for essential payloads of passengers and cargo.

The marine steam turbine appeared to be a very attractive source of power. This was a brilliant invention by the Hon. Charles Parsons, a talented engineer who was son of the Earl of Rosse. Parsons had first developed primitive turbines in the 1880s to generate electricity and, indeed, an early marine application of this design was installed on the CSP paddle steamer *Duchess of Hamilton*. (This utilised exhaust gas from the boiler to generate electricity for the vessel's lighting system.)

Steam turbines offered considerable mechanical and thermal advantages over reciprocating engines. They generate power by steam being forced through a series of rotary blades mounted on a drive shaft, encased in a steel

Early in her lengthy and distinguished career, the revolutionary turbine steamer *King Edward* lies at Ardrishaig on Loch Fyne. *(A. Ernest Glen collection)*

casting. The pressure of the steam deflected the blades and so imparted rotary motion and, in so doing, the steam expanded and fell to lower pressure. Thermally, the range of steam expansion was much wider than in a reciprocating engine with corresponding economies in fuel consumption and, as they had no cylinders and pistons, turbine installations were comparatively light in weight and compactly dimensioned.

Parsons realised that his ingenious invention could be used for the propulsion of ships and so in 1894 he formed a syndicate to invest in the construction of an experimental turbine-powered steam yacht which was named *Turbinia*. In 1897, this was demonstrated with spectacular success off Spithead at the Jubilee Fleet Review, where the vessel darted at great speed between lines of warships. This impressed the Admiralty so favourably that they immediately placed an order with Parsons Marine Turbine Company of Wallsend-on-Tyne for machinery to power an experimental torpedo boat which they named the *Viper*. This was driven by four propeller shafts, each fitted with two screws, the outer shafts being attached to high-pressure turbines with low-pressure turbines on the inner shafts. The *Viper*'s hull was of lightweight construction and, when combined with her powerful machinery, she reached a speed of over 37 knots in 1899.[180]

Simultaneously, another Tyne shipbuilder and munitions supplier, Armstrong, Whitworth & Company, speculatively constructed a turbine-powered destroyer named *Cobra* for the Royal Navy and she managed to

reach 35 knots. She could have gone faster still were it not for the fact that the stokers could not keep pace with her boilers' consumption of coal. She too boasted a very light hull construction and, most unfortunately, this proved to be her undoing – and also that of the *Viper*. Within six weeks in 1901, both vessels foundered. Firstly, the *Viper* ran aground off the Channel Islands following a navigation error and her hull split open. Next, the *Cobra* broke in two in heavy swells off Flamborough Head with the loss of all but 12 of her crew and several Parsons employees who were on board to help supervise the turbine machinery.

Meanwhile, Charles Parsons had turned his attention to the development of turbine-powered merchant ships and he delivered a number of technical papers to interested audiences on this subject. Having attended one of his lectures, Archibald Denny of William Denny & Bros of Dumbarton decided to seek support from various Clyde steamer owners to finance the construction of a turbine-powered Clyde steamer but, at first, none was willing to assist him financially.

In the end, William Denny & Bros formed a syndicate with the Parsons Marine Steam Turbine Company and the independent Clyde steamer operator Captain John Williamson (whose elder brothers James and Alexander were respectively marine superintendents of the Caledonian Steam Packet Company and Glasgow & South Western Railway fleets). Denny, Parsons and Williamson each contributed £11,000 to the cost of the

Above: An inter-war view showing the *King Edward* disgorging her passengers at Tighnabruaich with the *Lord of the Isles* lying off her stern. Note that the *King Edward*'s lifeboats have been repositioned. *(A. Ernest Glen collection)*

Right: The recently-completed *King Edward* at speed off Gourock. *(A. Ernest Glen collection)*

Below: The first *Queen Alexandra* departs Gourock in April 1908 during a brief Clyde career that was cut short by a serious fire. The steamer was subsequently rebuilt for further service in Canada. *(A. Ernest Glen)*

Below right: The Caledonian Steam Packet paddle steamer *Duchess of Fife* at Rothesay. *(A. Ernest Glen collection)*

vessel, the hull design of which was based on that of the successful Denny-built CSP paddle steamer *Duchess of Hamilton*. Indeed, to avoid risk should turbine propulsion prove unsuccessful for any reason, the framing of the new steamer was arranged in such a way that she could be converted to paddle power with reciprocating machinery, and sponsons could be fitted to the hull's sides. Of course, this never happened and the *King Edward*, as the vessel was named, proved an outstanding and enduring success. Completed in 1901, she was to remain in service for no less than half a century.[181]

The Royal Navy's experimental turbine-propelled warships had been fitted with Yarrow high-pressure boilers but on a Clyde steamer, built for commercial purposes, economy was more important than excessive speed and so conventional double-ended boilers were installed. A triple-screw arrangement was chosen with a high-pressure turbine to turn the centre shaft and low-pressure turbines on the two outer shafts. Of notably clean and modern appearance, the *King Edward* carried the simple black and white livery of John Williamson's fleet. Indeed, he was given first refusal to purchase her outright at the end of her maiden season once she had proven herself in service.

In a canny move, Williamson entered into an agreement to deploy the *King Edward* in cooperation with the G&SWR's steamer fleet. The vessel would operate from Glasgow to Greenock (Prince's Pier), Fairlie and Campbeltown. Greenock and Fairlie were key G&SWR coastal destinations, however, the Company was debarred from sailing to Campbeltown with their own steamers as it lay out with the operational remit they had been granted by Parliament. By working in conjunction with John Williamson, the G&SWR could extend the range of their destinations reachable from Glasgow by combined rail and steamer services.

The *King Edward* ran her initial trials in June 1901 reaching 18.66 knots. After minor adjustments and hull cleaning, she attained 19.7 knots on subsequent trials. Her propellers were then exchanged for a larger set and, on a third trial run she managed to reach 20.57 knots. Following these tests, on 28th June, she made a special cruise for invited guests, during which the CSP's *Duchess of Hamilton* was encountered in Kilbrannan Sound undertaking a special charter for the Institute of Naval Architects. The two vessels raced – and the *King Edward* won by a considerable margin.[182]

Not only was the turbine steamer faster and with better fuel economy than a paddle vessel, but she was also much quieter and smoother. Unlike paddle steamers, which had a distinctive surging motion, accompanied by the sonorous rumbles and clanks of single or compound expansion machinery, turbine propulsion was nearly silent with only a slight high-pitched whirring sound in the background. Being driven by screw propellers, there was however the possibility of cavitation affecting the hull's aft body. This phenomenon is caused as the propellers rotate and water pressure changes rhythmically on the hull's underside. When operating at speed, some cavitation could be felt towards the *King Edward*'s stern.

Another consequence of turbine power was that the steamer's machinery was largely hidden from view. Hitherto, on all Clyde paddle steamers, the engine protruded into the saloon deck amidships with open viewing galleries on either side. On cold or wet days, these galleries provided warm spots in which to shelter and, besides, the action of the mighty pistons driving a paddle steamer's crankshaft was a hypnotic sight – especially as such engines were always highly polished and embellished with painted ornamentation. On the *King Edward*, in contrast, the compact turbines were below continuous expanses of decking, and so the technological spectacle of marine propulsion in the raw was lost to the public's gaze.

Turbine machinery was, however, the *King Edward*'s only experimental feature. In terms of layout and internal appointments, she followed the best practice in Clyde steamer design of her era – albeit with much more generous space amidships for public circulation.

The *King Edward*'s inaugural season was an outstanding success – so much so that in October 1901 Captain John Williamson accepted the offer of William Denny & Bros to build a larger fleet mate. Launched in April 1902 as the *Queen Alexandra*, she entered service at the end of May after a series of trials during which speeds of nearly 22 knots were recorded. The *Queen Alexandra* took over the *King Edward*'s roster and the older vessel then switched to serve Tarbert, Ardrishaig and Inveraray, competing successfully against the ageing paddle steamers *Iona*, *Columba* and *Lord of the Isles*. While MacBrayne's *Columba* retained her unique mystique – and the lucrative Royal Mail contract – the *King Edward* nonetheless won a significant slice of the passenger market to Loch Fyne.

Next, the Caledonian Steam Packet Company decided that they too should have a turbine steamer as flagship to replace the coal-guzzling paddle vessel *Galatea* which, in any case, required re-boilering. Benefiting from West Central Scotland's growing prosperity, the parent Caledonian Railway's ambitious and astute management were keen to embrace the latest and best emerging design thinking. Their crack express trains to Carlisle (and London Euston), operated jointly with the London & North Western Railway, and their 'Grampian Corridor' expresses to Aberdeen were unparalleled in a Scottish context in terms of speed and comfort. Their brilliant Locomotive Superintendent, J.F. McIntosh, designed railway engines that were so magnificent to the eye that crowds gathered on the platform ends of Glasgow Central station to watch them depart. Such was the public's enthusiasm that occasionally police assistance was required to maintain order and safety.

The Caledonian's station architecture was equally progressive, their grandest schemes of the era usually resulting from collaboration between the 1901 Exhibition architect James Miller and their own Chief Engineer, Donald Matheson. One significant project was the doubling of the track on their Wemyss Bay branch and the construction of a new station and steamer pier there twice the size of the existing structure. Completed in 1903, Miller's design, with its sweeping expanses of glazed roofing and fully enclosed promenade from station concourse to steamer berth, was the height of Edwardian elegance.[183]

No doubt following consultation with his brother John on the performance of the *King Edward* and *Queen Alexandra*, the CSP's Marine Superintendent James Williamson gained board approval for the ordering of a new vessel based upon the *King Edward*'s design from William Denny & Bros. In the meantime, the CSP took delivery of two further paddle steamers – the John Brown-built *Duchess of Montrose* (1902) and, from Fairfield Shipbuilding and Engineering, the very long-lived *Duchess of Fife* (1903) but these were similar in conception to their existing vessels.

Their new Denny-built turbine steamer *Duchess of Argyll* ran trials in May 1906 and subsequently entered service between Ardrossan and Brodick, where her ability to reach speeds of over 20 knots, coupled with her relatively moderate consumption of coal, gave the CSP two welcome advantages over the G&SWR's *Glen Sannox*. Externally and within, the *Duchess of Argyll* was among the most elegant of Clyde steamers, the stylish

180 Paterson, 1969, pp154-155.
181 Paterson, 1969, pp157-160.
182 Paterson, 1969, p159.
183 MacIntosh, 2009.

Above: The Caledonian Steam Packet Company's turbine steamer *Duchess of Argyll* in her original condition with open forward mooring deck and large saloon windows. *(A. Ernest Glen collection)*

Right: The master of the *Duchess of Argyll* surveys the scene from the port bridge wing. Attached to the deck railing is an advertisement for an evening cruise by the steamer. *(Jim MacIntosh collection)*

Below: The Glasgow & South Western Railway's turbine steamer *Atalanta*. *(A. Ernest Glen collection)*

Below right: Elegantly dressed passengers arrive by train at Wemyss Bay Station and Pier, one of the Caledonian Railway's two steamer gateways to the Clyde resorts. *(Jim MacIntosh collection)*

A painting by the great railway poster artist Norman Wilkinson and issued by the Caledonian Railway to promote its steamer services, featuring the **Duchess of Argyll** in a condition in which she never actually appeared, with a plated-in forward mooring deck and large forward saloon deck windows. Goat Fell on Arran broods in the background while a yacht is about to cross the steamer's wake. *(Jim MacIntosh collection)*

CSP livery accentuating her sleek hull lines and well-proportioned silhouette.[184] Inevitably, her introduction caused the G&SWR to order a turbine steamer of their own.

In the meantime, turbine propulsion had been fitted to William Denny-built steamers operating across the Dover Strait and even to a John Brown-built trans-Atlantic liner for Cunard, the *Carmania* of 1905. This vessel was fitted with machinery manufactured by Parsons in Newcastle. As Cunard wished their next generation of very large trans-Atlantic liners also to be turbine-powered, John Brown & Company decided to establish their own turbine manufacturing division. To gain expertise, they built an experimental set of turbines of size and power output similar to those of existing Clyde turbine steamers. Once John Brown had used these to train their staff and had tried various experiments, they became surplus to requirements and so they were offered to the G&SWR should they order a steamer from the yard.[185]

A contract was signed in 1905 and the new vessel was completed the following summer as the *Atalanta*. Smaller, slower and less stable than existing Clyde turbine steamers, she also suffered some initial teething difficulties, first being used as necessary on a variety of G&SWR routes. A new North British paddle steamer, the *Marmion*, followed from A. & J. Inglis in 1906, it being necessary to use paddle propulsion due to the lack of water depth at Craigendoran Pier.

Teutonic fashionability

By the turn of the century, Germany was emerging as the most serious industrial rival to Britain's hegemony. Not only was Germany a leader in heavy engineering, but it also excelled in the emerging light industries,

manufacturing electrically-powered consumer goods for the home, a new phenomenon upon which Britain's industrialists largely failed to capitalise. Furthermore, Germany gained an early lead in fashion clothing, music and interior design – three areas of 'creative industry' in which Britain has more recently proven successful. In port cities throughout Europe – from Helsinki in the North to Palermo in the South Germanic 'Jugendstijl' became the favoured mode of decorating amongst the young and fashionable sons and daughters of the *haute bourgeois* merchant class (Charles Rennie Mackintosh is, of course, the best-know exponent of this aesthetic in Glasgow). Germanic light classical music, such as polkas and waltzes, was enjoyed by discerning couples promenading in public parks and in the grander restaurants, hotel ballrooms and variety theatres, where German musicians were employed for extra authenticity and cosmopolitan glamour.

In the 1900s, the most elegant of the railway-owned Clyde steamers likewise came to employ German musicians to entertain their passengers. Usually quartets of Bavarians or Württemburgers, they played popular light classical selections. In the months leading up to the First World War, however, many suspected that these musicians were unquestionably naval spies, who would report every sighting of a warship back to Berlin.

On the less salubrious steamers operating from the Broomielaw to cater for their clientele, a mix of traditional Scottish and Irish music, interspersed with the latest music hall favourites, was favoured.

The Williamson and Buchanan fleets

The Broomielaw was the long-established starting-point of trips 'doon the watter' for those who preferred to experience the sights and sounds of the upper Clyde to embarking at a downriver port.[186] During the new

184 Paterson, 1969, pp59-60.
185 Johnston, 2000, p115.
186 In 1927, the central Glasgow Clyde steamer berths were moved to the south side of the river and the North bank berths were given over to coastal steamers to Ireland etc.

Above: The officers and crew of the *Duchess of Argyll*, whose tasks ranged from stoking coal to preparing and serving sumptuous luncheons and dinners to First Class passengers. *(Jim MacIntosh collection)*

Right: The G&SWR's *Atalanta* at Dunoon Pier. *(A. Ernest Glen)*

Below: The second *Lord of the Isles* (with her promenade deck extended fully forward in the manner of the CSP's vessels) at Tighnabruaich. *(A. Ernest Glen collection)*

Below right: A stern-quarter view of the elegant *Duchess of Argyll* leaving Whiting Bay. *(A. Ernest Glen collection)*

An inter-war view of the second *Queen Alexandra* off Gourock. *(A. Ernest Glen)*

Buchanan Steamers' *Eagle III* approaches Renfrew Wharf in June 1914. Sailing from the Broomielaw, this popular vessel carried large crowds of day-trippers from central Glasgow to the main Clyde coastal resorts. *(A. Ernest Glen)*

century's first decade, improved sewerage disposal and treatment practices meant that gradually less raw effluent was dumped in the Clyde and so the quality of the river's water began slowly to improve, meaning that excursion traffic from central Glasgow experienced a revival and some renewed investment in better ships. As the Clyde yards were busy constructing not only mighty liners but also new Dreadnought warships – an ominous portent of the forthcoming First World War, there was much to excite the eyes of steamer passengers.

By this period, the steamers of the Williamson and Buchanan fleets were the most prominent in Glasgow's City Centre. In 1910, the Buchanan Company introduced their new *Eagle III* (with the numerals as part of the name), ordered from A. & J. Inglis, but subcontracted by them to Napier & Miller, who installed the final haystack boiler to be built for a Clyde steamer. Following some rebuilding by A. & J. Inglis to correct stability problems, she became a well-known and very popular vessel, synonymous with the Glasgow-Rothesay/Kyles of Bute service, giving heroic service in two World Wars, and sailing until 1946.[187] In comparison with the latest railway-owned steamers, however, the *Eagle III*'s saloons were less ornately appointed and this comparative austerity was reflected externally in her lack of scrollwork paddle box adornments. Although she carried a broad cross-section of mainly Glaswegian excursionists, her predominant clientele was of working class origin and she successfully provided this substantial market with a superior level of comfort and service in comparison with most of the older Broomielaw-based steamers. Reflecting on the *Eagle III*'s early years, a correspondent in the *The Dunoon Observer and Argyllshire Standard* recalled:

'It was the custom of the time for family groups to make the tour and equally customary for wealthier people to take their friends on an outing, which included lunch and afternoon tea on board. At that time a band was in attendance, and the writer well remembers, as a child, going on such an excursion as the guest of a well-known Dunoon benefactor. Music was of the period, and 'Hearts of Oak', 'The Guardship' and 'The Good Rhine Wine' were the popular

songs. When the vessel was returning and sailing home through the Kyles, the voice of Mr Ritchie, the purser, was heard adding his vocal refrain…'[188]

The rival Williamson fleet, run by Captain John Williamson, countered two years later when their new paddle steamer, the *Queen Empress*, was delivered by Murdoch & Murray of Port Glasgow. Also in 1912, Williamson acquired the Lochgoil & Inveraray Steamboat Company (formerly the Lochgoil and Lochlong Co.) and their famous *Lord of the Isles*, these vessels being additional to Williamson's regally named turbine steamers, *King Edward* and *Queen Alexandra*. The latter, built in 1912, was an almost identical version of their earlier *Queen Alexandra*, built in 1902, but badly damaged by fire in 1911. The burned carcass of the first 'Queen', however, had been rescued by Canadian Pacific Railways, and had crossed the Atlantic to Vancouver, where she re-emerged as the *Princess Patricia* to give excellent service as a much-appreciated 'Pacific Princess' on the Vancouver-Nanaimo run until she was withdrawn and scrapped in 1937.[189]

By the Edwardian era, the favoured nomenclature for the majority of the Williamson paddle steamer fleet had a mildly Gaelic flavour, represented in *Benmore*, *Kylemore*, *Strathmore*, all of them place names incorporating the Gaelic adjective *mòr* ('great'). Meanwhile, most of the Buchanan ships were named to reflect the popularity of the islands as tourist destinations – *Isle of Arran*, *Isle of Bute* and *Isle of Skye*, for example.

The Williamsons, Masters, owners and managers, have an unrivalled place of distinction in the history of Clyde steamers. In addition to their independent ventures, which offered variety for passengers and stiff competition for the railway fleets, the latter were the beneficiaries of the Williamsons' initiative, innovation and managerial skill. Indeed, it could well be said that the Williamsons, doubtless motivated by a touch of sibling rivalry, not only played a major part in developing Clyde steamer fleets before 1900, but also helped to shape their future by introducing the all-important turbine vessel.

187 Duckworth and Langmuir, 1990, p35.
188 The Dunoon Observer and Argyllshire Standard, 4th March 1967.
189 *Clyde Steamers*, No. 46, pp2-11.

Chapter Seven
The First World War and its Aftermath

During the first year of the war, the relatively easy-going Edwardian ways of living continued and one of the earliest slogans was 'Business as Usual'. By 1915, the rationing of supplies had begun when Germany imposed a blockade on Britain, its submarines attacking not only the Royal Navy but also merchant ships. Following the Battle of the Somme in July 1916, restrictions became more severe and in the spring of 1917, rationing was introduced.

Britain's ultimate victory in the First World War came at a terrible cost in terms of human lives and a generation of young men were either killed or written off as invalids (Scotland's loss was proportionately greater than that of the UK as a whole). This – and the economic cost of waging such a modern war of attrition – caused Britain to lose significant momentum, not least in naval architecture, shipbuilding and operational practices. Indeed, Britain's victory appeared to cement the pre-war *status quo* and so replacements for war losses tended to be little different from their pre-war predecessors; British coal-fired steamers with reciprocating machinery completed in 1920 were much the same as those delivered in 1910. In contrast, in the Scandinavian countries – particularly Denmark and Norway, which lacked coalfields – diesel propulsion was embraced and fleets hitherto dominated by steamships went over largely to diesel during the 1920s.

In 1914, a normal steamer service was maintained on the Clyde but, in February 1915 the *Duchess of Montrose*, *Duchess of Hamilton* and *Duchess of Argyll* were requisitioned, initially to serve as troop transports supplying the fields of battle across the Dover Strait. That September, the *Duchess of Montrose* and the *Duchess of Hamilton* were converted to minesweepers. The latter saw only the briefest military service, as a mine sank her off Harwich after only two months' duty. Alan J.S. Paterson poignantly observes that her

Formerly the pride of the CSP fleet, the ***Duchess of Hamilton*** looks drab in her wartime paint scheme at Southampton. Alas, she did not survive the conflict. *(A. Ernest Glen collection)*

During the course of the First World War, numerous Clyde steamers were requisitioned for naval service. Here, the *Duchess of Fife* is seen in wartime condition. *(A. Ernest Glen collection)*

The requisitioned CSP vessel *Duchess of Rothesay* in her wartime guise. *(A. Ernest Glen collection)*

sinking marked the end of an era:

> 'She had sailed for just over twenty-five years, a short span by the standards of steamers such as the *Iona* and *Lucy Ashton*, but it covered exactly the great years of the Clyde and its steamers. She would probably have been renovated for post-war service had she survived and could have been expected to continue sailing well into the 1920s. Fate decreed otherwise, however, and in one respect it was perhaps as well. This fine ship had been the pride of the Caledonian fleet for too long for those who knew her to contemplate lightly the prospect of her trudging round the firth in general service amidst the declining standards of a post-war world. Her best years were over when she went off to war where, like many of her human contemporaries, she perished, to the widespread regret of all who had known her in her prime. She had been the favourite of a lost generation and something of her high reputation died with her and those who had sailed in her. When she disappeared, something of the Clyde's old gaiety vanished for ever.'[190]

The *Duchess of Montrose* lasted until March 1917 when she too was lost while minesweeping off the French coast. In 1916, practically the entire CSP fleet was requisitioned and so Clyde services were reduced to a skeleton, operated by vessels chartered from various private companies. The G&SWR were more fortunate; their flagship *Glen Sannox* was briefly requisitioned as a troop transport, but quickly deemed unsuitable and returned to her owners. The remainder of the fleet served as minesweepers, the *Neptune* being blown up in April 1917 and the *Mars* sinking after being rammed by a destroyer. The *Mercury* had several lucky escapes, firstly having her stern blown off by a mine and thereafter losing her bow when another mine exploded in her path. Various NBR steamers were similarly requisitioned – including a new building, the *Fair Maid*, which was actually a near-sister ship of the *Waverley* of 1899 and therefore indicative of the NBR's conservative policy regarding ship design. Completed by A. & J. Inglis in 1916, she was sunk by a mine in November that year.

Following war losses, only a depleted Clyde steamer service was offered and the competitiveness of the Victorian and Edwardian eras never returned. The memory of war deaths and coping with the traumatised and walking wounded, coupled with wage inflation and associated industrial unrest, undermined Scotland's self-confidence and that of Britain as a whole. The many private railway companies were now less profitable and so in 1923 it was decided that, as they had cooperated during the war, they should be grouped into four large regional operators. Because the main

railways serving lowland Scotland – the Caledonian, North British and Glasgow & South Western companies – had been rivals and had long co-operated closely with English partners in running through-trains south of the border, there was reluctance about creating a unified Scottish railway. Instead, the Caledonian and Glasgow & South Western were combined with the London & North Western and Midland railways to form the London, Midland & Scottish Railway (LMSR), whose headquarters were in London. Nearly all of its locomotives were built in English works, rather than in Glasgow. Similarly, the North British was combined with various English companies to form the London & North Eastern Railway (LNER). (In the South and West of England, the Southern Railway and the Great Western Railway completed the so-called 'Big Four' of the inter-war era.)

These changes meant that the majority of Clyde steamer services originating from South Bank piers were now operated by the LMSR, while those from Craigendoran belonged to the LNER.

The first significant Clyde steamer built post-1918 was the *Glen Sannox*, delivered in 1925 by William Denny & Bros, a turbine-powered replacement for the famous G&SWR paddle steamer of the same name. In terms of design and layout, the new vessel was very similar to the CSP's turbine *Duchess of Argyll*, built almost 20 years previously – a sure sign of how much Scottish shipbuilding and engineering had stagnated since the Edwardian era.

Heavy industry in Scotland generally suffered serious decline in the 1920s and onwards into the 1930s, and innovation in most sectors was curtailed. Christopher Harvie trenchantly summarises the plight of shipbuilding:

> '…The yards were constrained by old equipment and the restoration of pre-war working practices, while modernisation was inhibited by the post-war inflation. Beardmore's, whose reconstruction ruined them, were appalled when their old machinery was eagerly bought up by their Clydeside rivals.
>
> But rivalry was not the rule: shipowners reserved berths or bought shares in shipbuilding firms, which had coped with wartime shortages by buying up steelworks. A tight system of vertical cartelisation ensued. For a time in the early 1920s Lord Pirrie presided over an effective amalgamation between Royal Mail Lines, Harland and Wolffs, Lithgows and Colvilles, which dominated the Clyde. Such cartels were probably inevitable, but checked innovation and diversification, and the trade slump caused the whole edifice to collapse.'[191]

The picture was similar in coal, steel, motor-vehicle manufacture and

190 Paterson, 1982, p92.

Above: The former G&SWR flagship *Glen Sannox* in the short-lived initial LMSR livery after the Grouping of the railways in 1923. *(A. Ernest Glen)*

Right: Inter-war Clyde cruising on a steamer of the Edwardian era: the *King Edward* departs from Tighnabruaich in the 1930s. *(Donald E. Meek collection)*

Below: The former Caledonian Railway turbine steamer *Duchess of Argyll* in her inter-war LMSR livery at Rothesay. *(A. Ernest Glen)*

Below right: The *Atalanta* undertakes minesweeping duties during the First World War. *(A. Ernest Glen collection)*

Above: The capacious Williamson-Buchanan flagship excursion steamer *Queen Mary* on trials off Gourock. *(A. Ernest Glen)*

Left: The recently-completed LMSR turbine steamer *Duchess of Hamilton* reverses out of Ardrossan harbour on a gusty day. *(A. Ernest Glen)*

Below: The Williamson-Buchanan turbine steamer *King George V* leaving Gourock in 1935. Strictly speaking, the *King George V* belonged to Turbine Steamers Ltd., but the consortium was very much part of the Williamson empire, and she is thus generally accepted as a 'Williamson-Buchanan' vessel. *(A. Ernest Glen)*

textiles. National disgruntlement led to nascent Communism on 'Red Clydeside', fomented by John MacLean and others. The emergence of radical political groupings like the Moscow-funded National Minority Movement, 'helped to raise the political temperature in the months before the General Strike of 4-12 May 1926.'[192] Athough the swift capitulation of most workers led to widespread despair and to managerial supremacy, the long and determined stand of the coalminers, which lasted until November, made its point by applying pressure where it hurt most – in matters of fuel supply. This affected the viability of coal-dependent shipping companies. The Wall Street Crash of 1929 further destabilised national economies and international trade.

Troubled though the period was, the latter-1920s were marked by a growing leisure culture, enjoyed at least by some. The development of the Clyde excursion fleet reflected this trend. In 1919, the two principal excursion operators from Central Glasgow – John Williamson & Company and Buchanan Steamers Ltd – merged to form Williamson-Buchanan Steamers Ltd. This combined fleet brought together popular paddle vessels such as the *Eagle III* (1910), the *Kylemore* (1897) and the *Queen-Empress* (1912) with the turbine steamers *King Edward* and *Queen Alexandra*. William Denny & Bros delivered a new turbine vessel, the *King George V*, during the late summer of 1926. She was the first passenger steamer fitted with Parsons' high-pressure turbines, the arrangement of which was unusual. Four turbines powered the port propeller shaft while the starboard shaft was worked by three turbines using boiler steam plus a fourth turbine using steam already passed through the port side turbines. To supply steam at sufficiently high pressure to the turbines, two navy-type Yarrow boilers were installed, working at 550lb and with an exceptionally high steam temperature of 750 farenheit. On trials, the *King George V* reached 20.78 knots – but there were rumours that she could actually reach nearer 25 knots. In service, her state-of-the-art steam plant was less successful than its designers had expected. After a tragic accident in which two engineers were scalded to death, she was reboiled in 1929 and again in 1935 with a single conventional boiler working at 200lb of pressure.

The *King George V*'s passenger accommodation was less ornate than on her Edwardian fleet mates, but her superstructure was largely enclosed, meaning that she was a more comfortable ship in inclement weather. Indeed, her layout set the pattern for the three remaining large Clyde turbine steamers delivered towards the end of the decade. These were the LMSR's *Duchess of Montrose* (1930), *Duchess of Hamilton* (1932) and Williamson-Buchanan's *Queen Mary* of 1933.

Built by William Denny & Bros, the *Duchess of Montrose* was the Clyde's first one-class excursion steamer and so her accommodation was of a uniformly high standard. This reflected changing social trends in the wake of the First World War in that the social standards of average steamer passengers from Gourock were probably less dissimilar than they had been in the Victorian and Edwardian eras. Leisure time was now centred more on relaxation, rather than on the display of class privilege. The luxury of space and a broader range of facilities to suit different tastes on board a one-class steamer was a big attraction. The *Duchess of Hamilton* was of very similar appearance to the *Montrose*, but was built by Harland & Wolff.

The Denny-built *Queen Mary* was an altogether more substantial vessel – indeed she was the most capacious Clyde steamer, with space latterly for 1,820 passengers as opposed to the 1,310 of the CSP 'Duchesses'. Certainly the finest vessel for many years designed to sail from Central Glasgow, her regular 10am departures for Dunoon and Rothesay were invariably well

patronised. Unlike the 'Duchesses', she was a two-class steamer, possibly reflecting the greater social diversity of her Glaswegian clientele. Unusually, her First Class accommodation was in the forward half, the idea being to give good views ahead from the restaurant and smoking saloon. Her superstructure was extensive, her decks extending aft nearly to the stern, affording relatively generous space, even on crowded departures. In appearance, the *Queen Mary* was slightly more progressive than her LMSR contemporaries, her plated-in bulwarks and aft-facing lifeboat davits lending her a slightly Art Deco air, emphasised by her striking black and white livery.[193] After only a couple of seasons, the *Queen Mary*'s name was modified to *Queen Mary II*; this was to allow Cunard-White Star Line to use her original name for their new trans-Atlantic liner, then under construction at the John Brown shipyard in Clydebank.

Rationalisation of shipyards and shipping companies in the 1920s made an impact on ship types and propulsion, as the drive for economy and efficiency opened the door to diesel engines. These came into prominence chiefly through the example of Royal Mail Lines and Harland and Wolff. On the high seas, it increasingly looked as if the future belonged to diesel. Revolutionary motorships such as the *Britannic* and the *Georgic* joined the White Star Line, the *Asturias* and the *Alcantara* (later re-engined with steam turbines, because of diesel-induced vibration) joined Royal Mail Lines, and Irish Sea shipping witnessed the arrival of the typically straight-lined, low-funnelled *Ulster Monarch* and her sisters.

Motor propulsion began to penetrate the Scottish west coast fleets through the post-1927 MacBrayne connection to the wider, innovative world of Royal Mail Lines and, especially, Coast Lines. MacBrayne's had introduced paraffin 'oil engines' to the islands in the early 1900s, through the *Comet* (built 1905, acquired 1907), the *Scout* (1907), and the *Lochinvar* (1908), but at that stage, the company had no policy for motorisation. This came of necessity, and in the context of a growing emergency. MacBrayne's had been struggling to keep afloat in the post-war years, complaints about its services were increasing, and various enquiries into the state of the company had been conducted. Ship replacement was becoming urgent. As if the 1920s could possibly become any worse, David MacBrayne Ltd suffered the loss of three of their principal ships in 1927. Firstly, the Stornoway-Kyle of Lochalsh mailship, *Sheila*, ploughed on to rocks near the entrance to Loch Torridon on New Year's Day, secondly, the veteran paddler *Chevalier* went aground irretrievably on Barmore Island, near Tarbert, Loch Fyne and, at the end of her season at Oban, the much-loved, round-Mull paddler, *Grenadier*, caught fire in somewhat mysterious circumstances. The ship's former Master, Captain Archie MacArthur, who was still sailing post-retirement as an 'extra Master' on a special, but somewhat fraught, arrangement with the company, was killed in the blaze.

Although MacBrayne's had increased the number of their shareholders very substantially over the preceding decade, they were apparently daunted by the cost of replacement vessels, and, smarting from criticism, David Hope MacBrayne withdrew from the negotiation of the 1928 mail contract. In those challenging circumstances, a knight in shining armour emerged in the person of Sir Alfred Read, Chairman of Coast Lines Ltd, who had succeeded in wresting his company free from the teetering edifice of Lord Kylsant and Royal Mail. Coast Lines and the London, Midland and Scottish Railway each took a 50 per cent share in the new company, which was reconstituted as David MacBrayne (1928) Ltd. The LMSR Chairman Sir Josiah Stamp was disinclined to assume a position of authority, and Read took the helm.[194] Without Read's purposeful, visionary leadership, it is

191 Harvie, 1998, pp39-40.
192 Harvie, 1998, pp93-94.
193 Orr, 1976.

Above: MacBrayne's cruise-ship *Lochgarry* is pictured at Ullapool. Built in 1898 as the *Vulture* for G. & J. Burns, and renamed *Lairdsrock* following Burns' merger with Laird's, she was acquired by MacBrayne's in 1937. Requisitioned for war service, she sank off Rathlin in January 1942. *(A. Ernest Glen)*

Right: The *Lochness* was the first new vessel to be built when David MacBrayne (1928) Limited was formed. The last steam-powered passenger vessel to be built by MacBrayne's, she maintained the Mallaig-Stornoway service until she was replaced by the diesel-engined *Loch Seaforth* in1947. *(A. Ernest Glen collection)*

Below: The Art Deco pier buildings at Fort William, seen in the 1950s with a fleet of MacBrayne buses awaiting a steamer's arrival. *(A. Ernest Glen)*

Below right: The similarly modern-looking pier building at Port Ellen, Islay, pictured here in the latter 1960s. *(A. Ernest Glen)*

Above: The *Lochfyne*, built by Denny's, Dumbarton, for MacBrayne's in 1931, made history as the first diesel-electric passenger vessel in the British Isles. She is seen here leaving Gourock on trials in the grey hull briefly favoured by the reconstituted company for its first ships. *(A. Ernest Glen collection)*

Right: Two diesel-engined motor ships, *Lochmor* and *Loch Earn*, were built for MacBrayne's by the Ardrossan Dockyard Company in 1930. Their rather square sterns and squat profiles are evident in this photograph of the launch of the grey-hulled *Lochmor*, which was assigned to the service from Mallaig and Kyle to the Small Isles, Harris, and North and South Uist. She remained in service until 1964, when she and the *Loch Earn* were sold to Greek interests. *(A. Ernest Glen collection)*

Below: When the motor ship *Lochfyne* was first delivered, she was put on public display in Glasgow alongside MacBrayne's oldest vessel, the paddle steamer *Glencoe* which, thereafter, was sent for scrapping. *(A. Ernest Glen)*

Below right: The diesel-engined *Loch Earn* approaches Tobermory, while the *Lochbroom* leaves the bay. *(Donald B. MacCulloch)*

difficult to know what would have become of Hebridean passenger and cargo services after 1930.

Despite the protests of conservatives and romantics, the noise and vibration of diesel engines were set to replace the gentle thump of the old steamships. Before his new motor ships appeared, however, Sir Alfred Read oversaw the building and introduction in 1929 of the first proper mini-liner for the Stornoway-Mallaig service – the steam-powered *Lochness*, a splendid-looking ship with a high forecastle, tall funnel and derricks on the fore and main masts. Built by Harland and Wolff, Govan, she served Lewis with distinction until the arrival of the new motorship, *Loch Seaforth*, in 1947. Thereafter she undertook the Inner Isles service from Oban. MacBrayne's first purpose-built, diesel-powered passenger vessels arrived in 1930, with the building of the *Loch Earn* and the *Lochmor* by the Ardrossan Dockyard Company, then owned by Coast Lines. Departing from the traditional black hull, the two sisters initially appeared in grey hulls with red stripes, thereby somewhat resembling miniature Union-Castle liners. In spite of loud, noisy engines and ponderously slow speeds, these somewhat ungainly sisters greatly improved existing MacBrayne services to the Outer and Inner Hebrides, although they were long remembered for their inadequate accommodation and lack of appropriate shelter in stormy conditions, as described in this diary entry:

'The *Lochmor* was late in sailing (Monday). The threatened gale had started. It was with difficulty that the ferry boat at Eigg got alongside. Then the *Lochmor* took shelter along with other vessels at Rum. After 6pm. About an hour after midnight the Captain in his prudence decided to ride the gale to Canna rather than risk his ship being driven on the reefs, and he hardly got under way when the

Passengers huddle round the warm funnels of the *Saint Columba* on a cold, wet day on the Clyde. *(Donald B. MacCulloch)*

German cargo vessel, which was anchored at the stern of the *Lochmor*, was wrecked.

No one who was aboard will forget that trip. There was the lady who rolled to the floor and lay soaked in a pool of brine for long, holding on to the leg of a table while her body tossed with the boat. Like the rest of the women she prayed and promised… The *Lochmor* could not get into Lochboisdale nor Lochmaddy and only by the grace of God managed Tarbert as darkness fell (Tuesday).'[195]

Nevertheless, the 'terrible twins' remained essential components of the MacBrayne network, giving yeoman service until their departure to Greece with the arrival of new car ferries in 1964.

MacBrayne's Clyde services were soon to feel the sharp edge of restructuring. As happened with Hebridean veterans such as the splendid *Claymore* of 1881, the famous *Iona* and *Columba* were sent for scrapping, and moving elegies were composed by their affectionate admirers:

'Old-fashioned by now she [the *Iona*] certainly was, but the classical beauty of her long hull, the rich colours of the MacBrayne funnels, and the smartness of her appearance made an unforgettably dignified and striking impression, especially against the backcloth of

Crowds board the LMSR turbine steamer *Duchess of Montrose* at Largs Pier in 1938. In the background can be seen the then-new Art Deco Nardini restaurant and ice cream parlour - today still a glamorous and popular attraction on the town's waterfront. *(Ian Johnston collection)*

steamer predecessors, she first and foremost exemplified an engineering solution rather than an aesthetic one.

Prior to her introduction into regular service in 1931, the *Lochfyne* was displayed triumphantly at the Broomielaw alongside the 85-year-old *Glencoe*, which was dispatched for scrapping shortly thereafter. In the 1930s, there was little sentimentality about such old ships – the *Lochfyne* was supposed to show how far MacBrayne's had progressed in the timespan since the *Glencoe*'s construction. The *Lochfyne* operated between Greenock, Gourock and Ardrishaig in winter, and was based at Oban in summer, although, with the arrival of the turbine steamer *King George V* at Oban in 1936, she became best known on the Clyde-Tarbert-Ardrishaig run.

In 1934, the *Lochfyne* was given a little sister, the *Lochnevis*, which was similarly diesel-electric powered. The single-funnelled *Lochnevis* benefited from the lessons learnt through the *Lochfyne*'s 'mistakes' as her diesel-electric machinery rested on vibration-absorbing spring-plates. The dapper *Lochnevis* proved to be fast and versatile on a variety of West Highland and Hebridean services, and was well suited to the carriage of livestock.

In spite of such radical innovation, MacBrayne's retained a place of honour for turbine steamers. In 1935, it received the *Queen Alexandra* and the *King George V* from Turbine Steamers Ltd. Both became iconic members of the fleet, the latter being long associated with the round-Mull cruise from Oban to Staffa and Iona, a service which she performed with distinction until withdrawn in 1974.[197] On transferring to MacBrayne ownership, the *Queen Alexandra* was given a new lease of life as the *Saint Columba*, together with enhanced passenger accommodation – and three funnels rather than her previous two. This overt signal of MacBrayne supremacy in the 'contest' for the Clyde came just as the Cunard Line's famous three-funnelled *Queen Mary* finally emerged from John Brown's yard at Clydebank. The *Saint Columba* distinguished herself on the Glasgow-Ardrishaig service and, from 1947 until her withdrawal in 1958 she linked Gourock and Ardrishaig. The tide was seemingly on the turn for the railway companies.

In addition to their modern-looking motor vessels and their stately second-hand turbine steamers, MacBrayne's also invested in some strikingly up-to-date architecture for their pier buildings. In particular, those at Fort William, Tobermory and Port Ellen (as well as some smaller buildings) were replaced with new edifices in the fashionable 'streamline moderne' style.[198] Notwithstanding a wet and windy climate, this aesthetic of flat roofs, pastel-painted stucco facades, metal-framed Crittall windows and curvaceous balconies was widely used throughout Scotland in the latter 1930s. It came to symbolise progress and modernisation – virtues particularly desirable as Scotland's industrial economy struggled to shake off the ongoing depressive effects of the 1929 Wall Street Crash. Furthermore, as its inspirations were nautical – the semi-enclosed promenades of ocean liners – it provided an appropriate style for shipping-related buildings, even in a Hebridean context. MacBrayne's 1930s 'new look' was completed with striking advertising in the 'moderne' style using fonts without serifs and colourfully stylised 'jazzy' representations of the land and seascape, much as was seen on contemporary Clarice Cliff ceramics.

Clyde modernisation

By the 1930s, the steamers operating year-round ferry services on the Firth of Clyde were ageing. Most dated from the late-Victorian and Edwardian eras and, in the interim, developments in ship design and

some of the finest scenery in the Western Highlands. It was in these waters that I made the first voyages of my life on board the *Iona*…

On an early spring day in 1936 I stood for the last time on the deck of the *Iona* as she lay in the dock of Arnott, Young & Co (Shipbreakers) Ltd at Dalmuir. She and her great consort, the *Columba*, had been withdrawn at the close of the previous summer, to the widespread regret of all who had known them. The *Iona* had sailed for seventy-two years, a record unlikely to be approached by any modern ship. When she was new, the American Civil War was still in progress, Louis Napoleon was Emperor of France and Bismarck had not yet achieved the unification of Germany; in her last months, a Europe only recently recovered from the ravages of the First World War was under new threat from Hitler's Third Reich. What a difference lay between the world of her youth and old age, between the high noon of the Victorian era and the uncertainties of the 1930s.'[196]

As the old stalwarts were sent to the breakers, further new MacBrayne motor ships appeared on the Clyde. In fact, the Clyde was treated to an even more ingenious version of the diesel engine, namely the diesel-electric engine. This novel arrangement appeared in the *Lochfyne*, built by Denny's for MacBrayne's in 1931, and noteworthy as the first such passenger ship in the United Kingdom. The *Lochfyne* was a miniature version of much larger ocean-going diesel-engined liners such as the Pacific Steam Navigation Company's *Reina Del Pacifico* and the White Star-owned *Britannic* and the *Georgic*. In line with their grand template, she sported two funnels, the forward funnel being a dummy. Her diesel-electric arrangement was intended to enhance control by providing a sharper response from the electric engines which turned the screws. Although this was achieved, it was at the expense of quiet running, as the ship suffered from stentorian engine-noise and horrendous vibration, as well as deck 'clutter' which required extra vigilance on the part of passengers. Unlike her Victorian paddle

194 Robins and Meek, 2008, pp101-107.

195 Unascribed quotation in Skewis, 1962, p24.

196 Paterson, 1982, p23.

197 Until 1965, the *King George V* landed passengers by launch at Staffa. Thereafter, she cruised off the island.

Above: The LMSR turbine steamer *Marchioness of Graham* leaves Ardrossan in the latter-1930s. *(A. Ernest Glen)*

Right: The former Williamson-Buchanan steamer *Queen Empress* passes the Water's Neb on the Clyde in the latter-1930s. *(A. Ernest Glen)*

Below: The diesel-electric paddle steamer *Talisman*, seen here off Dunoon in as-delivered LNER condition, was a remarkable combination of new machinery and old methods of propulsion. *(A. Ernest Glen)*

Below right: The *Comet*, acquired in 1906, was David MacBrayne's first paraffin-powered ship. Her innovative machinery was followed in the *Scout* and the *Lochinvar*. *(A. Ernest Glen collection)*

Above: A rare colour photograph, dating from 1938 and showing the LMSR paddle steamer *Jupiter* leaving Dunoon. *(Ian Johnston collection)*

Right: The LNER paddle steamer *Jeanie Deans* in her latter-1930s condition with a grey hull and lengthened funnels arriving at Dunoon. *(Ian Johnston collection)*

Below: The launch of the LMSR paddle steamer *Mercury* at the Fairfield Shipbuilding & Engineering Company's Govan yard on 16th January 1934. *(A. Ernest Glen collection)*

Below right: The LMSR paddle steamer *Caledonia*, seen off Gourock in 1938. *(Ian Johnston collection)*

propulsion elsewhere had been momentous. Britain and its allies may have won the First World War, but it was in Germany that developments in engineering progressed a-pace during the 1920s. It was on German Bodensee (Lake Constance) passenger vessels that the most advanced thinking had been applied. In the latter-1920s, paddle steamers there began to be displaced by a new generation of MAN diesel-engined motor ships. These used a new type of propeller unit designed and manufactured by Voith-Schneider. This consisted of a spinning steel plate, flush with the underside of the hull and fitted with a group of angled blades pointing downwards into the water, the direction of which could be changed by a ratchet system, creating a powerful thrust in any desired direction. The first vessels to use this system were the *Kempten*, the *Augsburg* and the *Ravensburg* (all delivered in 1931 to Deutsche Reichsbahn).[199] Voith-Schneider propellers would have been ideal for cross-Clyde vessels – but it was not for the best part of another half century until they were adopted there.[200]

While MacBrayne's had some success with their new motor ships, the LMSR and LNER's responses to the need to replace older Firth of Clyde vessels generally favoured traditional and well-proven paddle steamers over possible modern and more economical alternatives. There was a good reason for this conservatism, however, as the LNER's main steamer terminus Craigendoran Pier was surrounded by shallow water. Consequently, suitably commodious screw-propelled vessels would be unable to call there.

The LNER's famous *Jeanie Deans*, ordered from the Fairfield Shipbuilding & Engineering Company of Govan, appeared in 1931. The 'Jeanie', as she was affectionately known, was the largest paddle steamer to operate from Craigendoran, and the first three-crank triple-expansion vessel built on the Clyde for service on the Firth. She was also fast, achieving a highly respectable 18.5 knots on trials. Her profile, however, was none too pleasing at the outset, and may well suggest that ship-designers had suffered a loss of design perspective in the rocky and unsettling 1920s. Heightening of her funnels, and rebuilding of deck accommodation, enhanced her profile before the Second World War. Rebuilding after the war endowed her with two equal-height elliptical funnels, as well as new deck and lifeboat arrangements. In this guise, she operated successfully until 1964, when she was bought by a group of enthusiasts, trading as the Coastal Steam Packet Company, for operation from London, and renamed *Queen of the South*. She left the Clyde in November 1965 for this duty.

The LNER's second new vessel of the 1930s, the *Talisman*, built by A. & J. Inglis in 1935, was considerably more innovative. 'She was the first direct-acting diesel-electric paddle vessel in the world, and the largest Diesel-propelled paddle boat.'[201] The use of diesel-electric propulsion for their new ship suggests that the LNER was influenced to some degree by MacBrayne's experiments with the *Lochfyne* and the *Lochnevis*. Like the *Lochfyne*, the *Talisman* suffered from loud noise and vibration. Furthermore, her external profile was less than pleasing at the outset and, even in later years, after post-war rebuilding, her 'boxy' deckhouses tended to recall her experimental origins. Her greatest virtue was an important reduction in

fuel consumption. For 100 miles sailing she used only 1.47 tons of liquid fuel, as compared with 11 tons of coal burnt by her predecessor for a similar run.[202] This virtue, however, had to be set against a disappointing record of serious engine trouble in her first years in service, raising some degree of uncertainty as to whether she could continue to sail. Nevertheless, sail she did until 1967, having survived more than one threat to terminate her existence at a much earlier stage.[203]

When it came to replacing the lower Clyde fleet, the LMSR's Steam Vessels Committee insisted that diesel propulsion ought to be investigated but, as the LMSR was a major consumer of coal to fire its many locomotives, it was decided instead to stick with traditional paddle steamers with expansion engines. For ferry work, these were relatively manoeuvrable (though not nearly as nimble as Voith-Schneider-propelled vessels) and their technology and handling characteristics were familiar to the LMSR's managers and crews. Between 1934 and 1937, no less than six new steamers were delivered – the paddle vessels *Mercury*, *Caledonia*, *Marchioness of Lorne*, *Jupiter* and *Juno* and the turbine *Marchioness of Graham*. All were Fairfield-built except the *Caledonia*, which was built by William Denny & Bros. Perhaps acknowledging that paddle steamers were obsolescent, these vessels' paddle boxes were disguised so as to resemble turbine ships, especially when viewed side-on. Their midships promenade decks were arranged with clear space across the sponsons and around the funnels so that a few cars could be driven directly on board by planks and parked on the deck for the duration of short Clyde crossings at certain tides only.

The *Marchioness of Lorne* was built for the Holy Loch route, on which she replaced the *Marchioness of Breadalbane*. In her prime, the latter had been capable of up to 17 knots, but her replacement could manage not much more than 12, meaning that sailing times were extended over what had hitherto been typical scheduling.

The 1920s and 1930s were a period of great uncertainty in national life, in Scotland and throughout the United Kingdom, and this is reflected all too clearly in the responses of Clyde and Hebridean shipping companies to the demands of fleet maintenance and renewal. On the one hand, it is apparent that when strong, interventionist leadership emerged much could be gained and new strategies could be developed. This is exemplified by the steadying hand of Sir Alfred Read on the tiller of the storm-tossed company of David MacBrayne. On the other hand, the political and economic instability of the era was reflected in responses from shipping companies and their naval architects that were in themselves ambivalent, 'jerky', and even slightly contradictory, with elements of (occasional) penny pinching revealing themselves through ship design. Recovery was slow overall, but it is still evident in the fleet renewals of the 1930s. Just as renewed prosperity seemed to be within their grasp, Clyde and Hebridean steamer operators were faced with the prospect of further destabilisation caused once again by war. The era of the car ferry was, however, on the horizon.

198 New cast iron pier structures at Tobermory, Fort William and Loch Aline were built by Scott's of Greenock and towed in kit form to the pier sites, where they were assembled and new pier buildings constructed.

199 Klaus von Rudloff, Claude Jeanmaire et al, Autoregemeinschaft Bodensee-Schiffahrt: Schiffahrt auf dem Bodensee, Archiv Nr 72/3 Band 3: Beginn der Motorschiffahrt, Verlag Eisenbahn, Villigen, 1987, pp39-41.

200 In the latter-1930s, the Red Funnel Isle of Wight ferry *Vecta* and the Southern Railway's Lymington were fitted with Voith-Schneider propellers, as was the LNER Tay ferry *Abercraig*.

201 Duckworth and Langmuir, 1972, p70.

202 Duckworth and Langmuir, 1972, p70.

203 Brown, 1980.

Chapter Eight

The Car Ferry Era

The roll on-roll off (ro-ro) ferry has been a largely unsung Scottish invention of the mid-nineteenth century. This notwithstanding, it would be over a hundred years from the maiden voyage of the ro-ro pioneer *Leviathan* across the River Forth from Granton to Burntisland until drive-on ferry services were introduced on the Firth of Clyde.

In comparison with the increasingly elegant passenger steamers of the second half of the nineteenth century, the *Leviathan* was a rather perfunctory-looking craft, designed to ship freight wagons loaded with Fife coal, vegetables from the fertile fields of Angus, fish from the North Sea and beef cattle to the markets of Edinburgh and points further south. Her design was highly innovative and her ability to move freight in great quantities and with minimal labour signalled the way ahead for sea-borne transport. During the ensuing century-and-a-half, the ro-ro ferry developed from being an experimental and marginal ship type into one of central importance in the transport of goods and passengers.

The *Leviathan* made her debut when the railway age was at its height and lines were fanning out all over the British Isles. The Edinburgh, Perth & Dundee Railway, however, had set itself the difficult task of establishing train services along Scotland's serrated East Coast, meaning that both the River Forth and the River Tay would, somehow, require to be bridged in order to reach Dundee. The roll on-roll off solution to this problem had first been suggested in 1845 by the railway's Chief Engineer, Mr Bateman, who exhibited drawings showing a flat-decked vessel with ten carriages being shunted aboard by a steam locomotive via a 1-in-12 ramp. Bateman's initial proposal was that the ferry should operate at Queensferry, where the River Forth was only three-quarters of a mile wide and much more sheltered than the four-and-a-half mile passage between Granton and Burntisland. However, as the railway had an established passenger steamer route between these ports, it was decided that this longer crossing was the better option. The design for the port infrastructure was the work of two of the most inventive railway engineers of the era – Thomas Grainger (1794-1829) and Thomas Bouch (1822-1880) – while the *Leviathan* herself was drawn up and built by Robert Napier at his Govan shipyard.

The *Leviathan* was a double-ended iron-hulled paddle steamer, measuring 172 feet in length and with a deck width of 34 feet between the paddle-boxes. What was so remarkable about Napier's design was how presciently he brought together all the basic design characteristics of the

An etching showing the shore arrangements for loading the *Leviathan*; smoke belches from the boiler house providing power to winch the platform up a ramp to adjust height depending on the tide. *(The Illustrated London News, Bruce Peter collection)*

modern ferry in that pioneering vessel. The hull was flat-bottomed and the train deck was entirely unobstructed to allow two trains to be loaded simultaneously on parallel tracks. On either beam, independently operated steeple engines and boilers allowed each paddle-wheel to be turned forward or in reverse, meaning that the ferry could manoeuvre very quickly and turn around practically within her own length. The bridge was held aloft on a gantry, spanning the train deck and giving a commanding view of the loading and unloading operations. Indeed, the *Leviathan* proved to be a tremendous success. *The Illustrated London News* observed:

> 'It must be very satisfactory to the directors…to have their labours brought to so successful a termination. We understand that it had no sooner been advertised that goods would be taken across the Forth without breaking bulk, than 400 tons of turnips were offered them as a commencement.'[204]

Later on, a second ferry was introduced across the River Tay, making use of the same features as had been pioneered on the Forth crossing. Shorter than the *Leviathan* at only 140 feet in length, the *Robert Napier*, named in honour of the engineer and shipbuilder, was delivered in the autumn of 1850. Later still, a third example of the type, named the *Carrier*, arrived in 1851 – but this was constructed by Scott's of Greenock rather than by Napier's shipyard. Three further ferries – the *Balbirnie* (1861), the *Kinloch* (1865) and the *Midlothian* (1881) – were added as demand grew. (The completion of the Forth Railway Bridge in 1890 rendered the ferry fleet surplus to requirements and, after 40 years of constant and reliable service, the *Leviathan* and her sisters were sold for scrap to P. & W. McLellan of Glasgow in August 1890.)

Following the *Leviathan*'s successful inauguration, similar train ferry services were developed in Denmark and Germany. It was only in the inter-war era, however, that car ownership grew sufficiently to warrant the construction of vessels dedicated to the carriage of road vehicles. As Europe's leading industrial powers, Britain and Germany, had lost momentum as a result of fighting the First World War, it was in North America, where Henry Ford had first mass-produced his Model T car in 1908, that a pioneering dedicated car ferry for operation in open water appeared – the Canadian Pacific-owned *Motor Princess* of 1924.

Fly-bridges and turntable ferries

Yet, long before 1924, the precursors of present-day vehicular ferries were appearing on the upper River Clyde. A chain ferry ('Lampits ferry') was introduced between Pettinain and Carnwath in upper Clydesdale as early as 1840, with the capacity to carry cattle and up to four horse-drawn carts. It was replaced by a more advanced model in 1905, which served the community until a bridge was built across the river ten years later. These rudimentary double-ended vessels, which were in effect 'fly-bridges' or 'floating bridges', may now also be regarded as 'innovatory'. Their design and use were, in truth, dictated by the urgent practical needs of predominantly rural and agricultural communities, less concerned with catering for well-to-do tourists than with conveying wheeled vehicles and draught animals across rivers for the benefit of the locality. According to the minister of Carnwath, the ferry brought 'immense comfort and accommodation to the inhabitants on both sides, as well as of the country in general'.[205] Risks with modes of carrying and operation could be taken on relatively short and sheltered stretches of water. On the upper Clyde, the Clyde Navigation Trust operated vehicular ferry services of only minutes' duration at Whiteinch (1890), Renfrew (1897) and Erskine (1903); initially, these carried mainly horse-drawn vehicles and foot passengers. The first-

mentioned used a remarkable craft with twin screws at either end of a rectangular hull upon which the entire vehicle deck was hoistable to offset the river's tidal range, while the latter two were chain ferries, meaning that they were physically attached to underwater guiding- and pulling-chains between the two slipways. The vessel serving the Renfrew ferry was wryly nicknamed 'HMS Back an' Fur'ard' during the Second World War.

In the West Highlands, various so-called 'turntable ferries', sometimes chain-driven, were introduced during the 1920s and 1930s. Each could carry two or four vehicles on a raised vehicle deck which could pivot so as to enable unloading at a 45 degree angle on to an adjacent slipway. These maintained a generations-old tradition, often with a 'ferry inn' and ferryman's house close to the jetty, and they replaced more basic craft, which normally loaded no more than one car by means of planks placed with one end on the gunwale of the boat and the other on the jetty. They were to be found principally on mainland sea-lochs, such as Loch Leven at Ballachulish, where the first car was carried in 1906, and a chain ferry with a car-carrying turntable was introduced in 1926, Loch Linnhe (Corran), Loch Duich (Dornie), and Kylesku (Eddrachillis Bay, Sutherland. They also appeared on more exposed firths and narrows, such as the Moray Firth (Kessock, also served by the side-ramp ferry, *Eilean Dubh*), Loch Carron (Strome Ferry) and Lochalsh (Kyle-Kyleakin). A turntable ferry was placed on the potentially treacherous stretch of water between Kylerhea (Skye) and Glenelg in 1934. The arrival of this ferry-boat, the *Kylerhea*, maintained and

Built in 1908, the **Vehicular Ferry No 3** had a hoistable deck, capable of maintaining a constant height relative to the quays at Finnieston and Govan on the Upper Clyde at any state of the tide. The vessel is seen here at Finnieston in the latter-1950s. *(A. Ernest Glen)*

modernised a crossing which had been of great importance to Skye and the Outer Hebrides as a transit-point for droves and drovers of West Highland and Hebridean cattle making their way to the Falkirk Tryst and other Lowland markets. The cattle were frequently compelled to swim across the narrows while roped behind a boat, but, in the early twentieth century, before the arrival of the *Kylerhea*, they were transported in a large wooden vessel known locally as 'the gabbart'.

The capacity of the diminutive *Kylerhea* was soon challenged by the increasing size of cars, such as the occasional Armstrong Siddeley. Professor Michael Gardner has kindly supplied a photograph taken by his late mother on 18th June 1936, when his grandfather, the eighth son of the Highland Railway's Station Superintendent at Inverness, took the risk of entrusting his 1935 Armstrong Siddeley saloon to the *Kylerhea*. 'My mother told me,'

204 'Illustrated London News', 12th February 1850.
205 Veitch and Gordon, 2009, pp212-221.

The present-day Kylerhea-Glenelg ferry service was inaugurated in 1934, following a campaign which was led by the (then) parish minister of Glenelg, the Rev. T. M. Murchison. In this fine picture taken in 1936, the *Kylerhea*, the first turntable ferry on the route, prepares to embark an Armstrong Siddeley. *(Professor Michael Gardner)*

writes Professor Gardner, 'that the ferrymen had told her that they had never carried such a large car before!' Happily, the ferry and the car crossed safely, and the car, now owned by Professor Gardner, remains in use today.[206]

In 2011, this historically strategic crossing is still served by an old-style turntable ferry, the *Glenachulish*, built in 1969 by Ailsa Shipbuilding, Troon, and now the sole survivor of the fleet which served Loch Leven before the present bridge was opened in October 1975. The Loch Leven (Ballachulish) fleet included the romantically named *Appin Chief* and *Maid of Appin*, which could carry between four and six vehicles. They looked splendid with their green hulls and red boot-topping, as they transported their vehicles in a spell-binding setting of hills, heather and blue sea, until the new Ballachulish bridge was opened in 1975. As Marie Weir notes, 'Between 1954 and 1974, the increase in traffic [at Ballachulish] was dramatic, with the number of vehicles carried rising from 42,000 to 204,000.'[207]

The Glenelg-Kylerhea crossing was the principal access point for Skye until 1897, when the arrival of the railway at Kyle of Lochalsh stimulated the development of the ferry between Kyle and Kyleakin, which through the patronage of the railways was soon to become the gateway to Skye. The LMSR acquired the ferry from the Highland Railway after 1923, and

subcontracted its operation to David MacBrayne Ltd. In 1945, however, the ferry returned to the LMSR, and from 1948 it became part of British Railways, operating with CSP crews. The vessels operating the Kyle-Kyleakin service developed in line with similar craft elsewhere, from plank-loading of individual cars in the early 1900s to turntables capable of handling two cars by the 1920s on the *Kyleakin* (1928), the *Moil* (1936), both wooden-hulled, and the steel-hulled *Cuillin* (1942).[208] The two-car ferries were eventually displaced in the post-Nationalisation climate of the 1950s by a series of robust steel turntable vessels, beginning with the *Lochalsh* and *Portree* (1951), and continuing with the *Broadford* (1954), *Lochalsh* (1957), and *Kyleakin* (1960).[209] The design approval for the *Lochalsh* came within the remit of British Railways' Naval Architects' Department. Their naval architects Don Ripley and Tony Rogan described her arrangement as follows:

'The road vehicles were carried on a bridge-type structure that was secured in a fore and aft line for transit, but rotated through 90 degrees in port and had to drop down prow doors to span the gap between ship and shore to allow the loading and discharge of vehicles.'[210]

206 Personal correspondence with Donald E. Meek, 12th April 2011.
207 Marie Weir, 1988, p140.
208 MacArthur, 1971, p102.
209 Danielson, 2007, pp122-3.
210 Ripley and Rogan, 1995, p18.

Above: The turntable ferry *Strome Castle* loads a car for the crossing of Loch Carron on a glorious day in the 1950s. The basic steering arrangements in the stern cabin are clearly visible. *(A. Ernest Glen)*

Right: At Kyleakin, within sight of the ruins of Castle Moyle, the crew of the ferry *Lochalsh* lift her ramp and prepare to swing the turntable, weighted with heavy summer traffic. *(A. Ernest Glen)*

Below: The *Lochalsh* begins her crossing from Kyle of Lochalsh, with the Stornoway motor ship, *Loch Seaforth*, in the background. *(A. Ernest Glen)*

Below right: At Kyle of Lochalsh, the *Kyleakin* awaits cars. *(A. Ernest Glen)*

The fully-laden *Kyleakin* heads across to Kyleakin, as one of her sister steers for Kyle of Lochalsh. *(A. Ernest Glen)*

These turntable vessels remained in service until the side-loading vessels *Portree* and *Broadford*, were introduced in 1965 and 1967 respectively, followed by the *Coruisk* in 1969. These, in turn, were superseded by the bow-loading *Kyleakin* (III) and *Lochalsh* (III) in 1970-71. Ownership of the service passed to Caledonian MacBrayne from 1973. In 1991, the 1970s bow-loading vessels were replaced by the similar but much larger *Loch Fyne* and *Loch Dunvegan*, which served until the Skye Bridge was opened in 1995. Thereafter, following a period of lay-up and attempts to sell them, the two ships were reassigned by Caledonian MacBrayne to the crossings at Fishnish-Lochaline and Colintraive-Rhubodach respectively, where they remain to the present. The precedent of decanting former Skye ferries to other

crossings was set when the 1957 *Lochalsh* went to Scalpay, Harris, in 1967. The 1965 *Portree* and the 1967 *Broadford*, converted from side-loading to bow-loading, were redeployed to the Colintraive-Rhubodach service in 1970-71. The 1960 *Kyleakin*, renamed *Largs*, and the 1969 *Coruisk*, similarly converted to bow-loading, undertook the service from Largs to what became Cumbrae Slip.[211]

The present-day Corran-Ardgour ferry, *Maid of Glencoul*, previously engaged at Kylesku, and her consort, the *Corran*, are owned by Highland Regional Council, and load their vehicles by means of side-ramps, which are off-set relative to the vessels' centre-lines. They compensate for the lack of a bridge across Loch Linnhe. It is ironic that, like their predecessors in upper Clydesdale more than half a century earlier, the majority of West Highland turntable ferries were being displaced after 1960 by the improvement of Highland roads and the building of bridges, a significant indication of the growing volume of vehicular traffic heading for the West Highlands, just when David MacBrayne Ltd, and later Caledonian MacBrayne, were introducing the first car ferries to the Hebrides. Despite the closure of several traditional crossing-points, however, and the depletion of the fleet which once served them, the story of Scotland's sea-loch ferries is one of slow but consistent development in response to ever-growing demand for the conveyance of vehicles. They are due just (but long-delayed) recognition as worthy members of a pioneering line of vehicular ferries which link the *Leviathan* and her kind with the present day.

The first short-sea car ferries

As car ownership continued to grow during the 1930s, ferries appeared on Scandinavian domestic routes and on the Dover Strait, but it was not

Guests in the Lochalsh Hotel, Kyle of Lochalsh, were often wakened by the scraping of ramps and the thumping of engines, as cars were loaded at the slipway. *(Bruce Peter collection)*

The LMSR Stranraer-Larne car ferry *Princess Victoria* operated only briefly before the outbreak of the Second World War. Here, she is pictured undertaking builder's trials off Skelmorlie. *(Ambrose Greenway collection)*

until 1939 that the first Scottish-registered ferry of a similar type entered service for the LMSR's Irish Sea route from Stranraer to Larne. The 2,197-ton *Princess Victoria* was built by William Denny & Bros of Dumbarton. A notoriously difficult crossing, exposed to south-westerly gales and made more challenging by strong coastal currents and shallow water, the route demanded a vessel of very robust design. With two 14-cylinder Sulzer diesels installed, the *Princess Victoria* was additionally the first large motor ship to be owned by a British railway company. As with the majority of ferries of the era, she sailed astern up to linkspans, which were adjusted with the tide to align perfectly with her belting. Like most of her Scandinavian counterparts, her vehicle deck was only partially enclosed at the after end – this being achieved by means of a guillotine-type door which shut from above. Therefore, to drain away excess water caused by spray washing over in rough weather, freeing ports were cut in the vehicle deck shell plating. The forward section of this was fitted with pens, enabling her additionally to carry livestock, which boarded through side-hatches, located towards the bow.[212]

In the spring of 1939, the LMSR began to formulate plans for a Gourock-Dunoon vehicular ferry. In recent years, the route's existing paddle steamer services had carried around 1,000 cars annually as deck cargo. Tide permitting, these were loaded over planks onto the steamers' paddle boxes and parked between the funnels. Although the LMSR's Board did not think that a dedicated car ferry would immediately be profitable, it

was nonetheless politic to pre-empt further vehicular traffic growth and so £35,000 was set aside as possible funding for one of two schemes. One proposal involved the building of ferry slips in the shelter of Gourock Bay and on Cowal either at Hunter's Quay or East Bay, closer to Dunoon. The new ferries considered by the LMSR's management would have been like those operated across the Solent to the Isle of Wight by the Southern Railway. Such a scheme, however, would require Parliamentary approval – potentially a tortuous process, especially in the uncertain months immediately preceding the outbreak of the Second World War.[213]

An easier alternative would be to construct a more conventional passenger steamer with vehicle-carrying capacity, capable of berthing at the existing piers at Gourock and Dunoon. Thus, the LMSR sought quotations for a 300-ton 12-knot vessel with accommodation for 400 passengers plus 20 cars. Due to the tidal range at each pier, the vessel would have an elevating platform at the forward end of her hull, much like the one on the Whiteinch vehicular ferry, operating upriver, and steam propelling machinery towards the stern, which would also provide power to lift the platform deck. The lowest tender to build the vessel was £51,000 and so the scheme was shelved. The outbreak of war in the autumn of 1939 meant that it was never revived.[214]

211 Duckworth and Langmuir, 1972, pp91-8.
212 The Motor Ship, August 1939, pp172-174.
213 MacArthur, 1971, p94.
214 MacArthur, 1971, p94.

Chapter Nine

The Second World War and Post-war Austerity

During the Second World War, a large proportion of the LMSR and MacBrayne fleets were requisitioned by the Government for naval service as mine sweepers and troop transports. This meant that, for the war's duration, only skeleton services were provided on the Clyde and to the Western Isles, these being run year-round by vessels often intended only for summer pleasure use and with unheated saloons. All initially were repainted in navy grey, later substituted for a time by a dull ochre and black livery, and they sailed with their windows boarded over to maintain blackout. Fully enclosed steel surrounds were fitted to their wheelhouses to protect their officers from attack. A protective boom was installed across the Firth of Clyde between the Cloch lighthouse and Dunoon to prevent enemy submarines from navigating surreptitiously upriver. So Clyde steamer services beyond this impediment were largely suspended throughout the war.

Alas, the recently delivered Stranraer-Larne ferry *Princess Victoria* became an early casualty of the war. In May 1940, an enemy mine sank her off the Humber when she was only 13 months old. Of the Clyde steamers requisitioned for military service, several were involved in the evacuation of Dunkirk in May 1940 – the LNER-owned *Waverley* being sunk under heavy fire. With her guns, *Waverley* fought enemy bombers and machine gunners for two hours but, as her steering gear was damaged, she could not steer a zig-zag course and therefore took a direct hit near the engine room, just after bringing down one of the bombers; thereafter, she sank in minutes and over 300 men were lost, some being killed by the air attacks. Her erstwhile Clyde companions *Duchess of Fife* and *Marmion* successfully evacuated large numbers of troops. Of the Clyde's newer steamers, the *Mercury* was sunk by a British mine on Christmas Day 1940 while the *Juno* was lost in 1941.

Leaving Gourock in 1945 in a drab and neglected coat of wartime grey paint and with most of her windows panelled over, the *Duchess of Hamilton* looks far from her typically pristine peacetime condition. (A. Ernest Glen collection)

MacBrayne's motor vessels *Loch Earn*, *Lochmor* and *Lochfyne* were spared to maintain lifeline services in the Hebrides and Clyde, but the excursion steamer *King George V* attended Dunkirk with distinction, as did the *Lochgarry*, while the *Lochnevis* was used as a minesweeper.

The Second World War in Europe ended on 8th May 1945, but it took a considerable time to return Clyde and Hebridean steamer services to normality. The Clyde fleet remained in grey, albeit with the LMSR's buff funnel livery restored but, following years of neglect, all vessels were rather dilapidated. Those requisitioned for military service were in the poorest condition and the elderly *Duchess of Rothesay*, *Queen-Empress* and *Eagle III* were so badly degraded that they were declared unfit for restoration and consigned instead for scrap. Five Clyde steamers were lost – the *Kylemore*, *Mercury*, *Juno*, *Waverley* and *Marmion*[215] – and with a sharp upswing in passenger numbers, the LMSR and LNER were hard-pressed to cope in the immediate post-war years when services were reduced.

The LMSR's veteran *Duchess of Fife* was however renovated for further service though not fitted with a new boiler and, along with the turbine steamers *King Edward* and *Duchess of Argyll* and the LNER paddle steamer *Lucy Ashton* which had been in constant use on the Clyde during the conflict, the pre-First World War era was still represented in the Clyde steamer fleet of the latter-1940s. Major reconstructions of the Craigendoran-based 1930s LNER vessels *Jeanie Deans* and *Talisman* were carried out and a new paddle steamer, the *Waverley*, was delivered in 1947 by A. & J. Inglis of Pointhouse to the LNER to serve the Arrochar route plus Rothesay and the Kyles of Bute. The *Waverley* was originally planned in 1938 and, from the promenade deck upwards, her drawings were used in early 1946 to provide a model for the post-war rebuilding of the *Jeanie Deans*.

Though of handsome appearance and robust construction, the *Waverley* perhaps symbolised how far behind the design of vessels for Clyde services had fallen by the end of the Second World War. Following the conflict, Britain was exhausted and bankrupt; merely returning to some semblance of normality was enough of an effort, never mind experimenting with anything new or innovative. As a coal-fired steamer with a triple-expansion engine, the *Waverley* was little different from her surviving inter-war fleet mates – except that her passenger accommodation was of basic design and thus reflective of post-war hardship and difficulties in obtaining construction materials.

In the post-war era, exponential rises in the costs of fuel and staff wages greatly pressured the railway companies' managements. Although the LNER did examine the possibility of building the *Waverley* as a motor ship, the initial cost of a steamer was found to be lower. In the longer term, however, their conservatism with regard to ship design and propulsion became increasingly problematic as coal-fired steamers were greedy on fuel in comparison with motor ships of which there were only two large examples in the Clyde fleet – the *Lochfyne* and the *Talisman* – and both had experienced significant teething troubles. Britain remained a coal economy, however, and there was no pressing desire to modernise following the exhausting years of warfare; merely keeping the steamer fleets together and providing basic essential services as best as possible was apparently enough of a challenge. During the war, British naval architects were fully engaged with military matters and so there was no opportunity to advance ferry design. By the war's end, there was a pressing need to restore the services previously offered and so, as a workable design for the *Waverley* was already available, the LNER used it.

In the Western Isles, MacBrayne's new motor ship *Loch Seaforth*, built by Wm Denny & Bros of Dumbarton, belatedly appeared on the Mallaig-Kyle of Lochalsh-Stornoway route in December 1947, her construction having been delayed by difficulties in sourcing materials. Their original intention had been to order her in 1938-39 but, due to the war and its aftermath, she was actually the best part of a decade late when delivered. Her design was a small-scale version of numerous Irish Sea overnight vessels built both during the 1930s and subsequently in the 1950s. A tall forecastle protected against high swells, then there were cargo holds and accommodation for 500 in two classes occupying the vessel's aft two-thirds. Her First Class lounge on the Boat Deck was notably attractive with large picture windows to give panoramic views of the passing scenery.

On the Clyde, it was not until 1948 that the steamer fleet regained anything like the pre-war standard of upkeep – but catering took longer to restore to 1930s standards. In his history of the Caledonian Steam Packet Company, Iain C. MacArthur cites Geoffrey Grimshaw's recollections of Clyde steamer catering in the difficult post-war years of austerity:

'Catering suffered severely as a result of the war; but main meals of some sort could be had in all the ships even during the worst period of wartime and post-war food rationing... Quantities were not great, and quality far short of the pre-war standard, but passengers could have a three-course lunch consisting of soup, fish or meat with potatoes and sweet for 2s 6d. The price was increased to 3s 6d from 1 June 1946 and there followed thereafter a long and painful recovery extending over several years. By the beginning of 1951, the catering was still short of the standards both of pre-war and recent years; but it was well beyond the stage at which the main course of lunch served on board *Duchess of Fife* in April 1947 consisted of wartime M&V (tinned meat, vegetables and gravy). As late as June 1951 bacon and egg for high tea was sufficiently rare to be remembered... Like the dining saloons the tearooms deteriorated during the war. On occasions there was almost nothing

Above: The stately *Duchess of Fife* puts her engines astern and uses her paddles as 'brakes', as she pulls into Wemyss Bay after a speedy arrival, shown by her splendid wake. *(Donald B. MacCulloch)*

Right: Craigendoran Pier in the summer of 1947 with, left to right, the renovated *Talisman* and *Lucy Ashton* and the bow of the new Waverley, all in their post-war LNER livery. *(A. Ernest Glen collection)*

Below: The restored *Jeanie Deans* at speed in the Firth of Clyde in June 1947. *(A. Ernest Glen)*

Below right: The newly introduced LNER paddle steamer *Waverley* makes a stirring sight arriving at Rothesay in June 1947. Sixty-five years later, this magnificent vessel continues to delight passengers with her regular schedule of summer excursions. *(A. Ernest Glen)*

The new Clyde fleet

For the BTC, modernising Britain's estuarial and continental shipping services was a top priority and so a substantial new building programme was instituted. Clyde services were to benefit from the introduction of no less than seven new vessels – all of very different design from those constituting the existing fleet. Change was necessary as British Railways' Clyde services were incurring losses due to fares remaining close to pre-war levels while operational costs had increased exponentially. The Clyde excursion fleet, in particular, carried a high proportion of working and lower-middle class day-trippers and so increasing fares was not an attractive option if this clientele was to be retained. Vessels operating point-to-point services were equally inefficient and so a radical re-think was required. For starters, in 1950, the entire Clyde fleet became one class, a belated recognition on the railway's part in the changing social order of the post-war era; having fought together to achieve victory in the war, why should passengers be divided by class in their leisure time and frustratingly restricted to only part of a steamer's accommodation?

In February 1951, the BTC's Chairman, Lord Hurcomb, announced a £1 million modernisation of the Clyde fleet with four new diesel-powered passenger ferries to be built for rail-connected services to Dunoon, Rothesay and Millport and, in addition, three new car ferries for direct Gourock-Dunoon, Wemyss Bay-Rothesay and Fairlie (Ardrossan)-Brodick services. In the end, the cost of this programme increased to £1.3 million – a fact blamed by the BTC's management on the effects of the Korean War. The investment in new tonnage allowed the most elderly members of the Clyde steamer fleet to be withdrawn, the veteran turbine pioneer *King Edward* and the similar *Duchess of Argyll* being the first to go after the 1951 summer season. The paddle steamer *Duchess of Fife* and the turbine *Glen Sannox* followed them to the breakers in 1953.

As most Clyde shipyards had full order books, two of the four passenger ferries were designed by and ordered from Messers Yarrow & Company of Scotstoun, a builder more commonly associated with naval vessels and so, attractive as they were, the class did rather resemble minesweepers. While Yarrows themselves delivered the *Maid of Ashton*, the building of her three sisters was subcontracted, the *Maid of Argyll* and *Maid of Skelmorlie* coming from A. & J. Inglis of Pointhouse, located upriver from Yarrows, and the *Maid of Cumbrae* from Ardrossan Dockyard Ltd. The new vessels were compact and efficient and with their British Polar diesel engines enabling speeds of over 15 knots to be achieved. Inboard, they looked somewhat like

Following her launch from Denny's yard in Dumbarton in 1947, the *Loch Seaforth* is towed to the fitting-out basin by a steam tug. (Donald E. Meek collection)

but tea; by the later war years all the tearoom amenities, such as small pots of jam and sandwiches, had disappeared. Tea bread was of indifferent quality and its supply was uncertain.

The food situation was particularly bad during the 1946 season when the resumption of sailings to Campbeltown, Inveraray and Arran via the Kyles resulted in a greatly increased demand for main meals. The Superintendent Steward did not appear to realise that, under the system of supplementary permits operated by the Ministry of Food, a large increase in meal service entitled the caterer to a corresponding increase in rationed commodities. [216]

Following the Labour Party's landslide 1946 election victory, a policy of nationalisation was implemented, the idea being that the Government was in the best position to invest in Britain's neglected national and industrial infrastructures. Labour believed that the creation of large state-owned corporations would eliminate waste caused by commercial interests duplicating provision – a position diametrically opposed to the market-led policies which have held sway in Britain since the late-1970s. As part of the policy, the Transport Act of 1947 advocated the nationalisation of Britain's railways and associated shipping services under a new authority, the British Transport Commission (BTC), which came into being in January 1948. In Scotland, this meant that the LMSR and LNER fleets were brought together under BTC control as part of the new British Railways. All vessels were painted in what had been the LMSR's livery (albeit with red boot topping, rather than white) and so the old North British/LNER red, white and black funnels disappeared from the Clyde scene. As the LMSR owned 50 per cent of shares in MacBrayne's, this too became a partially state-owned business upon the railway's nationalisation.

A key aspect of the Labour Government's policy was a modernising socialist belief in centralised planning. This was to affect all aspects of British life – from the appearance of towns and cities to the development of industry and transport infrastructure. Even the Government's and local authorities' appointed planning experts could not have foreseen the profound changes which would impinge upon the very structure of British society during the ensuing decades. In the latter 1940s, it was taken for granted that, in West Central Scotland, a large working class, engaged in manual labour, would exist in perpetuity and, therefore, patterns of work and leisure would remain not much changed from the recent past. (The idea that within two decades very large numbers would holiday abroad was unimaginable at a time when steamers still carried up to 4 million excursionists per annum to the popular resort towns around the Clyde Coast).

This 1960s view from Oban's Railway Pier shows the *Lochnevis* lying at the North Pier, with the fishing-boat *Argosy* in the foreground. Fishing-boats registered in ports like Lossiemouth and Fraserburgh were a familiar sight in Oban, especially at weekends. (Bruce Peter collection)

Above: In this fine picture, the arrival of the *Loch Seaforth* at Mallaig (from Stornoway) is greeted by enthusiastic spectators, as she is manoeuvres towards the pier with the aid of a bow spring, the standard method before the days of bow-thrusters. Note the fish-boxes at the right of the image. *(Tom Shanks)*

Right: The *Loch Seaforth*, inbound from Stornoway, powers through the narrows of Kylerhea on her way to Mallaig, while the Kylerhea-Glenelg turntable ferry makes one of her regular crossings. *(Tom Shanks)*

Below: The *Lochfyne* sparkles in the sunshine, as she arrives at Dunoon. *(Tom Shanks)*

Below right: On the bridge of the *Lochfyne*, Captain McCallum rings the port telegraph, while a privileged 'guest' gazes over the bridge bulwark, and a young couple on the deck do likewise. A Royal Navy submarine can be seen in the distance. *(Tom Shanks)*

This rare 'action shot' of the busy foredeck of a MacBrayne motor ship was taken on board the *Lochnevis* at Port Ellen, Islay. The sailor on the right is about to link the fourth chain which will allow the ship's forward-facing derrick to lift a wheeled container filled with canvas bags (probably containing mail). Note the hatches, which have been removed to allow access to the 'tween-deck, stacked on the left, and the rope-holders beside the windlass. *(Tom Shanks)*

floating buses with rows of forward-facing fixed seating, but their large windows and effective heating made them relatively pleasant for short Clyde crossings. At weekends and off-peak times, they went cruising. As light refreshments and snacks were available from a small tea-bar, such trips to the Holy Loch, for example, were marketed as 'Café Cruises'. Yet, few doubted that the 'Maids', as they were known, were far inferior as excursion ships to their elegant pre-war-vintage turbine steamer fleetmates. The 'Maids' short hulls gave a lively ride and their diesel engines caused vibrations. Moreover, their compact dimensions meant that they lacked the luxury of space and on busy trips they felt crowded.

Serving respectively Arran, Bute and Cowal, the new Clyde car ferries were given these names (a policy reviving the nomenclature of the CSP's Clyde and Campbeltown Steam Packet Company subsidiary). As the ferry routes were rail-connected, as well as carrying road vehicles, these vessels were also required to transport passengers arriving by train in considerable numbers.

The design of these new ships was different from what the LMSR had imagined for Clyde ferries in the latter 1930s. Rather than being steamers with aft-located machinery and vehicle space forward, they were instead twin-screw motor ships with their engines forward and vehicle access two-thirds aft. As well as carrying cars and some commercial vehicles, they also transported livestock and some general cargo, for which purpose derricks were installed at the stern. To cope with varying tides, an electric lift was fitted between the side ramps, utilising the same technology as on Royal Navy aircraft carriers for raising aircraft from the hanger to the flight deck. Cars could be parked forward and aft of this installation – although the forward section was somewhat constricted by the large engine casing, around which vehicles had to drive. Power was provided by two Polar-Atlas diesels, giving a 15.5-knot speed.[217]

The first of the new ferries, to be named the *Arran*, was ordered from William Denny & Bros of Dumbarton; her sisters, the *Bute* and the *Cowal*, were contracted to Ailsa of Troon, where the *Arran* was additionally fitted out. In common with all BTC new buildings, these ferries were designed by their builders working to speed and capacity specifications supplied by the BTC's London-headquartered Shipping & International Services Department. Externally, their design gave few clues that these were vessels of the 1950s. Their superstructures had the same vertical-fronted appearance as their inter-war fleetmates and their funnels also followed 1930s design conventions whereas Scandinavian and North American ferries of the same period tended to be streamlined to distinguish them as modern and different from existing passenger-only tonnage.

Interiors were also left largely to the shipyards and these too reflected 1930s standards. No wonder the railway design commentator Brian Haresnape observed that:

'The lounges [on BTC-owned vessels of the 1950s] had the same stolid comfort that commercial hotels offered on dry land… The smoke rooms, bars and lounges…were curiously masculine in their furnishings – intended for the robust mariner rather than the frail and travelsick, old or young… What was missing was a sense of reality, a sense of the winds of change that were blowing in post-war Europe.'[218]

The *Lochfyne* adds a splash of colour to the scene, as she passes Rubha Bàn. *(Tom Shanks)*

The ferries could carry 650 passengers, the majority in a deckhouse forward of the vehicle ramp, containing a lounge with rows of fixed benches and a tea bar with space for 38. Below the vehicle deck, there was a bar similar to the claustrophobic and smoky 'below decks' drinking dens found on many of the Clyde steamer fleet. Indeed, the passenger accommodation was cramped and spartan with steep staircases and little more than the most basic facilities, after all, these were vessels intended only for short crossings of under one hour's duration. Outdoor deck space was relatively generous with much of the Boat Deck open to passengers; unlike the 'Maids', there was even a forward-facing view from below the bridge, enabling passengers to enjoy the panoramic sweep of islands, mountains and sea as they crossed

215 Mullay, 2008, pp.120-1.
216 MacArthur, 1971, pp115-116.
217 The Motor Ship, February 1954, pp492-494.
218 Haresnape, 1982, pp99-100.
219 MacArthur, 1971, p135.

In British Transport Commission livery, the *Jeanie Deans* is leaving Hunter's Quay following the nationalisation of rail and associated shipping services. *(A. Ernest Glen)*

the Firth of Clyde.

J. Leslie Harrington, British Railways' Chief Officer (Marine and Administration), whose wife launched the *Arran*, observed of the new vessel: '*Arran* is more than another new ship. She is a novel ship and the embodiment of much ingenuity to cater not only for passengers and cargo but also for motor vehicles and containers.'[219] Reflecting the grim reality of post-war austerity conditions, Harrington continued: 'The beauty and grace of travel yesteryear does not take us far today. Even relative values have changed. *Arran* would cost as much as the combined price of *Duchess of Montrose*, *Duchess of Hamilton*, *Marchioness of Graham*, *Marchioness of Lorne* and *Caledonia*, five of the present Clyde fleet built between the wars.' Indeed, the *Arran* had cost British Railways £260,000 – but her two near-sisters built by Ailsa of Troon were a little cheaper. Harrington's acceptance that 'beauty and grace' were no longer priorities – or even worth serious consideration reflected the economic reality and political priorities of the era. Unfortunately, this mindset has continued to afflict public sector design output in Scotland until relatively recently. Indeed, it is only within the last decade that there has been any acknowledgement that elegance and utility might be related and, furthermore, that visually attractive public environments and services could be an effective means of improving people's quality of life.

Yet, austere as they were, there is no doubt that the new Clyde car ferries were necessary and welcome and that they were innovative in the narrow context of Scottish domestic shipping services. Indeed, upon her introduction, the *Arran* aroused great curiosity, not least among seasoned observers of the Clyde steamer scene. In his substantial history of the Caledonian Steam Packet Company, Iain C. MacArthur quotes Ian McCrorie, who recalled that:

'Monday 4 January 1954 was fine... The Dunoon folk had turned out in force to witness her arrival – there were no pier dues on this occasion – and cheered loudly as she approached. Lord Inverclyde, representing the Scottish Tourist Board, cut a white ribbon to allow the first car, driven by the Secretary of the RSAC, to pass from the ship to the pier. The car ferry era had begun. *Arran*'s appearance, especially her two protruding Samson posts, suggested that she was

a cargo carrier but once inside one realised that she catered also for passengers in her lounge with upholstered bus-type seating, in her small but cosy bar, and in her tearoom which actually did provide lunches and high teas during the first season.

I remember hurrying down to Gourock Pier on that first day as fast as my bike could take me as soon as the school bell sounded at four o'clock. I was fascinated by the novel and efficient way in which cars were loaded and unloaded. Each time the lift came up or down

On board the *Jeanie Deans* coming into Dunoon. *(Tom Shanks)*

Above: The *Talisman* in BTC livery leaving Dunoon. *(A. Ernest Glen)*

Right: The *Jupiter* at Wemyss Bay Pier in the mid-1950s. *(A. Ernest Glen collection)*

Below: The BTC-owned Loch Lomond steamer *Maid of the Loch* of 1953 was the final paddle steamer built for railway-connected services in Scotland. *(A. Ernest Glen)*

Below right: The *Maid of Ashton* catches evening sunlight as she speeds off the Kyle coast. *(A. Ernest Glen)*

Top: The *Queen Mary II* off Greenock in 1953 in BTC livery. When the famous Cunard-White Star trans-Atlantic liner was being built, the Clyde steamer's name was altered to allow the Cunarder to be called *Queen Mary*. *(A. Ernest Glen)*

Above: Following re-boilering, the *Queen Mary II* re-entered service for the 1957 season with only one much wider funnel, somewhat resembling such recent ocean liners as Cunard's *Caronia*. Here, she is seen at Rothesay in the latter-1950s. *(A. Ernest Glen)*

Right: The new car ferry *Arran* is shown off Gourock shortly after delivery. *(A. Ernest Glen)*

Below: The *Arran* again, this time approaching Gourock Pier. *(A. Ernest Glen)*

Below right: Driving aboard the *Arran* at Dunoon pier; the 'ABC' ferries' combination of side-ramps, a lift and turntables enabled them to load at existing pier facilities at each state of the tide. *(A. Ernest Glen)*

it carried a load of anything up to five cars, and so cars waiting to go on board did not have to stand by till all the cars on board had come ashore. A one-way system operated below with the help of a turntable at the forward end of the garage, and I soon realised that this meant that the first car on board the ferry was also the first off. On the lift itself there were also two large turntables which were hand or foot operated. Two or three seamen grabbed the front or rear of the cars and with a stepping movement of the foot propelled the turntable around.'[220]

When the *Cowal* subsequently entered service, *The Glasgow Herald* reported prescient observations made by the Scottish Tourist Board's Chairman, Thomas Johnston, about the expected growth of Scotland's tourist industry and the role of the new car ferries in promoting tourism's development:

'Spectacular gains by the Scottish tourist trade, whose revenue had now reached the phenomenal figure of £51 million, and by the nationalised Clyde steamer fleet, which two years ago resembled 'a transport liability', were reported in Rothesay yesterday... The foresight of the British Transport Commission in their replacement programme had produced a transformation in Clyde services. 'We have only scratched the surface of the possibilities of tourism' said Mr Johnston. 'Beyond all doubt, tourism is now one of our major industries... The Clyde Coast, as one face of Scotland's tourist appeal, and the role now being played by the resorts and the British Transport Commission, had to be considered against the background of a generation not likely to be content with holidaying near their own homes.

Earlier, Mr Johnston praised the great public experiment conducted with 'initiative, foresight and genius' by the Transport Commission in revolutionising the resources of the Clyde steamer fleet. They had proceeded with great courage to cut the transport freight rates from Gourock to Dunoon for cars and lorries by 62 per cent for single and 72 per cent for return journeys. Vehicles carried had risen from 247 in the first eight months of last year to 17,906 for the corresponding period this year (1954). By 27 September, that figure had increased further to 21,000 and it was with interest that they watched what impact would be made by the new Wemyss Bay to Rothesay service.[221]

The advent of motoring holidays had consequences for the type of accommodation and catering offered to visitors to the Clyde resorts. Hitherto, hotels and boarding houses had tended to offer a 'full board' tariff to visitors arriving by steamer and typically staying for a week. In a speech made at the *Cowal*'s inauguration luncheon, Provost C.M. Black of Dunoon observed that:

'The motorist on holiday was a bird of passage, and while they hoped to persuade him to remain within their boundaries for a week at least, and use Dunoon as a centre for touring, they must be prepared for a new type of business – the provision of bed and breakfast and even an odd meal for motorists passing through.'[222]

From the outset, the new car ferries were a great success. Their economical diesel propulsion and large capacities in comparison with the paddle steamers enabled fares to be slashed from between 23s to 51s 8d

The *Cowal* approaches Gourock pier in sunny morning light. *(A. Ernest Glen)*

depending on the vehicle's weight to between 15s and 20s, based upon its horsepower. (From 1958, prices were calculated based on vehicles' lengths, rather than the power of their engines, a more typical measure used by the wider car ferry industry.) While the ferries generally found favour, there were complaints about their cramped passenger spaces, rows of bus-like seats and vibrations from their diesel engines. They were, however, reliable and their saloons were well heated and draught-free, comforts rarely found on the older members of the steamer fleet. Moreover, their economy in operation helped to boost the Caledonian Steam Packet Company's receipts and in 1955, 51,000 cars were carried across the Firth of Clyde. Excellent summer weather, meanwhile, ensured that the steamer fleet carried record numbers of passengers and, altogether, 4 million people travelled on the Company's vessels that year.[223]

For the ferries' officers and crews, work was more repetitive and monotonous than on the remaining Clyde excursion fleet. As well as carrying passengers and cars, the ferries transported substantial quantities of livestock in pens towards their sterns and also general cargo. This meant that they constantly required hosing clean. Yet, as Ian McCrorie, by this point working as Assistant Purser, recalled:

'You could tell the time of day...by glancing at the car deck. The first run in the morning...was characterised by the bread van on the lift and innumerable barrow loads of parcels and fish. And so the day went on with strawberries on the 12.10, the British Road Services lorry on the 13.10 and families and prams on the 14.00, the glorious band of cleaners coming back from a day's work on the 17.30, the bowler hats on the 18.10 and drunks at 20.35.'[224]

The introduction of the new Clyde ferry fleet preceded a gradual loosening of centralised control from the BTC in London to its various subsidiaries. In parallel, the Caledonian Steam Packet Company's 'lion rampant' pennant appeared again on mastheads instead of British Railways' house flag. Thereafter, the jerseys worn by the ferries' deck crew were replaced with ones embroidered with 'C.S.P. Co.', rather than 'BR.' Consequently, officers on MacBrayne's cargo-ships operating from Glasgow

220 Ian McCrorie cited in MacArthur, 1971, p136.
221 Glasgow Herald, 2nd October 1954.
222 Glasgow Herald, 5th January 1954.
223 MacArthur, 1971, pp140-141.
224 Ian McCrorie cited in MacArthur, 1971, p151.

to the Hebrides via the often stormy waters off the Mull of Kintyre joked that this stood for 'Can't Sail Past Cowal.'

As car ownership increased rapidly during the mid-1950s, it became clear that the Caledonian Steam Packet Company would require a fourth, considerably larger car ferry for deployment on their busy route to Arran. In March 1955 an order worth £468,000 was placed with the Ailsa Shipbuilding Company of Troon for a 1,107-ton, 18-knot ferry, capable of carrying 1,107 passengers, 40 cars and general cargo. Although delivery was slightly delayed by a shipyard strike, fortunately she appeared in time for the 1957 summer season. An attractive and generously proportioned vessel, she was to prove enduringly successful. The *Glen Sannox*'s superstructure was elegantly streamlined and her silhouette tapering towards the stern, accentuated her appearance of forward-movement. Inboard, she had space for 1,100 passengers and her facilities included a dining saloon and an observation lounge, as well as a tearoom and a public bar beneath the vehicle deck. A new innovation was the specification of fibreglass inflatable life rafts and so there were only two conventional lifeboats, enabling a considerable weight saving and freeing up extra deadweight capacity for passengers and cargo.[225]

Yet, notwithstanding her unprecedented size, the *Glen Sannox* remained a multi-purpose vessel primarily transporting foot passengers arriving at Fairlie and Ardrossan by train, some cars and occasionally crane-loaded general cargo. Although several observers thought that she was too big and therefore had cost too much to build, within little over a decade, the opposite proved to be the case – particularly with regard to her vehicle capacity. The *Glen Sannox* was, however, a long-lived and popular Clyde and West Highland ferry with 30 years' operation to her credit. After withdrawal, she served another decade as a Red Sea pilgrim ship before stranding on a reef off Jeddah in Saudi Arabia where she remains as an abandoned hulk.

New ships for the Hebrides

The vessels of the Victorian era lasted remarkably long in the Hebrides and West Highlands. David MacBrayne Limited had sent some of their best-known veterans to the breaker's yard in the 1930s, and had introduced state-of-the-art motor ships, but there were curious survivals, particularly within the cargo-carrying sector, which ensured that the diesel-engined motor ship did not immediately supplant the old order. McCallum, Orme & Company Ltd. was finally wound up in 1947, but its faithful steamships had one last fling. At the end of their lives, the *Dunara Castle* and the *Hebrides* the last representatives of a long and venerable line of Hebridean cargo-passenger steamships – passed briefly into the ownership of David MacBrayne Limited. They were complemented in their antiquity by MacBrayne's *Lochgorm*, formerly Burns and Laird's *Lily*, later their *Lairdspool*, built in 1896. Acquired by MacBrayne's in 1936, the *Lochgorm* was dispatched to the breakers in 1951.[226] Youthful travellers in the early 1950s, who were able to make the journey from Glasgow to the islands on the *Hebrides*, were astonished to find themselves on board a vessel which was overwhelmingly anachronistic, representing the grandeur, as well as the spartan frugality and basic engineering, of a much earlier day. The legendary *Dunara Castle* served the islands until 1948, while the *Hebrides* continued until 1955, when her demise was regarded as the end of an epoch. The passing of the *Hebrides* was commemorated in the letter columns of *The Scotsman* in the following *fin-de-siècle* salute from the pen of R. Gowans, Barnby-on-the-Marsh, Howden, East Yorkshire:

> 'I have travelled with livestock on most of the ships now in service in the west in all sorts of weather, and it is my honest opinion that none of the newer vessels are as quiet, or as good in a sea, as the *Hebrides*, *Dunara Castle*, or *Lochgorm*, and most certainly none are as

good-looking. There must be many who, like myself, will miss the splendid high teas served in saloons rendered magnificent with burnished brass, plush settees, and brightly polished mahogany, and there is no denying the fact that a herring or ham and eggs do not taste the same when a ship is powered by some form of oil engines, and the rattle and vibration of these is a poor substitute for the rhythmical and gentle thump of the old steam ones.'[227]

'Good looks', appropriate to the era, emerged, even if the steam enthusiasts and sections of the public at large might not have recognised them as such (the *Glen Sannox* was nicknamed 'Moss Heights', referring to new high rise flats at Cardonald). The consciously styled and more elegant lines of

the *Glen Sannox* were also to be found in the new vessels built for David MacBrayne Ltd in the first half of the 1950s. Post-war austerity appeared to ease gradually, and, with such long-awaited relief in the air, this somewhat penurious, even penny-pinching, company allowed the naval architect's hand a gentle flourish which resulted in some flowing lines and smooth curves, instead of the blunt angularities and straight edges of the 1930s and 1940s.

The first MacBrayne vessel to show traces of a more stylish design brief was the cargo-ship *Loch Carron*, built by the Ardrossan Dockyard Company and launched in 1951. The *Loch Carron* was remarkable for her splendid sheer, which rose gradually from midships to bow, and which was balanced aft by a neat taper and restrained elevation, rounded off with a well-proportioned cruiser stern. Her accommodation was aft, in one block, with a series of portholes on each side; there were two lifeboats on the Boat Deck, while aft of the bridge stood a rather squat motor ship funnel.

The configuration of the bridge and wheelhouse, on the same level as the Boat Deck, was somewhat unusual, as they were surmounted by a flying-bridge, with green canvas cloths. Precisely why the flying-bridge was deemed necessary has never been clear. The designers may have anticipated that the *Loch Carron* would find herself operating in narrow seaways, such as those at Kallin, North Uist, and especially Loch Skipport, South Uist, which were still used regularly by cargo-vessels in the 1950s. When leaving such lochs, the ship would have gone astern for much of the way and so a flying-bridge might have been regarded as a navigational advantage, permitting a clearer view of the course astern. On the other hand, the rising forward sheer of the ship, especially when relatively light of cargo, could have encouraged the naval architects to err on the side of safety by providing a higher navigational platform.

The *Loch Carron*'s cargo-handling gear consisted of a forward mast with two derricks, the one fore and the other aft, which served a hold each. When the ship was at sea, the derricks normally rested in their crutches,

Above: This fine colour image, probably taken in the very early 1950s, shows the former Stornoway mail steamer, *Lochness*, now on the Inner Isles run and lying at Oban's Railway Pier, with the *Loch Earn* berthed astern. The *Lochness* was sold on the arrival of the *Claymore* in 1955. *(A. Ernest Glen)*

Right: The last of MacBrayne's traditional mail ships, the *Claymore*, built by Denny's, Dumbarton, in 1955, shows off her modern domed funnel as she enters Lochboisdale on a fine evening. The *Claymore* was sold to Greek owners in 1976, and was rebuilt as a day-cruise vessel. *(A. Ernest Glen)*

Below: The elegant lines of the car ferry, *Glen Sannox*, are seen to advantage in this image. *(A. Ernest Glen)*

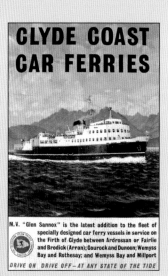

CLYDE COAST CAR FERRIES

M.V. "Glen Sannox" is the latest addition to the fleet of specially designed car ferry vessels in service on the Firth of Clyde between Ardrossan or Fairlie and Brodick (Arran); Gourock and Dunoon; Wemyss Bay and Rothesay; and Wemyss Bay and Millport.

DRIVE ON DRIVE OFF – AT ANY STATE OF THE TIDE

The cargo-boat *Loch Carron* enters Gott Bay to make her last call at Tiree in September 1976. *(Donald E. Meek)*

The MacBrayne cargo boats, *Loch Ard* and *Loch Carron* (ahead), lie together in Queen's Dock, Glasgow. *(A. Ernest Glen)*

and would be raised speedily by their winches and topping-lifts as soon as the ship was at the quayside. The mainmast, placed on the aft superstructure, was later lengthened, adding to the vessel's well-balanced profile. The slender lines of the *Loch Carron* seemed almost to contradict her raison d'etre but she subtantially modernised the conveyance of break-bulk cargo to the Hebrides. She could accommodate four passengers, often Glasgow gentlemen in tweed suits, who always enjoyed the leisurely voyage down the Clyde from Kingston Dock, round the Mull of Kintyre, and outwards to the islands. Cargo deposited at Kingston Dock could be conveyed to its various Hebridean destinations within a week.

The next new vessel to arrive in the Hebrides was the 1,024-ton passenger and mail ship *Claymore*. Built by William Denny & Bros, Dumbarton, and launched in March 1955, she was essentially a further development of MacBrayne's 1930s diesel-powered vessels. Similar in layout and speed to the *Loch Earn* and the *Lochmor*, she nonetheless incorporated numerous improvements in structure and style. She could be identified immediately by her Samson post and derrick, which were positioned well forward, but most obviously by her large domed funnel with prominent front vents, situated precisely amidships. Together with her all-metal wheelhouse, with its streamlined front, the *Claymore*'s superstructure was thoroughly contemporary in appearance. The specific source of inspiration was the French Line's trans-Atlantic liner, *Flandre*, which had been launched in 1952 when the *Claymore*'s overall design was being determined.

The internal layout of the *Claymore* reflected both the needs of the Hebrides and a surprisingly, if not anachronistically, class-conscious approach to passenger status in the mid-1950s. Forward, in the Tween Deck below the hatches, cargo of all kinds – break-bulk, animals and vehicles – could be accommodated. Animals on the hoof could be driven through the ship's forward shell doors, by means of a walkway below the level of the piers, or (in the case of individual animals) lifted on board by derrick and horsebox. Five cars, at a pinch, could be accommodated on the Fore Deck, where they would be deposited by derrick and nets (and, if necessary, nudged under the winch drums), and five more on the Tween Deck, if there was no other cargo. Beneath the Tween Deck was the lower hold, covered

by a large metal-hinged hatch which was opened by the derrick.

The Tween Deck led to the Main Deck, where the alleyways went aft, past passenger cabins, to a splendid restaurant, with marquetry panels and paintings, white tablecloths and silver service. On the Upper Deck, forward, was the First Class saloon, with comfortable armchairs and tables. To port was the Second Class saloon, and to starboard, the bar and ticket office. Even the stair between the Upper and Main Decks was divided by class, with Second Class feet going to port, and First Class feet to starboard – the distinction signified by an inscribed brass plate on each side. It was always a source of wonder to a passenger that such a distinction could be maintained with respect to the soles of one's shoes. Well hidden on the Lower Deck aft was the Steerage – a dingey little den, with red sofas, much used by the ship's less salubrious clientele, ranging from noisy Oban High School pupils heading home for breaks, to well-lubricated Hebrideans, who required to be stabilised in horizontal positions by some *aqua vitae* prior to riding the treacherous Atlantic waves. Those overnight passengers with some money to spare could book berths in the small cabins or larger state-rooms, with their neat bunks and white linen.

The *Claymore* was distinguished not only by her funnel, but also for her vibration, which was more than evident in all parts of the ship. The cause of the problem was basic under-engining, with the installation of four-cylinder Sulzer diesels, instead of five- or six-cylinder versions, which would have reduced the timing and provided a much smoother output. Four-cylinder engines were regarded by the company as quite sufficient to maintain the *Claymore*'s schedules, which required a relatively slow overnight sail from Barra to Tiree on the inward run to Oban. Dire warnings, issued by the stand-by Chief Engineer while the ship was still on the stocks at Denny's, were brushed aside, with predictable results. The vessel's service speed was 12 knots, but, with throttles fully open, she could just about manage 14 – and become a floating earthquake. This capability was tested on one occasion – and on one occasion only – in the Sound of Mull, when the officers and engineers decided to give her full power. As the oscillations increased to unprecedented heights, ticket-racks fell off their mountings, panels and screws loosened, and plates (of all kinds) shook themselves to the point of fracture. On the *Claymore*'s arrival in Oban, news of her unofficial

225 The Motor Ship, August 1957, pp223-225.
226 Cambell and Fenton, 1999, p24.
227 Letter dated 28th June 1955. We owe this reference to the kindness of Mrs Priscilla Scott.
228 This incident was described to Donald E. Meek by the first Chief Engineer on the *Claymore*.
229 Skewis, 1962, p24.

MacBrayne's very last steam-powered vessel, the cargo-boat *Loch Frisa*, lies in the East India Harbour, Greenock. *(A. Ernest Glen)*

Sound of Mull trials (and their consequences) reached the ears of the company's Glasgow office. A manager was dispatched immediately to check the extent of the on-board devastation and to prohibit any further irresponsible speeding of this kind. Relations between Oban and Glasgow were not always sweet.[228]

The White Paper of 1952, specifying the building of the vessel that became the *Claymore*, also specified the building of another cargo-vessel to replace the 1898-vintage *Hebrides*. The new cargo-ship was the *Loch Ard*, built by Ferguson Bros, Port Glasgow, and launched into the Clyde almost fully fitted out and ready to sail in 1955. The *Loch Ard* was of a similar configuration to the *Loch Carron*, but broader and more substantial looking. She had a bipod mast forward (rather than a single mast), with robust derricks fore and aft, giving her lifting capability of up to 16 tons. Her superstructure aft was taller and more compact than that of the *Loch Carron*, and this gave her a very attractive appearance, matching that of contemporary broad-beamed diesel coasters. The *Loch Ard* partnered the *Loch Carron* for some years, taking cargo from Glasgow to the Hebrides on alternate weeks, but latterly she became the dedicated cargo-ship for Islay. The MacBrayne cargo-fleet was now five-strong, as the *Loch Carron* and the *Loch Ard* served alongside the *Lochbroom* (1946, acquired 1948) and the *Loch Frisa* (1946, acquired 1949, as the last steam-powered ship to serve MacBrayne's) and the *Loch Dunvegan* (built 1946, acquired 1950).

By the early-1960s, the days of the traditional passenger-cargo vessel were numbered in the Hebrides. The *Loch Earn* and the *Lochmor* had been in service for 30 years, the *Lochiel* (West Loch Tarbert-Islay) for 21 years, the *Lochnevis* for 26 years, and the *Loch Seaforth* for 17 years. Within ten years, the *Claymore* herself was thoroughly outmoded, but she struggled on bravely with the Inner Isles service until 1975, assisted in car-carrying by the cargo-ship *Loch Dunvegan*, which was placed on dedicated car-runs to supplement the *Claymore*'s capacity on Saturday afternoon sailings to Tiree. In 1976, after lay-up in the East India Harbour, Greenock, the *Claymore* was sold to Greek (Kyrtados) interests, and sailed to the Aegean as the *City of Andros*. Soon her Hebridean cargo-handling features were removed, her bow and stern extended and her Bridge Deck lengthened aft. Restyled as a cruise-ship and renamed *City of Hydra*, she served Cycladic Cruises on their itineraries to the Cyclades, and was regularly to be seen at Hydra and other island destinations. She remained active as a cruise-ship until the mid-1990s, before being consigned to the notorious ship graveyard at Elefsis Bay, north of Piraeus. There she sank in late 2000, a battered remnant of her former self, taking with her the last vestiges of the old Hebridean mail ship era.

The derrick-loading cargo-vessels were similarly outmoded by the growing demands of car ownership. The *Loch Frisa* was sold in 1963, the *Lochbroom* and the *Loch Ard* in 1971, and the *Loch Dunvegan* in 1973. The *Loch Carron* made her last sailings in late 1976, soon after the *Claymore* had gone to Greece.

In retrospect, it is clear that, during the 1950s, MacBrayne's had little or no proactive strategy for improving routes or schedules, and that it still adhered to the course set by Sir Alfred Read in the 1930s. What was revolutionary in 1930 was decidedly out of fashion by 1960, and facilities remained basic, as an observation from 1962 indicates:

'It is common for the passenger to have to choose between a sparred bench on the open deck and a corner of a smoky lounge smelling of alcohol. The Outer isles route is the worst, but the Inner Isles and Stornoway services by no means provide comforts suitable for an eight- to twelve-hour journey.'[229]

Ships replaced after 1945 with government assistance were, on the whole, much improved, 'classier' versions of earlier models, with better accommodation and facilities, including stronger derricks and horseboxes. However, investment in what really would have changed the schedule – greater engine power – was minimal. Speeds were remarkably slow, most vessels clanking along at an average of 12 knots or even 10; the 'faster' Hebridean ships could manage perhaps 14 knots with a favouring wind and a helpful current. This was the era of early 4.00am rises to catch the ship for Oban, which left Tiree about 6.00am, and might reach Oban by mid-day. The same ship had left Castlebay, Barra, at midnight or thereabouts on the inward run, and had proceeded southwards through the Minch at half speed, so as to arrive in Tiree no earlier 5.00am – give or take an odd half-hour here or there. Engines were no more powerful than was needed, and what was needed was, seemingly, not speedy conveyance.

Foresight in the boardroom was on a par with the power (or lack of it) in the engine-room. When the *Loch Carron*, *Claymore* and *Loch Ard* were built in the first half of the 1950s, David MacBrayne Ltd had not anticipated that the tidal wave of car ownership would sweep through the Hebridean seas in less than a decade. That wave had already revolutionised ship design for the Clyde and it was about to do the same for the Hebrides. A complete reassessment of the rationale for the MacBrayne fleet was urgently required, and, by the early 1960s, a new vision was being articulated powerfully. The celebrated 'Road to the Isles' would now travel not only towards the sea, but also over the sea.

Chapter Ten
Rail to Road Restructuring

By the latter 1950s, major social changes were under way. Following the ending of rationing in 1955, an economic boom benefited an expanding middle class who saw owning a car as a badge of new-found wealth and social status. British Railways (and their associated shipping services) remained steam-dominated with all that implied in terms of grime and unreliability. The British Railways' Modernisation Plan, announced in 1955, envisaged the gradual replacement of steam by diesel and electric traction but, by the time that the first new trains were delivered in 1958, the switch from rail to road was in progress and the rapid growth in car ownership gave a sense of freedom and personal betterment with which the railways had great difficulty in competing.

In December 1958 the Conservative Prime Minister Harold Macmillan opened Britain's first motorway, the M6 Preston By-pass, and his controversial Secretary of State for Transport, Ernest Marples was strongly supportive of the development of a nationwide network.[230] The Scottish Office saw the construction of motorways and dual carriageways as being vital to future economic and social development. Indeed, so fervent was this ideology that Scottish new towns were deliberately located away from railway lines so as only to be readily accessible by car. The 1963 White Paper 'Central Scotland – A programme for development and growth' described the priority given to the development of main road trunk routes within the investment plans for the period until 1969.[231] In all, £57 million was directed to road building over a five-year planning period, with £44 million in grants to local authorities. Some 209 miles of dual carriageway and motorway were planned to be in use by 1970, with a further 80 miles

Brodick Pier in the mid-1960s with the *Glen Sannox* in British Rail monastral blue hull livery and the modern motor 'puffer' *Glenshira* in the foreground. *(Tom Shanks)*

LMSR and LNER owned shares in Scotland's leading bus operator, Walter Alexander & Sons, when the rail network was nationalised in 1948, the government inherited these shareholdings. Later, in 1949, the Alexander family sold the remainder of their shares to the BTC. The various nationalised Scottish bus operators - Alexanders (Midland), Alexanders (Fife), Alexanders (Northern), Scottish Motor Traction, Scottish Omnibuses Ltd and Highland Omnibuses Ltd – were restructured to become collectively known as the Scottish Bus Group. By the end of the decade, this restructuring would have profound consequences for the future control of steamer and ferry services on the Clyde and to the Hebrides.[234] Until 1973, MacBrayne's continued to operate their own network of bus services, connecting with their ships. Their bus fleet mainly consisted of smallish vehicles, each with a mail compartment to the rear of the passenger saloon. Strikingly turned out in a red, cream and green livery embellished with a silhouette of a Highlander on each side, they were a familiar sight parked at piers throughout the West Highlands. Thereafter, the MacBrayne bus fleet was absorbed into Highland Omnibuses Ltd.

The 1960s was a difficult decade on Clydeside. The year of 1963 was the first of several crisis years for shipbuilding as yards struggled to compete with considerably more modern and efficient facilities in Germany and the Far East. Empty order books in Scotland were one obvious sign of the beginnings of de-industrialisation. Wage inflation and labour unrest were two further manifestations of change – and these had consequences for the remaining Clyde steamer fleet. The surviving turbine and paddle vessels were obviously ageing. The *Scottish Daily Express* of 22nd May 1964 reported that the Caledonian Steam Packet Company intended to cut seven services, withdrawing three steamers at the end of the summer season; next to this was an article headlined 'John Brown's Fight Jap Prices.' The CSP's General Manager, Alex Stewart, was quoted as saying:

'Increasing Continental travel, aided by direct air charter flights, is bringing holidays abroad more than ever within the reach of the average purse, and short distance holidaymakers who once traditionally went to the Clyde are travelling further a-field.'[235]

It was explained that passenger numbers had slid from 4,367,173 in 1959 to 3,582,303 in 1963 – and it was the excursion steamers, not the car ferries, which were responsible for this trend. Meanwhile, in the *Weekly Scotsman*, it was observed that:

'A sail doon the glottal-stop 'wa'er' was for a century one of the most noted habits of the Glaswegian. But now the weans prefer the candy-floss atmosphere of the Isle of Man, the glitter of Blackpool, and the sun of France, Belgium and Holland – facts which are reflected in the annual loss of £300,000 a year on the Clyde services… It does look like the end of an era when the Clyde was a playground for the mightiest industrial conurbation in Britain.'[236]

The threat of strike action by crews 'because of the way the negotiating committee was treated by the bosses' at the Glasgow Fair that year can only have negatively affected the CSP's earnings. In the end, the strike was averted, but it was symptomatic of the decline of the Clyde excursion fleet.[237]

With the exception of the *Waverley*, all the steamers dated from the

completed by 1972.[232]

Meanwhile, the BTC was haemorrhaging increasing amounts of money as heightened fuel and labour costs further undermined the still steam-dominated railway network. In a drastic move, Macmillan's Government wound up the BTC in 1962, replacing it with a series of smaller units, including a new British Railways Board. This was chaired by Dr Richard Beeching, a chemist brought in from Imperial Chemical Industries with a remit to stem the railway's losses by whatever means were necessary. In practice, this meant that around a third of the railway network would be closed down as uneconomic, with the Highlands of Scotland being particularly badly affected. Beeching imagined only a core Inter-City express passenger and freight network remaining but, in the end, several key rural lines – including routes to the West Coast steamer ports of Oban, Mallaig and Kyle of Lochalsh – survived the 'Beeching Axe.'[233]

Simultaneously, Scottish bus services were re-organised. The majority of these had initially fallen under BTC control in the latter 1940s. As the

230 Charlesworth, 1984, pp25-28.
231 Central Scotland – A programme for development and growth, 1963, pp2-15.
232 Central Scotland – A programme for development and growth, 1963, pp17-18.
233 Allen, 1966.
234 Booth, 2000, pp13-28.
235 Scottish Daily Express, 22nd May 1964.
236 Weekly Scotsman, 28th May 1964.
237 Scottish Daily Express, 15th June 1964.

Above: The paddle steamer *Waverley* sporting a monastral blue hull and lions rampant on her funnels in Rothesay Bay in the mid-1960s. *(A. Ernest Glen)*

Right: The *Jeanie Deans* was withdrawn before the new British Rail corporate identity was extended to the hulls of the Clyde steamer and ferry fleet. Here, the ageing steamer is seen in Rothesay Bay in the early 1960s. *(A. Ernest Glen)*

Below: The MacBrayne bus fleet was an important part of the Company's operations in the 1960s. Here, two Willowbrook-bodied Bedford VAS buses are operating a private charter. *(A. Ernest Glen)*

Below right: Viewed from another steamer, the blue-hulled *Maid of Argyll* streaks through Rothesay Bay. *(Tom Shanks)*

1920s and 30s. As labour relations deteriorated, their standard of upkeep also became generally poorer. Wood-effect scrumbling on the deckhouses was painted over in white and, instead of polished bright work on the deck railings black paint was crudely applied to save the crews from expending effort on ongoing maintenance. Thus, at the very moment when the travelling public's expectations were increasing, what the CSP could provide was markedly scruffier than a decade previously.

The stately *Jeanie Deans* and the *Duchess of Montrose* – the oldest of the ex-LNER and LMSR fleets – were withdrawn, along with the small motor launches *Ashton* and *Leven* (which had been built to carry sight-seers in connection with the 1938 Empire Exhibition). This meant that, come 1967, there were a mere four steamers left on the Clyde – the *Caledonia* and *Waverley* stationed at Craigendoran, the *Duchess of Hamilton* at Gourock and the *Queen Mary II* in Glasgow. A fifth, the *King George V*, was based in Oban, operating cruises to Staffa and Iona.

In the 1965 season, a new colour scheme was applied to the entire CSP fleet. While British Railways' Chairman, Dr Beeching is best remembered for imposing draconian cuts on the rail network, he also believed that a new railway image was required to compete with luxury express coaches and jet airliners. The railway's old-fashioned heraldic imagery was jettisoned in favour of a modern 'double arrow' logo and a new 'monastral blue' livery (a rich green-blue shade which appeared to vary depending on lighting conditions). The new identity was devised by Jock Kinnear of the London industrial design firm Design Research Unit. Kinnear, incidentally, had only recently produced a similar graphic identity for Britain's motorway network.[238] As part of the re-branding, British Railways became British Rail – it being observed by many that the loss of the last syllable was somehow analogous to Dr Beeching's cutting away of a third of Britain's railway network.

For railway-controlled shipping, the new identity required that hulls be painted blue rather than black and funnels would be red with the 'double arrow' on each side. The CSP's directors were not enamoured with this new scheme – especially as red funnels would make their ships less easily distinguishable from those of MacBrayne's, Burns & Laird Lines and the Isle of Man Steam Packet Company. While the CSP accepted that hulls should be blue (though a different shade from the colour used in Caledonian Railway days), they resisted red funnels and so instead buff was retained and the need for a corporate logo was resolved by applying red lions rampant – hardly the modern image British Rail's London management had in mind, but at least with a distinct Scottish character. While the CSP's car ferries looked attractive in this new scheme, the remaining steamers appeared decidedly uncomfortable but their English counterparts, which adopted the British Rail red funnel and 'double arrow' logos, looked so much worse!

Ferries for the Hebrides

By 1964, the move from rail-connected passenger and cargo steamer services to road-connected car ferries reached the Hebrides. David MacBrayne received £2 million from the Secretary of State for Scotland using powers granted by the Highlands and Islands Shipping Act of 1960 to commission no less than three new 2,104-ton ferries. These were to serve their Uig to Lochmaddy and Tarbert (Harris), Mallaig to Armadale and Oban to Craignure and Lochaline (Morvern) services. The first two routes were intended jointly to form a bridge to the Outer Hebrides via Skye, where the road from Armadale to Uig had been newly upgraded, while the

third route responded to increasing vehicle traffic to Mull.

Each of the new ferries could accommodate 600 passengers and up to 50 cars, using a loading system similar to the Clyde ferries *Arran*, *Bute*, *Cowal* and *Glen Sannox*. Rather than embarking vehicles aft of the superstructure, the MacBrayne solution developed the design principles established on their passenger and cargo motor ships *Loch Seaforth* and *Claymore*. Thus, the superstructure covered the hull's aft two-thirds and cargo access was via side openings in the bow quarters where the new ferries had ramps and turntables. Their 'interrupted' bow profile gave them a very distinctive appearance. Power was provided by twin eight-cylinder Crossley diesels, providing a 14-knot service speed.[239]

Unusually for MacBrayne's, the new ferries were ordered from the Hall, Russell shipyard in Aberdeen, the first being delivered as *Hebrides* in April 1964 and making her debut on the Uig-Tarbert-Lochmaddy route. Next came the *Clansman* in June, serving Mallaig-Armadale, with the *Columba* following at the end of July for operation from Oban to Mull. Having been funded by the Scottish Office then leased to MacBrayne's, the ferries were registered in Leith, rather than Glasgow.[240] Another unusual aspect of their ownership was that they were designed with the intention of fulfilling a secondary emergency role as floating radioactive decontamination units to be requisitioned in the event of a nuclear attack. The fact that the Cold War was at its height and that the Cuban missile crisis had strained diplomatic relations between the Americans, their allies and the Soviets must have influenced the Scottish Office's thinking.

Inboard, the new ferries represented a considerable improvement over the inter-war tonnage they superseded. The layout of the passenger accommodation was very similar to the *Glen Sannox*, the Main Deck featuring a smoke room forward and a cafeteria aft with an observation lounge on the Boat Deck. Where the *Glen Sannox* had a bar ahead of the engine room beneath the vehicle deck, the MacBrayne ferries instead had some passenger cabins. As the Scottish Office was keen to expand Scotland's tourist industry, a high standard of design was required. It so happened that a young interior design student at the Glasgow School of Art called John McNeece was keen to design a passenger ship for his diploma year project and so, realising that the new ferries were in the early stages of construction, he contacted MacBrayne's with a view to taking on their passenger spaces as a 'live' project. This was accepted and so the vessels' otherwise fairly conventional hardwood and Formica panelled interiors were brightened by McNeece's modern furniture and fabrics. This work attracted the attention of the Council of Industrial Design in London, whose magazine *Design* featured a rather caustic deconstruction of Gaelic culture, written by the well-known journalist and broadcaster Magnus Magnusson:

'The three new MacBrayne's car ferries to the Western Isles that started operating during the summer shed an interesting sidelight on another aspect of design altogether. It is a curious fact that Gaelic culture in the Western Isles, although rich in verbal imagery and music, is totally non-visual. No painting, no sculpture; even the material culture, apart from tweed-making, is clumsy and barely functional. As a result, perhaps, the old ships that plied from the islands to the mainland were the dreariest and ugliest boats ever built; the bar was a hatchway below decks, a corner for hard peasant drinking without comfort. The new ferries, with their attractive interiors designed by McNeece and Fletcher, reflect a new movement – the movement of tourists to the islands. These boats are

238 Haresnape, 1983, pp119-122.
239 The Motor Ship, May 1964, pp51-53.
240 The Secretary of State for Scotland Michael Noble regretted that one of these vessels was not ordered from Wm Denny & Bros of Dumbarton. Had he known of their lack of orders, he would have encouraged the ordering of one of the three ferries from the yard.

designed to attract not islemen but mainlanders – and they mirror a different social attitude. It will be interesting to see if this new traffic has a stimulating effect on native design in the Western Isles.'[241]

As has been shown, tourism in the Hebrides was anything but new, but it was expected that, thanks to the new ferries, its significance to the islands' economies would increase greatly in future years. Additionally, the ferries appealed to islanders themselves, and local affirmation of their qualities was evident from the outset. The *Columba*, according to Sir Charles Maclean of Duart, was 'the most comfortable and luxurious vessel ever to operate on the Mull run'. 'No one,' he stated, 'can grumble on the score of the passenger accommodation.'[242]

Scotland's side-loading ferries of the 1954-64 period were very different in concept from the vast majority of ro-ro vessels commissioned elsewhere in Northern Europe during this era. Most Scandinavian ferries of the period were bow- and stern-loading drive-through vessels, built to handle great throughputs of vehicles and berthing at newly established dedicated ferry ports. The operating environment in the Hebrides was far from ideal, with shallow harbours and landing facilities, and so what might be termed 'Hebrimax' dimensions had to be observed. As R.G. Robertson noted in 1969, a very substantial number of cars and passengers required to be carried on a shallow-draft hull:

'Although the car ferries were not very large ships, their design was by no means easy as in the West Highland trade there are so many diverse, and mutually conflicting, requirements to be satisfied. Light draught being the overriding consideration, space was made available for 50 cars...[and] for 870 [*recte* 600] passengers...all on a length of 235 feet and a draught, fully loaded, of nine feet.'[243]

Furthermore, Clyde and Hebridean piers and harbours were conceived in an earlier era, and so bringing vessels capable of carrying road vehicles to use these facilities proved a stiff challenge, not least because the pier owners often were not the ferry operators. In most cases, existing piers required strengthening, while the one at Uig needed a 15-metre extension before the *Hebrides* could call there. Furthermore, Clyde and Hebridean ferries served sparse and dispersed rural communities, whereas those elsewhere in Europe and North America usually provided 'sea bridges' on major trunk roads and across fjords, meaning that the case for large-scale investment in high-capacity port infrastructure and vessels was easier to justify. In fact, Scotland's West Coast ferry services are arguably unique in the western world in that they operate through treacherous waters with strong currents and widely varying depths, carrying relatively small numbers of passengers and vehicles to offset the costs of provision. In such an inhospitable context, the achievement of bringing a fleet of four new ferries to the Clyde plus three to the Hebrides within only a decade is all the more remarkable. Scotland's expanding network of Clyde and Hebridean routes served destinations at the very ends of transport arteries. These continue as vital lifeline services, however, and island life is highly dependent on their reliability and regularity.

Particularly in the Hebrides, MacBrayne's new car ferry services had a profound impact on the patterns of island life and habitation. They were accepted from the outset as a necessary improvement to the transport infrastructure. In its report of the arrival of the *Columba* at Iona, *The Oban Times* commented retrospectively:

'It is a pointer to the future success of the new ferry that since the introduction of the new services in May (four runs each way per day) the [*Loch Earn* and the *Lochmor*, filling the gap before the appearance of the *Columba*] have carried to and from Mull several thousand more passengers than travelled in the same period on that route last year.'

Anticipation of the *Columba* was adding to the growing volume of passengers, as well as of traffic. The *Loch Earn* and the *Lochmor* had even greater challenges when handling vehicles, and cars were sometimes 'forced to await the next run'.[244]

In short, the *Columba* and her sisters appeared just in the nick of time to relieve severe pressures within the Hebridean transport system.

This was more than evident when the *Hebrides*, the first of the three vessels to take up station, began to serve the route known as the 'Hebridean Triangle', with its apex at Tarbert (Harris). From 15th April until 31st December 1964, her first few months in service, she carried 47,325 passengers, 10,335 cars, and 754 commercial vehicles. In 1970 and 1971, the number of commercial vehicles carried by the *Hebrides* in the summer-autumn season was just over 2,000. The number of cars being carried leapt during the same periods, from 11,097 in 1967 to 18,736 in 1972. With the provision of car ferry services to Stornoway in the 1970s, the number of commercial vehicles carried on the 'Hebridean Triangle' declined somewhat.[245] Given such statistics, it is hard to understand how life in the Outer Hebrides had managed to function at 'normal' levels before the coming of the *Hebrides*. The car ferries were, of course, redefining Hebridean 'normality' in an age when motor vehicles had become a central part of the wider national transport system.

New routes and schedules were part of this process of 'normalisation' but not without challenges. In the case of the *Hebrides*, the long 'over-island route' through Skye from Kyleakin to Uig could cause problems for drivers heading to the Outer Hebrides. Pressure on the small car ferries serving the Kyle of Lochalsh-Kyleakin crossing could lead to delays and, initially, the *Hebrides* could be held up at Uig as she awaited cars known to be 'on the way'. Not infrequently too, cars would hurtle down the road to Uig with horns blaring and lights flashing, in an attempt to catch the Captain's ear or eye before he left the pier.[246] In the longer term, of course, vehicle-arrival and car-marshalling strategies were developed to ensure that loading proceeded in a seemly manner. The new arrangements were a far cry from the leisurely style of the older motor ships. The car ferry's schedule began to rule the waves, as well as life on the islands.

When sheep were to be transported, the vehicle hoist on a car ferry would be transformed into a temporary mechanical sheep-pen, with wire or wooden 'flakes' fixed to stanchions on the athwartship edges. The sheep would then be herded from the pier into the 'pen', assuming that they were co-operative. On many occasions, they were disinclined to obey orders, with the result that officers and crew could be seen running around the pier-head, waving their arms and their caps, in an attempt to coerce the recalcitrants gently aboard. Trouble could also be caused by cattle, for much the same reason. As a consequence, a car ferry could be two hours (or more) late when leaving an island pier. On arrival at a mainland port, when the animals had been discharged and were being driven to the mart on the hoof (as happened in Oban), the vessel would exude the odour of the

241 Design, September 1964, p40.
242 Oban Times, 6th August 1964.
243 Ships Monthly, April 1969, pp136-7
244 Oban Times, 6th August 1964.
245 Patton, 2009, p66.
246 Patton, 2009, pp63-4.

Above: The new MacBrayne-operated car ferry *Hebrides* in Uig Bay, Skye, during her maiden 1964 season. *(Bruce Peter collection)*

Right: The lounge bar on one of the three new MacBrayne-operated ferries; the interior design by John McNeece drew considerable praise and represented a major improvement over previous standards. *(Bruce Peter collection)*

Below: How cars were loaded before the car ferry revolution; a Ford Cortina is lowered onto the deck of the *Loch Seaforth*. *(Tom Shanks)*

Below right: The smoking saloon on one of MacBrayne's new car ferries. *(Bruce Peter collection)*

farmyard, which mightily assailed the nostrils of genteel tourists, rejoining their vehicles on the Car Deck. Immediate washing-down of the deck was essential. The 1964 vessels were restricted with regard to garage height, and it was only with the arrival of much larger car ferries that animals could be conveyed on board in floats, as was eventually demanded by EU regulations – a practice pioneered by the *Iona*, which carried cattle-floats on the Mallaig-Stornoway service as early as 1972.

With the creation of new routes came shorter voyage-times and more frequent services. Hebridean tourism also became more diverse. It was now possible to arrange package deals, 'island hops', which allowed the tourist to sleep in a berth on board a car ferry at Uig or Oban, and take the first next-day sailing to the preferred destination. There, the tourist could spend the day, before returning on an evening sailing. By using the other car ferry links it was, for instance, possible to undertake a relatively brief but satisfying circuit of Harris and Lewis. The old mail ship 'odysseys', with their slightly unpredictable schedules, were a thing of the past. The professional tourist, rigged out in tweeds, hats and telescopes, became an endangered species, as 'hairy knees and haversacks' began to dominate the ships' decks. Islanders, also dressed in less formal garb, soon became used to 'taking the ferry' to stock up in Oban or Inverness or Mallaig, still with a sense of going on a 'special' trip.

However inventive the first generation of car ferries may have been in their hydraulic systems for loading and unloading, their finish and furnishings retained an attractive touch of old-time elegance, with teak top-rails and traditional wooden buoyant seats. Even the tuneful Chadburn telegraph still rang out musically when the car ferry was arriving at, or departing from, a pier, and officers and crew wore navy-style uniforms. To match the rhythm of the times, however, the restaurant was gradually modified towards 'plastic service', to produce a lighter, 'faster' menu, while stewards were kept busy catering in the cafeteria for those who now preferred snacks to sit-down meals. Islanders and tourists began to mingle in a much more relaxed one-class environment.

On the whole, the new services worked well, and all have endured to the present. The only ship which did not appear to be quite suited to her designated route was the *Clansman*, which seemed altogether too large for the Mallaig-Armadale crossing. When caught in strong winds she inflicted several 'hard dockings' on Armadale pier. Indeed, all three car ferries presented new tests for their Masters when manoeuvring at constricted Hebridean harbours, as they were slow to answer the helm, and, with their high superstructures, suffered from windage difficulties. Their single rudders were largely ineffective, and their bow-thrusters were seriously underpowered. As a result, a Master had to make deft use of engines, helm and springs, as well as wind and tide, to bring the vessel on to, or off, a pier.

After a nomadic career and substantial rebuilding as a drive-though vessel (see below), the *Clansman* was the first to leave the fleet, going in 1984 to Torbay Seaways, Devon, to operate a proposed Torquay-Guernsey service, but was quickly re-sold to Maltese interests, and eventually served as a pilgrim carrier in the Middle East. Thereafter, the *Hebrides* was also sold to Torbay Seaways in 1985 to operate in her place. She became the *Devoniun*, before moving to the Adriatic where she linked Southern Italy and Albania until her engine room caught fire, forcing her permanent withdrawal from service.[247]

The *Columba* left the Oban-Craignure route in 1975 and switched to car ferry operations serving other islands, notably Coll and Tiree (with a call at

A 1960s summer deck scene on MacBrayne's *Columba* as she heads northwards through the Sound of Mull, with Lismore Lighthouse astern. *(A. Ernest Glen)*

Tobermory, Mull) and Colonsay, as well as undertaking mini cruises.[248] She maintained these routes until she was sold in 1989 when replaced by the new *Lord of the Isles* (see below). Substantially rebuilt as a small, luxury cruise-ship, named the *Hebridean Princess*, she continues to sail on Scotland's western seaboard in the ownership of Hebridean Island Cruises, presently a subsidiary of ex-P&O Chairman Lord Sterling's All Leisure Group. In 2006, and again in 2010, she deputised as Royal Yacht, conveying Her Majesty Queen Elizabeth and family members on special cruises to the Hebrides — a most exceptional achievement for a former MacBrayne car ferry. The *Hebridean Princess* has won a high reputation and her excellent condition reflects well not only on Hebridean Island Cruises and their staff, but also on Hall, Russell of Aberdeen. They produced three remarkable vessels, which, in most cases, fulfilled what was expected of them (and some more) as the first Hebridean car ferries.

247 Duckworth and Langmuir, 1987, pp148-51.
248 Duckworth and Langmuir, 1987, p151.

Above: A tranquil mid-1960s scene in Oban with the *Columba* between sailings berthed at the North Pier. *(A. Ernest Glen)*

Right: Over two decades later, the *Columba* is seen at Oban in 1988 - her final season in Caledonian MacBrayne service. Thereafter, the new *Lord of the Isles* replaced her and she was converted into the exclusive cruise ship *Hebridean Princess*. *(Bruce Peter)*

Below: The car ferry *Hebrides* ended her days operating as the *Illyria* between Southern Italy and Albania. After an engine room fire, she was dumped in a backwater in Elefsis Bay, where she is seen in 2004 berthed next to the former Belgian Dover strait ferry *Roi Baudouin*, latterly the Greek-owned *Georgios Express*. Both vessels have since been scrapped. *(Bruce Peter)*

The early summer of 1966 will be remembered in maritime circles largely because of the seamen's strike. In Oban, the Mecca of MacBrayne's operations, the *Claymore* lay idle at the Railway Pier, growing large amounts of marine vegetation below the waterline, and very much in need of a 'shave' by the time the strike ended. She again rattled her way northwards through the Sound of Mull in late June with the quartermaster at the wheel complaining of her more sluggish than usual performance. As the *Claymore* languished, others were taking action, not only to move a car or two quietly to the islands closest to Oban, but also to pioneer new approaches to car ferry development in the Hebrides. An Oban High School pupil (the teenage Donald E. Meek) and a few of the *Claymore*'s crew were sitting on the buoyant seats on the Boat Deck, enjoying the sunshine and a few yarns, when they noticed a small 'barge' entering Oban Bay, and steering astern of the *Claymore*. Resplendent in light blue hull colours, with the company name, 'Eilean Sea Services' (*eilean* being the Gaelic word for 'island'), in bold white lettering on her sides, the diminutive *Isle of Gigha* headed for Oban's South Pier and lowered her bow ramp on to the adjacent slipway. The teenager was fascinated, even amazed, and ran at top speed across to the South Pier to view this remarkable phenomenon. About half-a-dozen cars embarked, the bow ramp was pulled up, and the tiny vessel's propellers, invisible below her very flat bottom as they pulled her astern, created a creamy white wake on an otherwise emerald sea. He recollected that he had seen something similar when, in the mid-1950s, a large, grey Landing Craft (Tank) had beached like a massive whale on the silver sands of Gott Bay, Tiree, and had swung open its gaping mouth to deliver Royal Air Force vehicles for the island base there. The *Isle of Gigha* was a smaller version of the LCT. Now history was repeating itself,

Western Ferries' *Sound of Jura* Islay ferry is seen off Port Askaig in the early-1970s. (A. Ernest Glen)

but in the interests of commercial sea transport.

By 1969, the *Isle of Gigha*, now renamed *Sound of Gigha* and given a coat of bright red paint, had joined a new company, Western Ferries (Argyll) Ltd, which was stealing the headlines and revenue from the operations of David MacBrayne Ltd to Islay and Jura. As the *Hebrides*, *Clansman* and *Columba* continued to provide new and excellent service to islands north of Oban, the more southerly islands of the Inner Hebrides had been left to function as best they could with combinations of old-fashioned motor ships. On the West Loch Tarbert-Islay service, the *Lochiel*, built in 1939 as the last of the series initiated by Sir Alfred Read, was still swinging cars laboriously on and off her foredeck by means of a derrick. Coll and Tiree were 'making do' with the *Claymore*, supplemented by the Saturday service of the cargo-ship *Loch Dunvegan*, but by 1972 these islands had been treated to a 'new' replacement vessel – none other than the venerable *Loch Seaforth*, which, having been displaced by the car ferry *Iona* on the Stornoway-Mallaig run, was now wheezing her weary way between Oban and the Inner Hebrides. Worn out by the rigours of the northern Minch, the *Loch Seaforth* finally expired at Tiree in March 1973, when, having struck a rock at the southern end of the Sound of Gunna, her collision bulkhead gave way, and she sank alongside Gott Bay pier, blocking any further dockings for several months. The *Claymore*, already dispatched to lay-up, had to be recalled to perform the final honours for the traditional Oban-Tiree service with the assistance of a small ferryboat.

In 1967, when Western Ferries (Argyll) Ltd was established, the alternative they provided to MacBrayne's was much appreciated by islanders who were thoroughly weary of the latter's outmoded operations. The first vessel built for Western Ferries was the *Sound of Islay*, launched by Ferguson Brothers, Port Glasgow, in 1968. She has been described graphically by Captain Sandy Ferguson, who was initially her Mate, but was soon promoted to Master and then to Senior Master in the new company:

'The *Sound of Islay* was a small stern loading ferry capable of carrying 16 cars and with saloon passenger accommodation for 93. She was a very practical, if slow, vessel, her only fault being that she rolled like a cow in even a moderate sea... She was the first ever purpose built ro-ro ferry to operate a scheduled service on the West Coast of Scotland, and also the first ro-ro vessel on that coast not to be fitted with a hoist for side loading vehicles... The *Sound of Islay* was an immediate success. We were competing, if you could call it that, against the ageing derrick loading *Lochiel*, and were soon

Western Ferries' rather basic 'landing craft' *Sound of Gigha*, formerly the pioneering *Isle of Gigha* owned by Eilean Sea Services, is seen at Port Askaig. *(A. Ernest Glen)*

In her final season, the *Duchess of Hamilton* is seen sweeping out of Rothesay Bay in 1970. *(John Peter)*

carrying in excess of 90 per cent of the traffic to and from Islay...

It immediately became apparent that the *Sound of Islay*, whilst being ideal to start the service in opposition [to MacBrayne's], was far too small for the trade that quickly became available. The Board of Western Ferries Argyll were to be congratulated on so quickly acquiring ownership of a much larger Norwegian roll-through ferry, which was already under construction at the Ulstein shipyard in Norway.'[249]

The new vessel, *Sound of Jura*, which took up service in 1970, can be described fairly as the 'mother' of all drive-through car ferries to serve the Hebrides, though she operated mainly by using stern-loading only, because her short bow-ramp was not well suited to the Hebridean tidal range. Captain Ferguson, who was later to become Master of the new Caledonian MacBrayne car ferry *Iona*, and also the company's Marine Superintendent, was pleasantly surprised by her capabilities, despite such design faults as a lack of stabilisers:

'The *Sound of Jura* was, ton for ton, the best ferry I ever commanded. Considering that she was built in Norway at exactly the same time as David MacBrayne were building the *Iona* at Troon, the difference between the two was staggering... At that time Norway was miles ahead of the UK when it came to building ro-ro ferries, and that country could teach us a tremendous amount... Give MacBrayne's their due, they had stabilisers fitted to the *Iona*, but she was away behind the 'Jura' in just about every other respect.'[250]

Captain Ferguson was particularly appreciative of the bridge-control systems with which the *Sound of Jura* was equipped.[251] The 'Jura' remained on the Islay run until 1976, when she was suddenly sold by Western Ferries to Mexican interests, remaining in service, largely unchanged apart from hull colour, as the *Quintana Roo* until she was wrecked by Hurricane Wilma in 2005.

Western Ferries' departure from the West Loch Tarbert-Islay service around the same time occurred in the context of wrangles over the manner of allocation of government subsidies, which had benefited David MacBrayne Ltd, even when the service they provided was far from satisfactory. In addition to its outstanding, mould-breaking legacy of innovative car ferry design, Western Ferries left one fixed asset of great advantage to Caledonian MacBrayne in the longer term – the terminal at Kennacraig. This was more readily accessible by sea than the old West Loch Tarbert pier further up the shallow loch.

Above: The controversial CSP drive-through ferry *Caledonia* (ex *Stena Baltica*) in Ardrossan harbour during her maiden season on the Clyde. *(A. Ernest Glen)*

Right: The *Stena Nordica* at Stranraer on charter to British Rail; the vessel's success doubtless influenced the decision to buy the smaller *Stena Baltica* for service to Arran. *(Alistair Deayton)*

Below: The *Stena Baltica* during the initial stage of her conversion to *Caledonia*. *(Ian Quinn collection)*

Below right: A tractor hauls trolleys loaded with general cargo into the *Caledonia*'s vehicle deck at Ardrossan. *(A. Ernest Glen)*

In 1973, a sister company Western Ferries (Clyde) Ltd invaded the Firth of Clyde, inaugurating a new ferry route to Cowal from McInroy's Point outside Gourock to Hunter's Quay near Dunoon. Unlike the long-established, rail-connected Caledonian Steam Packet service, Western Ferries' operation was geared solely to the needs of motorists and operated initially by a pair of double-ended ferries bought second-hand from Sweden, the *Sound of Scarba* and *Sound of Shuna*. So positive was the customers' response that a third ferry, the *Sound of Sanda*, was introduced in 1974; this was originally the *Lymington*, built by William Denny & Bros in 1938 to traverse the Solent to the Isle of Wight.

While Western Ferries' cross-Clyde route proved an enduring success, their pioneering Islay service was closed down in 1976, unable to make money in the face of subsidised competition from a resurgent public sector ferry operation. The need for a 'joined-up' transport policy, alongside major cost-cutting, was among the factors which prompted a radical reorganisation of the MacBrayne model and that of the Caledonian Steam Packet Company on the Clyde. Ironically, the efficient operational principles imported to the west coast of Scotland by Western Ferries were wholly in tune with those informing this reorganisation.

Caledonian and MacBrayne restructuring

In 1969, the Caledonian Steam Packet Company celebrated 80 years of service. The New Year brought momentous changes as the Company was handed over by British Rail to a new Edinburgh-headquartered state transport authority, the Scottish Transport Group (STG). This combined the shipping services of the CSP and David MacBrayne with the Scottish Bus Group – a sure sign that road had overtaken rail as Scotland's dominant mode of transport. A new CSP Manager, John D. Whittle, and Company Secretary, James Kirkwood, were brought in from the Scottish Bus Group's Central S.M.T. subsidiary (serving industrial Lanarkshire, this was reputedly Britain's most lucrative bus company). They decided that neither the CSP's remaining steamers nor MacBrayne's passenger and cargo vessels had a future and that, as soon as financing could be arranged, the entire Clyde and Western Isles fleets would consist solely of car ferries. MacBrayne's *Lochfyne* and the CSP's *Caledonia* were withdrawn at the end of the 1969 season, and evidence of railway influence upon the CSP's fleet was banished with a return to black hulls rather than rail blue. At this point, the CSP lost control of their prestigious Irish Sea ferry route between Stranraer and Larne, this being retained by British Rail's Scottish Region.

In a further bid to cut costs while modernising the fleet, in 1966, the CSP began a policy of purchasing and chartering second-hand tonnage for Clyde services. The Tilbury-Gravesend ferry *Rose* was thus acquired to serve on the Largs-Millport route. Shortly thereafter, she was renamed *Keppel*, replacing the diesel-electric paddle vessel *Talisman*, which was consigned for scrap in early 1967.

Since January 1966, the CSP had chartered a modern Swedish-owned ferry named *Stena Nordica* to enable a two-ship service to be provided on the Stranraer-Larne route. Their own vessel was the *Caledonian Princess*, a stern-loading steam turbine-powered ferry, dating from 1961 and built by Wm Denny & Bros of Dumbarton. In comparison, the *Stena Nordica* demonstrated how relatively old fashioned and inefficient British ferry design was in comparison with recent developments in Scandinavia, where numerous examples of her type shuttled back and forth between Denmark,

Western Ferries' very small *Sound of Islay* in Campbeltown Loch. *(John Peter)*

Sweden, Norway and West Germany.

The *Stena Nordica*'s owner, Stena AB of Gothenburg, belonged to a business entrepreneur called Sten A. Olsson who typically built ships at low cost in declining shipyards desperate for orders – indeed, Stena soon gained a reputation for such hard bargaining that yards building vessels for its operations frequently went bankrupt during construction, or immediately after a Stena order had been fulfilled. Olsson often sold recently built ferries for a profit, then invested this revenue in yet more new buildings. The CSP's management were particularly impressed by the efficiency of the *Stena Nordica*'s drive-through vehicle deck, which could disgorge a full load of cars and freight in minutes whereas, on their own Clyde vessels, it was necessary to turn vehicles round on a turntable. As late as 1966, the CSP had been planning to commission a further pair of ferries with hoists and turntables, based on the already obsolescent *Glen Sannox* design.

Shortly thereafter, they concluded that, if a similarly arranged vessel to *Stena Nordica* could be obtained for the Ardrossan-Brodick route, there would surely be an opportunity for great efficiency savings – and an enhanced level of service to travellers. Indeed, the Scottish Transport Group's management made the expansion of car ferry services and the introduction of drive-through ferry services their top priority. To that end, it purchased Arran Piers Ltd from the family of the Duke and Duchess of Montrose in August 1969 so as to enable Brodick Pier to be rebuilt for ro-ro operation by end-loading ferries.

Later the same month, the STG Chairman, Patrick M. Thomas, announced that the 1,157-ton drive-through car ferry *Stena Baltica* had been bought for £660,000 and was expected to be operating between Ardrossan and Brodick by Easter 1970. Therefore, work commenced simultaneously on a ferry linkspan at Ardrossan; this was located to the south west of Winton Pier. However, the *Stena Baltica* was a smaller and rather more primitive ferry than the chartered *Stena Nordica*. Although belatedly delivered to Stena in 1966 following construction delays, she was actually the first car ferry the company had ever ordered. With space for 50 cars – but only 580 passengers – she offered only a little over half the capacity of

249 Ferguson, 2008, p43.
250 Ferguson, 2008, pp49-50.
251 The Department of Trade and Industry regulations for ship safety meant that the Sound of Jura was given winter certification for only a limited number of passengers and also summer restrictions regarding operation in strong winds were applied.

The *Sound of Jura* at Port Askaig in the early-1970s. *(John Peter)*

the *Glen Sannox*. Externally and within, she was typical of Scandinavian short-sea ferries of her era built for service in sheltered waters. The basic design was by her builder, a yard best known for constructing fishing trawlers but which had constructed only one previous ferry, the Norwegian-owned *Kraakerø*, delivered in 1964 and operating across the mouth of the Oslofjord between Sandfjord and Stromstad. The Danish naval architecture consultancy Knud E. Hansen A/S carried out superficial aesthetic modifications to give the *Stena Baltica* a more purposeful and harmonious silhouette. Inboard, twin medium-speed MAN diesels gave her a service speed of only 14 knots. Unlike existing Clyde ferries with larger and more powerful engines, these did not impinge upon her vehicle deck and her exhaust uptakes were routed through slim casings on either beam.

Although she could load and unload vehicles far more quickly than the side-loading *Glen Sannox*, this benefit was negated by crossings taking longer to complete.

Short, squat and with bluff hull lines, upon the *Stena Baltica*'s introduction on Stena Line's Gothenburg-Frederikshavn route, she quickly became notorious for her poor sea-keeping qualities and disturbing motion, as the Swedish shipping historian Anders Bergenek recalls:

'The *Stena Baltica* dated from a time when Swedish ferry entrepreneurs such as Stena were only beginning a long learning process about ferry design and operation, and so the ship was far from ideal in terms of design and layout. My mother travelled on her soon after she was delivered; she rolled alarmingly and everyone was

The *Glen Sannox* following conversion to stern-loading configuration approaches Fairlie. *(John Peter)*

The *Maid of Cumbrae*, also converted to a stern-loading car ferry, leaving Gourock. *(A. Ernest Glen)*

Above: The somewhat eccentric-looking *Iona* at Gourock Pier shortly after taking up the service to Dunoon. *(A. Ernest Glen)*

Right: The *Iona* departs Gourock for Dunoon. *(A. Ernest Glen)*

Below: The CSP car ferry *Arran* at West Loch Tarbert under charter to David MacBrayne to maintain the Islay service pending the completion of ro-ro linkspans. *(A. Ernest Glen)*

Below right: The Kyle of Lochalsh-Kyleakin vehicle ferry *Lochalsh*. *(Bruce Peter collection)*

seasick. A retired Stena captain, Einar Von Hofsten, once told me that a colleague who commanded the ship once thought that she would sink after a moderately large swell caught her stern and she suddenly lurched downwards and sideways. After only a short spell linking Gothenburg and Frederikshavn, she was chartered for four months to Lion Ferry to sail between Halmstad and Copenhagen. This route passes Kullen, a rocky outcrop on the Swedish coast, off which the sea can be quite choppy. Twice within weeks, lorries on her vehicle deck shifted out of place. Incidentally, her near-sister, the *Kraakerø*, was not allowed to carry commercial vehicles – but the Swedish marine safety authorities were more liberal than those in Norway.'[252]

Inboard, the *Stena Baltica* was comfortably appointed, her saloons having been designed in a modern Scandinavian manner by the noted Swedish interior architect Robert Tillberg, then best known for his work on the famous Clydebank-built Swedish-American flagship liner *Kungsholm*. Forward on her saloon deck was a cafeteria, with a lounge aft and a further bar above on Boat Deck. Alas, as her construction had been tightly budgeted and her owner desired to optimise revenue-earning space, her staircases were very steep and passages narrow. For example, the main exits to her Boat Deck were behind her twin funnels and the space was barely wide enough for one person to squeeze through at a time (there was also a constant stench of diesel there).

The *Stena Baltica* arrived on the Clyde on 10th January 1970 and was handed over to Scott-Lithgow of Greenock for conversion for operation between Ardrossan and Brodick. It was only then that the STG realised their foolishness in buying a Swedish ferry which did not comply with British safety standards regarding fire prevention and damage survivability. After four months' conversion work, she emerged on 26th May bearing the proud name *Caledonia*, entering service three days later with a temporary certificate. In order to cross shallow waters off Ardrossan at speed, her ballast was reduced to a minimum – and this was to prove detrimental to her already dubious sea-keeping capabilities. Following her initial summer season, she returned to Greenock for further reconfiguration so as to be granted a five-year certificate. In total, the conversion cost the STG £140,000. Given the very obvious decline of Clyde shipbuilding during the 1960s, the fact that a purpose-built vessel could have been built locally for not much more than the cost of acquiring and rebuilding the *Stena Baltica* into the *Caledonia* was a sore point for Clydesiders.

In service, the *Caledonia* proved no less controversial. During her inaugural summer season, her lack of passenger capacity in comparison with the *Glen Sannox* was immediately problematic. She felt crowded and her stairs and passageways were too narrow to let passengers move freely. Furthermore, as her small outside decks were enclosed with Perspex panels, the litter dropped by passengers did not blow overboard and, because her crew apparently failed to clean her between crossings, each day, her condition became increasingly scruffy. (The advent of cafeteria food, served in polystyrene cups and plastic dishes, as well as filter cigarettes, no doubt exacerbated litter problems on Clyde vessels in the post-war era; previously public environments were litter free not so much because Scots were tidier as because there was no litter to drop.) On the plus side, her saloons were considerably more modern and comfortably appointed than on any other Clyde vessel of the period and, on a quiet and calm weekday crossing, a pleasant experience could be had on board. To meet demand at peak times, it was necessary to supplement her with traditional steamer tonnage for the carriage of foot passengers.

Come the first autumn gales, the *Caledonia*'s poor sea keeping became all too obvious. The Ardrossan-Brodick crossing is particularly exposed and her behaviour had not improved since her time under the Swedish flag. Furthermore, as she had only four lifeboats, her winter passenger certificate was reduced to only 132, meaning that even out of season she sometimes struggled to cope with demand. A vigorous correspondence in *The Glasgow Herald* ensued, most commentators agreeing that, in foisting the *Caledonia* on the travelling public, the STG had proven to be out of touch with their customers' expectations. The Clyde steamers of the pre-First World War 'golden era' remained within living memory and, in comparison with these stately vessels, the second-hand imported *Caledonia* appeared to represent how far shipping in the West of Scotland had fallen.

The displaced *Glen Sannox*, meanwhile, was rebuilt at the stern with an enlarged vehicle deck and a stern ramp then placed on the Wemyss Bay-Rothesay service. This was part of a shuffle of ferries between the STG's Caledonian Steam Packet and MacBrayne fleets. Upon delivery, MacBrayne's large new Islay ferry, the *Iona* moved temporarily to the CSP's Gourock-Dunoon route, while the CSP's smaller side-loader *Arran* shifted north to serve Islay pending the delayed completion of ro-ro linkspans at West Loch Tarbert and Port Ellen (this was the first time that a CSP vessel had operated in MacBrayne territory).

This delay reflected one of the key difficulties in bringing ro-ro services to the Western Isles – piers and ferry berths were owned and maintained by various local authorities, rather than by the ferry operators themselves. At first, Argyll County Council, whose responsibility it was to develop a ferry berth in West Loch Tarbert, carried out test borings at Redhouse near the mouth of the loch but they quickly halted work on grounds of expense, even although the *Iona* was under construction at a cost to the Scottish Office of £740,000. Therefore, the STG had no option but to move the *Arran* to serve Islay as a temporary measure until Argyll County Council managed to complete the necessary port facilities to enable a ro-ro service to begin.

Other limiting factors impacting upon the design of ferries for Clyde and Hebridean routes are variable water depths, awkward currents and tidal races between the islands, constricted harbours and exposed piers. Consequently, the ferries and their associated infrastructure have required very specific and often ingenious design approaches. For example, restricting a vessel's length and breadth dimensions so that it can manoeuvre in a small harbour, or restricting its draft to navigate through shallow water, will have a knock-on effect on its deadweight capacity (or payload). This is because a shorter, shallower hull has less volume below the water and therefore less excess buoyancy. Furthermore, the need for sufficient free height in the vehicle deck to accommodate lorries and buses means that the superstructure will need to be far higher above the waterline than in previous generations of short-sea passenger and cargo vessels. This raises a hull's centre of gravity, making it less stable. To compensate, a broader and more bluff configuration could be proposed, but this would reduce speed, manoeuvrability, fuel economy, comfort and possibly safety as the vessel would tend to slam and roll more, perhaps causing cargo to shift and also putting extra pressure on the bow visor. Therefore, to design a successful 'Hebrimax' ferry involves making appropriate compromises between these various competing requirements so as to optimise capacity, performance, comfort and safety.

Delivered in May 1970, the *Iona* was in terms of layout and appearance a very different type of drive-through ferry from the *Caledonia*. Indeed, her design origins probably lay in the types of ferry then being delivered to operators on Norway's west coast – an environment rather similar to

252 Interview with Anders Bergenek by Bruce Peter by telephone, 8th May 2010.

132

The Island-class small ferry *Rhum* at Lochranza. *(Bruce Peter collection)*

Scotland's Western Isles. Built by Ailsa Shipbuilding of Troon, the *Iona* was rather fore square and eccentric looking, her superstructure being capped by a tiny dummy funnel. Initially this carried MacBrayne's livery but was quickly repainted yellow before the vessel entered service on the Clyde on charter to the CSP. Inboard, she was austere and verging on dingey; her bar was below the vehicle deck and, throughout, her rather constricted passenger spaces were finished in Formica and passengers sat on plastic-covered seats. Furthermore, she possessed very little by way of outside deck space and no forward-facing viewing deck. Arguably, she represented a nadir for Scottish public sector transport design. Nonetheless, she proved to be a useful and seaworthy ship, very well regarded by highly experienced Masters such as Captain Sandy Ferguson, and her career was lengthy, firstly on the Clyde and, from April 1972 on a variety of Hebridean routes.

Thereafter, two new double-ended ferries were built in Newport, Monmouthshire, for the five-minute Kyle of Lochalsh-Kyleakin route to Skye. The *Kyleakin*, which entered service in August 1970, and the *Lochalsh*, which appeared a year later, were the first ferries built for Scottish routes to use Voith-Schneider propulsion, over 40 years after the system had first been used commercially on ferries in Germany. Next, an eight-strong series of small bow-loading landing craft ferries was ordered from Lamont's of Port Glasgow. Known as the 'Island' class they were delivered between 1972 and 1976 for various MacBrayne and CSP secondary routes. Indeed, the first of the series, named the *Kilbrannan* and introduced between Lochranza on Arran and Claonaig in Kintyre was the last vessel to be delivered with a CSP yellow funnel as, from 1st January 1973, this firm ceased to exist as a separate entity.

The late 1960s and early 1970s were therefore a period of experimentation in enhancing car ferry design and provision on the Clyde

and in the Hebrides. Experimentation was conducted, however, in a context which acknowledged the urgent need for change, but was somewhat unsure of how change should be introduced and managed most effectively. Much required to be learned about the most suitable ship-designs, and how best to integrate these with existing harbour and port facilities, normally totally unsuited to the proposed form of 'progress'. Sadly, it was possible for the introduction of a modern car ferry, such as the *Iona* for the Islay run, to be stopped in its tracks by insufficient forward planning with respect to harbour facilities. The Scandinavian countries provided much-needed inspiration and useful models. These worked extremely well for Western Ferries, for example, but led to expensive mistakes, made in a spirit of ill-informed enthusiasm, as exemplified in the rebuilding of the *Stena Baltica* as the *Caledonia*. The learning curve was both steep and treacherous, but even more change was on the way.

The Island-class ferry *Coll* at Fishnish. *(John Peter)*

Chapter Twelve
The Caledonian MacBrayne Era

The first day of 1973 brought an inevitable merger to fruition between the Scottish Transport Group's Caledonian Steam Packet Company and David MacBrayne subsidiaries to form a single Clyde and Hebridean ferry company, Caledonian MacBrayne, headquartered in Gourock. All of the ferries and the three remaining excursion ships *Waverley*, *Queen Mary II* and *King George V* were transferred to this new operator. Yet, David MacBrayne Ltd also remained in existence and for a few more years operated mail and general cargo services from the Clyde to the Hebrides. When these were wound up in 1976, following the completion of better roads to remote places, David MacBrayne Ltd became dormant.

The merged company decided on a new funnel livery of red with yellow discs containing lions rampant – a combination of bright, modern colours and traditional imagery which still looks smart and dignified today.

Caledonian MacBrayne's management re-doubled their efforts to develop ferry services. Firstly, the *Clansman* and the *Arran* were rebuilt to increase their vehicle capacities. The *Clansman* was sent to Ailsa Shipbuilding at Troon in 1972 for a nine-month conversion, with the aid of a £1.5 million government grant. Her superstructure was raised, her hull was lengthened and new bow and stern doors were installed. This transformed her into a drive-through vessel, albeit one of rather strange appearance as she had a ridiculously long forward mooring deck while her superstructure covered only the aft half of her hull. Upon the completion of this work, she entered service between Ullapool and Stornoway, but as her speed was reduced to only 14 knots, she proved a sluggish performer on this route.

In contrast, the *Arran*'s conversion was more like the one previously carried out on the *Glen Sannox*, by which her aft hull was opened up to form a flat expanse of vehicle deck, accessed by a stern ramp. Meanwhile, several more new ferries were ordered. Firstly, a stern-loading vessel designated

The *Waverley,* the last paddle steamer on the Clyde, in her new Caledonian MacBrayne livery in 1973. *(Tom Shanks)*

taken out of service. First to go was the *Duchess of Hamilton.* Upon withdrawal, the lions rampant on her funnels were re-used on the *King George V.* Next, the *Waverley* was withdrawn in late-1973 and the *King George V* in 1974. Most fortuitously, the *Waverley* was sold to preservationists for the token sum of one pound. This generous and far-sighted gesture on Caledonian MacBrayne's part has enabled the paddle steamer to continue operating until the present as the last tangible link on the Clyde to the *Comet* of 1812. Following lottery-funded restoration, she now looks as good as new but her steam-expansion machinery makes her expensive to operate commercially and, with ever increasing oil prices, her future as a working ship will always face challenges. Finally, in 1977, Caledonian MacBrayne withdrew the *Queen Mary,* bringing to an end the Company's involvement in traditional Clyde steamer cruising.

Caledonian MacBrayne's many new purpose-built small and medium-sized ferries were better received than their larger converted drive-through vessels *Caledonia* and *Clansman.* While the former continued to attract torrents of criticism from Arran residents for her poor sea-keeping and over-crowded accommodation, the latter simply could not maintain reliable schedules on the Stornoway run and, besides, her deadweight capacity was barely sufficient for the number of heavy lorries she was expected to carry. Caledonian MacBrayne found the solution to these problems in Norway.

In the early 1970s, the Rederi A/S Alpha, which operated the Moss-Horten route across the Oslofjord in Norway, decided to open up a new international service from Tønsberg in Norway across the mouth of the Oslofjord to Strömstad in Sweden as this offered the potential to sell tax-free goods. For this purpose, they ordered a pair of 2,997-ton ferries, each capable of transporting 500 passengers and 120 cars, from the local Moss Rosenberg Verft. The first vessel, named *Basto V,* was delivered in April 1973. The new service could not have come at a less opportune moment unfortunately as the oil crisis had made fuel prices soar and, besides, traffic volumes were disappointing – even at the height of the summer season. That autumn, the route was closed down and the *Basto V* was first chartered out then advertised for sale.

Caledonian MacBrayne considered buying her to replace the sluggish *Clansman* between Ullapool and Stornoway but, while her size and layout appealed, their recent troubles in upgrading the *Caledonia* (ex *Stena Baltica*) to British standards gave them cause to think twice. They discovered, however, that the keel was about to be laid for a sister ship to the *Basto V* and so a contract was negotiated with the owner and builder to construct her according to British regulations so that upon completion Caledonian MacBrayne could acquire her. Most importantly, she was fitted with fin

for general work was commissioned from the Robb Caledon shipyard in Leith. Named the *Pioneer,* she displaced the *Arran* from the Islay route.

While the *Pioneer* was a conventional twin-screw ferry, Voith-Schneider propulsion was again specified for two new ferries for the Gourock-Dunoon Clyde crossing. Common sense would have suggested that, when ordering new tonnage, this route too should have been converted for drive-through operation but, as there was apparently insufficient funding available for an end-loading linkspan and associated pier infrastructure at Dunoon, stern- and side-loading vessels were ordered instead from Lamonts of Port Glasgow. The first of these was launched in November 1973 as the *Jupiter* and entered service the following March. With space for 40 cars and 690 passengers, she offered a much-enhanced service in comparison with the existing *Bute* and *Cowal.* Yet, having been conceived at a time of economic hardship and when public money had to be spread rather thinly to pay for several new ferries, the *Jupiter* provided only the most basic facilities. She was, so far as passengers were concerned, a floating bus with two saloons containing rows of fixed bench seating, one panelled in bright orange Formica and the other in blue – both very redolent of their period. Outside deck space was cramped and, as the bridge was on the Promenade Deck, there was no forward view. Her sister, the *Juno,* was completed in December 1974 and the two ferries went on to serve reliably for over 35 years. A third, slightly improved, example of the type, the *Saturn,* was built by Ailsa Shipbuilding of Troon for the Wemyss Bay-Rothesay route, and entered service in 1978. She had a superior hull form and her bridge was raised, enabling passengers once again to enjoy the view ahead. Due to their speed and manoeuvrability, the three ferries became popularly known as 'streakers'.

Between 1970 and 1977, the four remaining excursion steamers were

The turbine steamer *Queen Mary* in the Firth of Clyde in the mid-1970s. *(A. Ernest Glen)*

Above: On 27th November 1973 the newly-launched Gourock-Dunoon car ferry *Jupiter* is manoeuvred by a Cory tug at James Lamont & Co's Port Glasgow shipyard. *(A. Ernest Glen)*

Right: The *Glen Sannox* approaches Rothesay Pier in her new Caledonian MacBrayne livery. *(Bruce Peter collection)*

Below: The *Pioneer* awaits her launching at the Robb Caledon shipyard in Leith on 1st April 1974. *(A. Ernest Glen)*

Below right: The newly-launched *Pioneer* awaits a tow to the fitting-out berth for completion. *(A. Ernest Glen)*

The newly-introduced Gourock-Dunoon ferry *Juno* off Gourock Pier. *(A. Ernest Glen)*

stabilisers and cabin berths for 16 passengers.

Named *Suilven* upon delivery in 1974, the new ferry was a significant improvement over the *Clansman*, which moved south to displace the troubled *Caledonia* from the Ardrossan-Brodick route. She, in turn, switched to the relatively sheltered waters between Oban and Craignure on Mull. Meanwhile, the *Suilven* settled down to a lengthy and largely successful 21-year career shuttling back and forth across the Minch. When finally replaced in 1995, she was sold for further service to New Zealand. After a lengthy delivery voyage, she entered service across the Cook Strait between the North and South Island, still retaining her original name. Once again, her sturdy design was put through its paces in what are very tempestuous waters. In 2004, she was sold to Fiji, where she is still in service.

In spite of the relative success of the Norwegian-built *Suilven* on the Stornoway run, the design formula for Caledonian MacBrayne car ferries in the 1970s remained curiously unsettled. The *Pioneer*, which had taken up the Islay run in 1974, was quite different in design from both the *Iona* and the *Suilven*, and bore a resemblance to the Clyde 'streakers'. Her accommodation was in the forward section of the hull, while the remaining two-thirds consisted of a long, open car deck, finished off with a stern ramp. Her squared off funnels tended to give the impression that Lego blocks had been used in her construction. She had exceptionally shallow draft for a vessel of her kind, as if to ensure that Caledonian MacBrayne would not repeat the fiasco of the non-introduction of the *Iona* to the West Loch Tarbert-Islay service in 1970.

The *Pioneer* was followed in 1978 by the *Claymore*, also built by Robb Caledon, Leith, along very similar lines. The *Claymore* had a very tall forward superstructure, her bridge being so elevated that it caused some navigational difficulties for Masters who were used to viewing harbour landmarks from much lower altitudes, and on one occasion she grounded at Lochboisdale for this reason. Significantly perhaps, both the *Pioneer* and the *Claymore* were built on the east coast of Scotland at a time when the North Sea oil industry was getting into its stride, and it is probably more than a coincidence that their profiles resembled that of a typical oil-rig supply

vessel. Indeed, recently, after serving Orkney for Pentland Ferries between Gills Bay to St Margaret's Hope, the *Claymore* has been rebuilt as the Danish off-shore survey vessel, *Sia*, a role for which she appears to be very well suited. In Pentland Ferries' service, her fleetmate was the former *Iona*, which had become the *Pentalina-B*, until being sold in 2009 to Cape Verde interests. The *Pioneer*, on the other hand, has moved to Equatorial Guinea, where she continues to give good service as the *Brenda Corlett*, largely unchanged apart from her colour-scheme, and much appreciated by her current owners.

The *Pioneer* and the *Claymore* could be described as 'basic' in their approach to passenger provision, with cafeterias in their saloons. Their décor was much lighter than the dreary colour-schemes and dingey dens of the *Iona*, but the emphasis in their creation was not on internal aesthetics, but on providing soundly engineered technical solutions to the many challenges imposed by Hebridean waters and harbours. In that context, they were successful. Both vessels were stern-loading, and had hoists amidships, to cater for piers which had no appropriate slipways or linkspans. The installation of the *Pioneer*'s hoist, however, was a subsequent modification following her displacement from the Islay run in 1978 (with the eventual arrival of the *Iona*), to make her better suited to wider use throughout the network.

The rather mean passenger facilities of the *Iona*, *Pioneer* and *Claymore* probably reflected the austerity of the troubled 1970s, when the United Kingdom generally suffered from high rates of inflation and a sense of instability. The next generation of Caledonian MacBrayne ferries, built during the 1980s, when Margaret Thatcher's Conservative government was in power, were more generously proportioned than those of the previous decade, but their rather spartan passenger spaces continued to reflect Scotland's painful social change. Over time, the design of these vessels' overall layouts and silhouettes became better resolved, the accommodation blocks extending along the hull in a more integrated manner than in earlier attempts. Evidently, their principal designers and builders, Ferguson's of Port Glasgow, were successfully learning how to construct such ferries,

Above: The *Juno* at Dunoon Pier in the mid-1970s. *(A. Ernest Glen)*

Below: The *Arran* leaving Rothesay following her 1973 rebuilding as a stern-loading car ferry. An additional side-ramp has been fitted for use at the Dunoon and Rothesay linkspans. *(A. Ernest Glen)*

Below right: The launching of the new Rothesay ferry *Saturn* at the Ailsa Shipbuilding Company, Troon, on 30th June 1978. *(A. Ernest Glen)*

The 1978 *Claymore* speeds towards Oban en route from Castlebay in the summer of 1988. *(Bruce Peter)*

The Ullapool-Stornoway ferry *Suilven* in Loch Broom in the latter 1970s. *(Bruce Peter collection)*

something very new to them in the early 1980s.[253] Unfortunately, Caledonian MacBrayne's ability to provide a high standard of service was compromised by strained relations between management and unions, even although the ferries themselves generally ran punctually and were operated according to very high safety standards.

Some degree of conceptual uncertainty was evident in the matter of Car Deck design. There were designs with a central casing and a single funnel and ones with side casings and twin side-funnels. The latter have become the more common design and these were fitted to the *Isle of Arran*, built initially for the Arran service by Ferguson's, Port Glasgow, in 1984. The *Isle of Arran* was the first of the larger, more capacious car ferries ordered by Caledonian MacBrayne during the 1980s and 90s. While more spacious than the previous generations, her passenger accommodation was as basic as the 1970s vessels in its original configuration. Furthermore, as with all of Caledonian MacBrayne's fleet at that stage, it was not particularly well maintained. The passenger gangway was attached at promenade deck level where the first sight to greet those boarding was the ship's bins for galley waste. Ascending to the saloon deck, the cafeteria and lounges were panelled in grey Formica with tiled floors, fixed benches and bare fluorescent strip lighting. A large proportion of passengers appeared to be eating chips well dowsed with vinegar from polystyrene cups – and so the smell of chip fat and vinegar pervaded the ship. The outside decks were extensive and there were rows of red plastic benches – but these were invariably dirty and soon faded to pink. Yet, although ongoing maintenance was obviously required, the impression passengers got was that a large number of crew members spent much of their time doing nothing more than reading tabloid newspapers in their cabins. Caledonian MacBrayne's management evidently had difficulties in inspiring a sense of corporate pride in the face of resistance from the maritime unions.

Caledonian MacBrayne's appointment in 1983 of a canny new Managing Director, Colin Paterson, greatly advanced their development during his successful nine-year tenure. Even although the Conservative government fervently believed in privatisation, Paterson made the case persuasively for Caledonian MacBrayne's continuation as a state-owned business. He also lobbied successfully for funding to build a succession of substantial new ferries, thereby enabling a major fleet expansion and modernisation programme to take place.

The first of these ships was a new Oban-Craignure (Mull) ferry, the *Isle of Mull*, built by Appledore Ferguson, Port Glasgow, in 1987-88. She had central casing on her Car Deck and a single funnel of curiously angular design. Most unfortunately, upon launching, she was found to be seriously overweight and consequently she lacked deadweight capacity. As a remedial measure, her builder removed steel wherever possible, replacing piping with plastic and installing railings in place of solid bulwarks, for example. This enabled her to enter service as planned, replacing the *Caledonia*, but after one season, she went to Tees Dockyard for the insertion of a 5.4-metre midships section. As Norman Brown relates, 'Fergusons footed the bill – not only for all the work on the new section but for all the pier modifications it necessitated, because the boat was now longer than originally anticipated. Two of the yard's senior managers were sacked.'[254] Not only did this give her a greater payload but she also became the most spacious of the Hebridean car ferries of the 1980s, complete with the first children's play area on board. Thus, the solving of a potentially disastrous mistake enabled a significant design enhancement. Yet, at the outset, her passenger spaces lacked any sense of charm or elegance, her cafeteria being panelled in lurid yellow Formica with fixed plastic tables and chairs such as one would find in 'greasy spoon' cafés and fast food diners.

The somewhat larger *Caledonian Isles* was built specifically for the Ardrossan-Brodick service by Richards (Shipbuilders), Lowestoft, in 1993 and is reminiscent of the *Isle of Mull*, with similarly spacious accommodation. While her boat deck wraps around the superstructure, enabling passengers to enjoy a forward view as they approach Arran, unfortunately, her saloon deck windows are set so high that it is difficult to see out when seated in her saloons. Once again, Caledonian MacBrayne and their naval architects had produced a satisfactorily safe and robust solution from an engineering perspective, but one that failed to consider how passengers would experience the vessel from within. (Subsequent refurbishment work has, however, somewhat improved the *Caledonian Isles'* internal ambience.)

The *Hebridean Isles*, built by Cochrane Shipbuilders, Selby, in 1985, for the 'Hebridean Triangle', followed the *Isle of Arran* in sporting side-funnels, which were placed further aft, allowing the Car Deck to be completely clear of obstruction. Ferguson's of Port Glasgow also built the purposeful-looking *Lord of the Isles* in 1989, again with twin funnels but with a bridge

253 Norman Brown with Andrew Clark, 'Of Fergusons, ferries and "finish"', Clyde Steamers, No. 45 (Summer 2009), pp40-7.
254 Norman Brown with Andrew Clark, 'Of Fergusons, ferries and "finish"', Clyde Steamers, No. 45 (Summer 2009), p43.

The *Isle of Arran* approaches Ardrossan from Brodick in the late-spring of 1988. *(Bruce Peter)*

and forward features identical to those of the *Isle of Mull*, while her observation lounge on the Boat Deck is largely the same as that on the *Hebridean Isles*. Both the *Hebridean Isles* and the *Lord of the Isles* have hoists on their open-tailed Car Decks, but these are now largely redundant because of the construction of linkspans on all routes. These ferries display a chunky angularity due in part to their sturdy hulls being surrounded by substantial protective belting and to their ingenious combination of ramps and hoists for the loading and unloading of vehicles.

Car ferries constructed in the 1990s have dispensed totally with midships hoists, greatly improving their profiles. The *Isle of Lewis*, a splendid vessel built in 1995 by Ferguson's, Port Glasgow, for the Stornoway-Ullapool service, is a very much larger version of the *Lord of the Isles* with a spacious foyer and a fine restaurant and saloons, giving excellent views of passing seas and scenery. The *Clansman*, too, built in 1998 by Appledore Shipbuilders, Bideford, Devon, for the Inner and Outer Isles, is basically an enlarged version of the *Lord of the Isles*, but with a midships casing and a single funnel, rather like the *Isle of Mull*. The same profile appears on the *Hebrides*, again built by Ferguson's, which replaced the *Hebridean Isles* on the 'Hebridean Triangle' in 2001. To satisfy the buoyancy requirements of the latest safety regulations for hulls of restricted dimensions, the *Clansman* and *Hebrides* have exceptionally bluff bow profiles, as well as relatively shallow drafts. Consequently, they generate enormous bow waves even when sailing moderately slowly. Fuel consumption is increased, as their engines are worked harder to push such ungainly forms through the sea. The *Clansman*, which is used intensely on routes from Oban, has suffered several bouts of engine malfunction, perhaps a result of her compromised design. Thus, although Caledonian MacBrayne's larger vessels of the latter-1980s and 1990s have brought many benefits to the communities they serve, several have revealed shortcomings of one kind or another.

Thankfully, from the passengers' perspective, vessels built since the 1990s have placed greater emphasis on providing superior accommodation and décor than those of the 1980s. The least attractive internally is, perhaps, the *Clansman* which has a rather bleak, monotonous atmosphere on the Upper Deck, with rows of aircraft-style seating, though gradual refurbishing has greatly enhanced her ambience. The *Hebrides*, however, was the first Caledonian MacBrayne vessel to benefit from the employment of interior design professionals and so her public areas show a much higher degree of co-ordination, with a warmer finish. Catering outlets (which are in the forward sections on all ships since the *Lord of the Isles*) are of the 'self-service and plastic' variety but the quality of food and service has noticeably improved. Other welcome innovations have been shipboard art exhibitions and the sale of island produce such as gourmet foods in the ships' gift shops. Much credit for these enhancements is due to the positive discerning influence of Dr Harold Mills, who was appointed Caledonian MacBrayne's Chairman in 1997. The least attractive aspect of the ships of the 1990s from the passengers' perspective is the general lack of external deck space, particularly on the *Clansman* and the *Hebrides*.

As well as large ferries, Caledonian MacBrayne commissioned

The newly-completed *Isle of Mull* at Oban in June 1988. At the end of her inaugural season, she was withdrawn for lengthening to correct her insufficient deadweight capacity. *(Bruce Peter)*

Above: The *Caledonian Isles* arrives at Ardrossan during her 1993 maiden season on the Arran service. *(Bruce Peter)*

Right: An autumn morning scene in Loch Broom with the *Isle of Lewis* approaching Ullapool from Stornoway. *(Bruce Peter)*

Below: The *Clansman* swings round in Oban harbour between her sailings to the Inner Hebrides. *(John Peter)*

The *Isle of Lewis* amid the rugged mountain scenery of Loch Broom outward bound from Ullapool to Stornoway. *(Bruce Peter)*

numerous smaller ferries during the latter-1980s and early 1990s. These rather 'boxy' and utilititarian 'landing craft' included the double-ended 'Loch' class, comprising *Loch Striven*, *Loch Linnhe*, *Loch Riddon* and *Loch Ranza*, plus the similar *Loch Buie*, *Loch Tarbert*, *Loch Bhrusda* and *Loch Alainn*. As these vessels demonstrate, aesthetics are not always the principal issue when building a ship. Caledonian MacBrayne has occasionally been prepared to dispense with good looks in the interests of providing an efficient ship for a problematic crossing. A new double-ended ferry for the Mallaig-Armadale service, the 1,559-ton *Coruisk,* was delivered from Appledore Shipbuilders, Devon, in 2003. Due to her superstructure being high above the vehicle deck in order to allow trucks and buses to drive through below, as well as the need to provide crew accommodation, she is a somewhat ungainly craft, rejoicing in ironic nicknames like 'The Wedding Cake'. However, her passenger accommodation is notably attractively appointed. The *Coruisk* introduced podded propulsion to the fleet, although, in her first week in service, a computer failure caused her to ground and severely damage one of her propulsion units. Having settled into service between Mallaig and Armadale, with relief duties on the Clyde in winter, she has proved to be a very useful member of the fleet, and is well suited to the short Mallaig-Armadale crossing, which was for long a challenge to appropriate ship deployment.

The introduction of ever-larger car ferries over the last half century, but especially since 1980, has had major consequences for the islands served by the ships and the following trends are apparent. Firstly, there has been an enormous increase in vehicle traffic to the islands, consisting of cars and large lorries, as well as mammoth machines and mechanical parts for specific building projects (e.g., wind turbines) has taken place. Island infrastructure has been tested to its very limits and beyond. Such traffic has serious implications for island roads, especially in the Inner Hebrides. Nevertheless, it boosts island economies, and allows essential development to take place, especially in the field of 'renewable energy'. Secondly, the importing of very large quantities of mainland foodstuffs, leading to further

dependence on 'external' food sources, and thus reducing further the self-sufficiency of the islands, is apparent.

Nowadays, Caledonian MacBrayne's ferries operate to regular and reliable schedules to most, though not all, islands, allowing relatively speedy access to and from them. Schedules have become much tighter and faster, as a consequence of improved loading methods. A consequence has been a major increase in tourism and tourist-related vehicles (e.g. camper vans and caravans), following the introduction of pilot schemes for Road Equivalent Tariffs. This has, however, led to additional pressure on local authorities to enhance infrastructure to handle the ships and their carryings. This has implications for roads, piers, storage, and many tourist-related facilities.

Traditionalists have observed that ferries have helped speed up a gradual erosion of individual island characteristics. For example, Sunday sailings to and from Lewis were introduced in 2009, thus ending the island's unique status as the last where observance of the Sabbath extended to all aspects of public life. Yet, the 'mainstreaming' of islands as centres for major sports and cultural events, such as the 'Wave Classic' in Tiree in the autumn, and the Celtic Festival in Lewis in the summer have helped to promote a more buoyant economy in the islands, with a sense of being at the centre of contemporary life, rather than at the 'periphery'.

The most important overall aspect of the 'car ferry revolution' in the Hebrides, and also in the Clyde estuary, is that it has undoubtedly brought the islands even 'closer' to the mainland, and has caused them to become more dependent upon it. Arguably, this is not something to lament but to celebrate, as it has improved the 'quality of life' in the islands beyond measure. However, it implies that the standard of provision has to be maintained and enhanced into the future. If the quality of the ships or service is allowed to decline, given such major improvements in the last 30 years, it will have serious consequences for the western seaboard of Scotland and for the region's major industry, tourism.

Above: The *Hebrides* approaches her berth at Uig in the summer of 2010. *(John Peter)*.

Right: The *Coruisk*, which operates in summer between Mallaig and Armadale and, in winter, on the Clyde. *(John Peter)*

Below: Lochranza with the Claonaig ferry *Loch Tarbert* at the ramp in the summer of 2009. *(John Peter)*

Below right: The *Hebrides* motors into Uig Bay. *(John Peter)*

Chapter Thirteen
Tendering and Fleet Modernisation

Caledonian MacBrayne entered an even more demanding arena in the latter 1990s when they joined forces with the Royal Bank of Scotland to form NorthLink Orkney & Shetland Ferries. Subsequently they won the tender to operate subsidised routes from Aberdeen and Scrabster to Orkney and Shetland in 2002, superseding the incumbent operator P&O Ferries. As P&O's operation was carried out by ageing second-hand tonnage, NorthLink was obliged to build an entirely new fleet, consisting of two substantial overnight vessels, the 11,720-ton *Hjaltland* and *Hrossay* and a smaller shuttle ferry to link Scrabster and Stromness, the 8,780-ton *Hamnavoe*. All three vessels were designed by the Finnish consulting naval architects Deltamarin and constructed by Aker Finnyards at Rauma in Finland. In terms of design sophistication, these ferries represented a significant paradigm shift in comparison with even the most recent units of the Caledonian MacBrayne fleet.

A radical re-organisation of Caledonian MacBrayne's corporate structure was subsequently required to meet the Scottish Government's interpretation of European Union regulations for subsidised transport services; these would be put out to competitive tender on a regular basis. To prevent cherry-picking by private sector entrepreneurs of only the most

The first of a new generation of Caledonian MacBrayne ferry; built in Poland by Remontowa at Gdansk, the *Bute* finally brought drive-through operation to the Wemyss Bay-Rothesay route and a much enhanced level of comfort, service and style. *(Bruce Peter)*

lucrative services, the Scottish Government planned to put Caledonian MacBrayne's routes out to tender as a single network. Meanwhile, a judgement in Germany relating to subsidised bus services there appeared to show that, if certain criteria were met, the need for competitive tendering could be avoided altogether. Some Scottish legal opinion argued that Caledonian MacBrayne did indeed meet these criteria and consequently in December 2004 the Scottish Parliament voted by a majority of one against ministers' tendering proposals. Having consulted with the European Union and the UK Government, however, it was decided that in failing to proceed with the tendering process, European law would indeed be infringed and therefore between the autumn of 2005 and 2007, an intensive and expensive bureaucratic process was conducted.

In order to give other bidders a fair chance of success, Caledonian MacBrayne was split into a ship-owning division called Caledonian Marine Assets Ltd (CMAL) and a ferry operating company, initially known as CalMac Ferries Ltd; both new companies were fully owned by the Scottish Government's ministers. The latter would be required to submit a tender which would be evaluated against those of rival bidders. The plan was that whoever won the tendering process would use the fleet of ferries now owned by CMAL. Given that fuel and crew wages are the two greatest expenses for any ferry operator, in preparing their tender, CalMac Ferries Ltd had little room for manoeuvre and so, to cut costs, it was decided that the best strategy would be to register CalMac Crewing Ltd in the Channel Islands to reduce liability to taxation. For a state-owned business to feel obliged to do such a thing emphasised for many the ludicrous nature of the tendering process – and it was subsequently revealed that the entire exercise cost the taxpayer around £15 million to complete. In the end, the only two commercial sector bidders – V Ships and Western Ferries – withdrew from the process and so its outcome was that in October 2007 CalMac Ferries Ltd won a six-year contract to operate Caledonian MacBrayne's services. At this point, CalMac Ferries Ltd was absorbed into another long-dormant public sector shipping company, David MacBrayne Ltd, which also controlled the NorthLink Ferries routes to Orkney and Shetland. So far as users of Clyde and Hebridean ferry services were concerned, operations continued to be marketed using the popular and well-established Caledonian MacBrayne identity.

Meanwhile, the design of two new ferries for the busy Wemyss Bay-Rothesay service across the Firth of Clyde, the 2,612-ton *Bute* and *Argyle*,

Above: The second of the new Wemyss Bay-Rothesay ferries, the *Argyle*, enters Rothesay Bay. The two sisters are externally distinguishable at a distance by *Argyle* having two large forward-facing windows on each bridge wing, whereas *Bute* only has one. *(Bruce Peter)*

Right: The *Bute* heads away from Rothesay Pier. *(Bruce Peter)*

Below and below right: Inboard, the *Bute* and *Argyle* are attractively appointed. Here, we see the Argyle's aft saloon and her midships hallway café. *(Bruce Peter)*

The new generation of NorthLink ferries for services to Orkney and Shetland set a high standard for comfort and design and this was subsequently emulated in the Caledonian MacBrayne fleet. Here, the *Hrossey* is seen at Lerwick in June 2009. *(Miles Cowsill)*

involved a detailed public consultation exercise to gauge their customers' needs. At last, a new linkspan was built at Rothesay, meaning that drive-through operation could take place, rather than the time-consuming three-point turns required by motorists on the 'streakers'. In the early morning and evening, the route carries many commuters who connect at Wemyss Bay with train services to Glasgow. The remainder of the time, a mix of locals and tourists form the bulk of the traffic and so the ferries were designed to meet both groups' needs. Thus, they were designed with a great deal of comfortable indoor seating, but also with large windows to give panoramic views in all directions and extensive sun decks with even a forward-facing viewing area below the bridge.

The contract to build the *Bute* and *Argyle* was awarded to the Remontowa Northern shipyard in Gdansk, Poland and they were delivered in 2005 and 2007 respectively. In terms of fit and finish, these vessels are obviously far superior to the majority of their Clyde-built fleetmates. Indeed, once they settled into service, they proved to be very popular with regular travellers and tourists alike.

The great acclaim of these ferries put Remontowa in a prime position also to win the order from CMAL for a new Islay ferry. Deltamarin's design for the *Hamnavoe*, in particular, became the reference ship for this vessel which was largely drawn up 'in house' by Caledonian MacBrayne's own technical staff. Between this work commencing and the vessel being built, the CMAL-David MacBrayne split took place and, while her operator stated that she would be named *Pioneer*, her owner CMAL decided to hold a competition to choose a name. The winning choice was *Finlaggan*, an attractive Islay name harking back to the power centre of the Lordship of the Isles on that island and never previously carried by any past MacBrayne steamer or ferry.

As the *Finlaggan* took shape in Gdansk, it became clear that her silhouette would be largely traditional – but her detailed design is far more sophisticated than any existing large Caledonian MacBrayne vessel. Her hull configuration is better optimised to give her superior sea-keeping characteristics and fuel economy than the *Clansman* and *Hebrides*. Also, she is the first of the fleet with clam shell-type bow doors, which open outwards and to the sides, rather than a lifting visor.

The *Finlaggan*'s dimensions are only a little greater than the existing Islay ferries. Yet, her measuring 5,209 tons versus *Hebridean Isles*' mere 3,040 reflects the fact that she has a much more substantial superstructure while her slightly increased breadth is vital in achieving a capacity of 88 cars on

five parallel lanes plus a retractable mezzanine. The hull's extra width has required CMAL to rebuild the berths and linkspans at Kennacraig, Port Askaig and Port Ellen, meaning a significant additional investment in infrastructure over and above the *Finlaggan*'s £22 million cost. Propelled by two Wärtsilä diesels, her service speed is around 16.5 knots and her captains report that, in comparison with existing tonnage, her bow thrusters have a remarkably instantaneous effect in pulling her away from piers, even against strong winds and opposing tides.

Passengers embark into a spacious 'ferry square' amidships on the lower saloon deck. The centrepiece of this is an illuminated abstract sculpture, set amongst comfortable leather armchairs, settees and tables. Moving aft, there is a large multi-purpose lounge divided into a series of more intimate sections with comfortable couches and chairs in the centre and reclining seats on either beam. Overlooking the stern is a curving expanse of panoramic windows. The décor uses muted dark brown and grey shades with soft lighting and a variety of matching carpet and upholstery patterns. For those used to Caledonian MacBrayne's older ships, the leap in quality is remarkable.

Finlaggan is the first ferry designed to comply with Lloyd's Register of Shipping Crew Accommodation Comfort notation regarding the elimination of noise and vibration in the crew's quarters. This has been achieved by a combination of tactics, ranging from resilient engine mountings to filling void spaces between the machinery spaces and the vehicle deck with insulation. Most intriguing of all is the fitment of a layer of special ceramic sound deadening panels on the steel plating of the casings on either side of the vehicle deck immediately below the deck head. They act as dampers, preventing vibration from transferring upwards into the superstructure.

Eco-ferries

The Scottish Government wishes to reduce the nation's carbon footprint by 20 per cent by 2020 and this has forced publicly owned companies in Scotland to examine closely their operational practices. CMAL's Small Ferries Research Project was funded by the European Union. Analysis of the fleet has shown that the greatest saving could be achieved by prioritising the replacement of small ferries on very short crossings as these spend half of their time loading and unloading with their engines running and, between accelerating and decelerating, only briefly achieve maximum efficiency on the power utilisation curve in the middle of each crossing.

To examine the problems of small ferry operation and to generate the design criteria for a new generation of 'eco-ferry', CMAL looked at energy consumption on Caledonian MacBrayne's Sconser-Raasay route. They found that, in each 24-hour cycle, the existing ferry spent a quarter of the time using only between 6 and 12 per cent of the available power and 40 per cent of the time using power levels of up to 15 per cent of the available power. This meant that, on average, only 22 per cent of the power generated was used to propel the ship and most of the rest was wasted.

Their solution was to propose a diesel-electric system, enabling the engines to run at very low speed with lithium ion battery banks added to the DC links in the propulsion motor drives. This would allow the vessel to operate in either diesel + generator, diesel + battery or battery-only modes. The technology is already well established and reliable in applications on terra firma. The first surface ship employing a similar system is a tug at Long Beach in California.

CMAL hope initially to commission the building of four ferries of this type for the Sconser-Raasay, Tarbert-Portavadie, Gigha-Tayinloan and Lochranza-Claonaig routes, with Scottish & Southern Energy supplying power to charge their batteries. In the longer term, up to 16 of the class may be commissioned, CMAL expecting a need for possibly 11 and the others to

Operating from Kennacraig to Port Askaig and, from 2012, also to Port Ellen, the *Finlaggan* brings a much higher standard of comfort - and significantly increased capacity - to the Islay routes. Here, she is seen off Port Askaig in November 2011. *(Bruce Peter)*

operate in Ireland. Negotiations commenced in March 2011 and an order for two vessels was placed in October 2011 with Fergusons of Port Glasgow. Although CMAL have carried out detailed design research and even carried out tank testing of a model in Hamburg to prove the viability of their proposal, the eventual builder and turnkey suppliers will be expected to provide their own complete design, based on CMAL's specifications.

CMAL are in a better investment position than was expected as transport was given a 7 per cent increase to a total spend of £109 million per annum in the Scottish Government's most recent budget (in which severe cuts were imposed in other areas). Planning for the long-term, CMAL estimate that they will need to spend £604 million on vessels between now and 2022 and £180 million on upgrading port facilities. Such upgrading – purposefully executed before (rather than after) the arrival of new ships – will hold the main key to any further significant improvement in ferry design and provision for the Clyde and the Hebrides.

Henry Bell, back in 1812, faced the challenge of bringing a single steamship into being for commercial purposes. He succeeded where others had failed, and showed them the way. He anticipated that the steamship would transform the world, and he was right, as the history of marine transport in the Clyde and the Hebrides, outlined in this book, clearly testifies. Progressing from wood to iron, and then to steel, in the fabric of their hulls, and from steam to diesel engines in their modes of propulsion, ships have altered the regions which they have served, and continue to serve, beyond anything that Bell could have imagined, even in his most visionary moments. In the process, ships became not only indispensable parts of the areas that they served but also subject to the pressures exerted by the very societies which they were transforming. No longer are they the exclusive possessions of individuals or companies; they have become the

shared tools of government, economy and society, to be shaped and reshaped as required. Harbour facilities, depth of water and the general operating environment – to say nothing of the ever-increasing range of safety regulations and financial constraints – also influence design. The dynamics of shipping are thus complex, complicated and challenging.

For these reasons, while helping to promote the transformation of society, ships also act as indicators by which we can measure the changing economic circumstances, moods, aspirations, and priorities of a nation. That is borne out fully in the 200 years of maritime history between the launching of the *Comet* and the present day operations of Caledonian MacBrayne.

Onboard, the *Finlaggan* is rather more sumptuously appointed than any previous member of the Caledonian MacBrayne fleet. *(Bruce Peter)*

Books

Allen, G. F., *British Railways After Beeching*, Ian Allan, London, 1966.

Anderson, I. F., *Across Hebridean Seas*, Chatto and Windus, London, 1937.

Atkinson, R., *Island Going to the Remoter Isles, Chiefly Uninhabited, off the North-west Corner of Scotland*, Collins, London, 1949.

Booth, G., *Glory Days: Scottish Bus Group*, Ian Allan, Shepperton, 2000.

Bowman, A. I., *Kirkintilloch Shipbuilding*, Strathkelvin District Libraries and Museums, Glasgow, 1983.

Bowman, A. I., *Symington and the 'Charlotte Dundas'*, Falkirk District Council, Department of Libraries and Museums, Falkirk, 1989.

Bowman, J. E., *The Highlands and Islands: A Nineteenth-century Tour*, ed. Elaine Barry, Allan Sutton, Gloucester, 1986.

Brown, A., *Talisman: The Solitary Crusader*, Alan Brown, Johnstone, 1980.

Cambell, C. and Fenton, R., *Burns and Laird*, Ships in Focus Publications, Preston, 1999.

Cameron, H. (ed.) *Na Bàird Thirisdeach*, The Tiree Association, Glasgow, 1932.

Central Scotland – A programme for development and growth, HMSO, Edinburgh, 1963.

Charlesworth, G., *A History of British Motorways*, Thomas Telford Ltd, London, 1984.

Cooper, D., *Road to the Isles: Travellers to the Hebrides 1770-1914*, MacMillan, London, 2002.

Danielson, R., *Railway Ships and Packet Ports*, Twelveheads Press, Truro, 2007.

Deayton, A., *Steamers of the Clyde: The White Funnel Fleet*, Tempus Publishing, Stroud, 2003.

Devine, T.M., *The Great Highland Famine: Hunger, Emigration and the Scottish Highlands in the Nineteenth Century*, John Donald, Edinburgh, 1988.

Devine, T.M., *Clanship to Crofters' War: The Social Transformation of the Scottish Highlands*, Manchester University Press, Manchester, 1994.

Duckworth, C. L. D. and Langmuir, G. E., *West Highland Steamers*, fourth edition, Brown, Son & Ferguson, Ltd, Glasgow, 1987.

Duckworth, C. L. D. and Langmuir, G. E., *Clyde River and Other Steamers*, Brown, Son & Ferguson Ltd, Glasgow, 1990.

Dunlop, J., *The British Fisheries Society 1786-1893*, John Donald, Edinburgh, 1978.

Durie, A. J., *Scotland for the Holidays: Tourism in Scotland c1780-1939*, Tuckwell Press, East Linton, 2003.

Ferguson, S., *From Burma to Barra: The life and times of a Marine Superintendent*, Ardminish Press, Isle of Gigha, 2008.

Fox, S., *The Ocean Railway: Isambard Kingdom Brunel, Samuel Cunard and the Revolutionary World of the Great Atlantic Steamships*, Harper Collins, London, 2003.

Gardiner, R. (ed.), *The Advent of Steam: The Merchant Steamship before 1900*, Chatham Publishing, London, 1993.

Gardner, M. L. G., *The History of Finsbay Lodge, Harris: Life and Fishing in a Hebridean Isle*, Michael Gardner, Bradford, 2008.

Gaskell, P., *Morvern Transformed: A Highland Parish in the Nineteenth Century*, Cambridge University Press, Cambridge, 1968.

Gaskill, H. (ed.), *The Poems of Ossian and Related Works*, Edinburgh University Press, Edinburgh, 1996.

Glasgow Victoriana: Class Photographs by Thomas Annan, Ayr, undated.

Graham, E., *Clyde Built: Blockade Runners, Cruisers and Armoured Rams*, Birlinn, Edinburgh, 2008.

Gray, M., *The Highland Economy 1750-1850*, Oliver and Boyd, Edinburgh and London, 1957.

Haldane, A. R. B., *The Drove Roads of Scotland*, House of Lochar, Colonsay, 1995.

Haresnape, B., *Sealink*, Ian Allan, London, 1982.

Haresnape, B., *British Rail 1948-1983: A Journey by Design*, Ian Allan, Shepperton, 1983.

Harvie, C., *A Floating Commonwealth: Politics, Culture, and Technology on Britain's Atlantic Coast*, Oxford University Press, Oxford, 2008.

Hunter, C., *Oban – Past and Present*, Charles Hunter, Oban, 1993.

Johnston, I., *Ships for a Nation, John Brown & Company Clydebank 1847-1971*, West Dumbartonshire Libraries and Museums, 2000.

Kinchin, P. and Kinchin, J,. *Glasgow's Great Exhibitions 1888 1901 1938 1988*, White Cockade, Bicester, 1988.

Levitt, I., 'The Scottish Office and St Kilda 1885-1930: a steamer too far', in Randall (ed.), *Decline and Fall*, 51-63.

MacAonghais, Iain, *Duain agus Orain*, C. Mac-na-Ceàrdadh, Glaschu, 1875.

MacArthur, I. C., *The Caledonian Steam Packet Co Limited: An Illustrated History*, Clyde River Steamer Club, Glasgow, 1971.

MacIntosh, J., *Creating an Edwardian Railway Masterpiece: The Caledonian Railway's Wemyss Bay Station*, Caledonian Railway Association and Friends of Wemyss Bay Station, 2009.

Mackay, J., *The St Kilda Steamers: A History of McCallum, Orme & Co.*, Tempus Publishing, Stroud, 2006.

Mackenzie, J. M., *Diary 1851*, Acair, Stornoway, 1994.

McCrorie, I., *Caledonian MacBrayne: Ships of the Fleet*, Caledonian MacBrayne, Gourock, 1977.

McCrorie, I., *Caledonian MacBrayne Hebridean & Clyde Ferries: The Fleet*, Ferry Publications, Ramsey, 2010.

McPhun: *Steam-Vessels in the Service of Clyde*, Glasgow, 1835.

Meek, D. E., *Steamships to St Kilda*, Islands Book Trust, Lewis, 2010.

Mullay, A. J., *For the King's Service: Railway Ships at War*, Pendragon Publishing, York, 2008.

Murchison, T. M. (ed.), *Prose Writings of Donald Lamont 1874-1958*, The Scottish Gaelic Texts Society, Edinburgh, 1960.

Napier Commission Report, 1884

National Abstract of Statistics, AF48/28

National Abstract of Statistics, AF 42/7522

National Abstract of Statistics, BT2/15517

National Abstract of Statistics, BT2/481

New Statistical Account of Scotland.

O'Hara, G. C., *Ironfighters, Outfitters and Bowler Hatters*, Clyard Novella Ltd, Prestwick, 1997.

Oakley, C. A., *The Second City*, Blackie & Son Ltd, London and Glasgow, 1946.

Orr, R. M., *Queen Mary*, Caledonian MacBrayne, Gourock, 1976.

Osborne, B. D., *The Ingenious Mr Bell: A Life of Henry Bell (1767-1830), Pioneer of Steam Navigation*, Argyll Publishing, Glendaruel, 2001.

Paterson, A. J. S., *The Golden Years of the Clyde Steamers*, David & Charles, Newton Abbot, 1969.

Paterson, A. J. S., *The Victorian Summer of the Clyde Steamers*, David & Charles, Newton Abbot, 1972.

Paterson, A. J. S., *Classic Scottish Paddle Steamers*, David & Charles, Newton Abbot, 1982.

Paterson, L., *The Light in the Glens: The Rise and Fall of the Puffer Trade*, House of Lochar, Colonsay, 1996.

Patton, B., *A MacBrayne Memoir*, Brian Patton, Foulden, 2009.

Peter, B., *Knud E. Hansen A/S: Ship Design through Seven Decades*, Forlaget Nautilus, Frederiksværk, 2007.

Peter, B. and Dawson, P., *The Ferry: A Drive-through History*, Ferry Publications, Ramsey, 2010.

Raasay House Weather Tables, 1851-59. Raasay Heritage Trust Archives.

Ramsay, F. (ed.), *John Ramsay of Kildalton*, Peter Martin Associates Ltd, Toronto, 1969.

Randall, J. (ed.), *The Decline and Fall of St Kilda: Proceedings of an international conference organised by the Islands Book Trust in August 2005 to mark the 75th anniversary of the evacuation of St Kilda*, Islands Book Trust, Lewis, 2006.

Reed, L., *The Soay of Our Forefathers*, Birlinn, Edinburgh, 2002.

Ripley, D. and Rogan, T., *Designing Ships for Sealink*, Ferry Publications, Kilgetty, 1995.

Robins, N., *The Cruise Ship: A Very British Institution*, History Press, Stroud, 2008.

Robins, N. S., and Meek, D. E., *The Kingdom of MacBrayne: From Steamships to Car-ferries in the West Highlands and Hebrides 1820-2005*, Birlinn, Edinburgh, 2008.

Robson, M., *St Kilda: Church, Visitors and 'Natives'*, Islands Book Trust, Lewis, 2005.

Simper, R., *Scottish Sail: A Forgotten Era*, David & Charles, Newton Abbot, 1974.

Smith, A., *A Summer in Skye*, Samson Low, Marston & Co. Ltd, London, n.d.

Storey, L., *Muinntir Mhiughalaigh*, Clàr, Inbhir Nis, 2007.

Symington 2003: *The First Practical Steamboat: William Symington and the Charlotte Dundas*, Grangemouth, 2003.

Thomas, J., *The Skye Railway*, The History of the Railways of the Scottish Highlands, Vol. 5, David St John Thomas, David & Charles, Newton Abbot, 1990.

Thomas, J., *The Callander & Oban Railway*, The History of the Railways of the Scottish Highlands, Vol. 4, David St John Thomas, Nairn, 1991.

Topographical and Historical Gazetteer, I, 1842.

Veitch, K. and Gordon, A., 'Traditional Ferries', in Veitch, K. (ed.), *Transport and Communications: A Compendium of Scottish Ethnology*, Vol. 8 (Edinburgh, 2009), pp212-221.

Walker, F. M., *Song of the Clyde*, John Donald, Edinburgh, 2001.

Weir, M., *Ferries in Scotland*, John Donald, Edinburgh, 1988.

Whittle, J., *Speed Bonny Boat: The story of Caledonian MacBrayne Ltd under the Scottish Transport Group 1969-1980*, Saltire Publications, Newbridge, Midlothian, 1990.

Williamson, J., *The Clyde Passenger Steamer, Its Rise and Progress During the Nineteenth Century from the Comet of 1812 to the King Edward of 1901*, James MacLehose and Sons, Glasgow, 1904.

Journal articles
Brown, N., Clark, A., 'Of Fergusons, ferries and "finish"', *Clyde Steamers*, No. 45 (Summer 2009), pp40-7.

Dawson, P., 'Robert Tillberg: Reflections on a remarkable career', Designs 04, ShipPax, Halmstad, 2004, pp90-95.

Fraser G. MacHaffie, 'A Queen goes to Victoria', *Clyde Steamers*, No. 46 (Summer 2010), pp2-11.

Meek, D. E., 'Smoking, Drinking, Dancing and Singing on the High Seas: Steamships and the Uses of *Smùid* in Scottish Gaelic', *Scottish Language*, 25, Glasgow, 2006, pp46-70.

Meek, D. E., 'Early Steamship Travel from the Other Side: An 1829 Gaelic Account of the *Maid of Morven*,' *Review of Scottish Culture*, 20 (2008), pp57-79.

Newspapers and periodicals
An Gaidheal.
Clyde Steamers.
Design.
The Dunoon Observer and Argyllshire Standard.
The Oban Times.
The Glasgow Herald.
Illustrated London News.
The Kaleidoscope.
Marine Register of Deaths.
The Motor Ship.
The Queen.
The Railway Engineer.
Scottish Daily Express.
Ships Monthly.
The Weekly Scotsman.
West Coast Times.

Theses
Skewis, W. I., 'Transport in the Highlands and Islands', unpublished Ph.D. thesis, University of Glasgow, 1962.

Acknowledgements

Donald E. Meek's contribution to this book is based partly on a chapter originally published in K. Veitch (ed.), *Scottish Life and Society: Transport and Communications*, A Compendium of Scottish Ethnology, Vol. 8, John Donald in Association with the European Ethnological Research Centre, Edinburgh, 2009, pp227-73. We are grateful to the European Ethnological Research Centre for permission to reproduce and expand the original chapter.

Our especial thanks to Miles Cowsill and Nicola Green of Ferry Publications for producing this book; our thanks to John Peter for scanning and preparing the photographs, to Ian Hall for checking the manuscript for accuracy, to Ann Glen for reading the manuscript, to Captain Norman Martin for his very helpful comments on our account of the post-1970 fleet, and to Caroline Hallworth for copy-editing the manuscript. Ian Somerville and Iain Quinn gave invaluable assistance with identifying ships and locations in the illustrations.